Diversity and
Public Administration

Diversity and Public Administration

Theory, Issues, and Perspectives

Edited by

Mitchell F. Rice

M.E.Sharpe
Armonk, New York
London, England

Library of Congress Cataloging-in-Publication Data

Diversity and public administration : theory, issues, and perspectives / edited by Mitchell F. Rice.
    p. cm.
Includes bibliographical references and index.
ISBN 0-7656-1431-6 (cloth : alk. paper)
    1. Civil service—Personnel management. 2. Diversity in the workplace. I. Rice, Mitchell F.

JF1658.D58 2004
352.6′08—dc22   2004002827

Printed in the United States of America

The paper used in this publication meets the minimum requirements of
American National Standard for Information Sciences
Permanence of Paper for Printed Library Materials,
ANSI Z 39.48-1984.

∞

BM (c)   10   9   8   7   6   5   4   3   2   1

Contents

Figure and Tables

Figure

Tables

Acknowledgments

This book would not have been possible without the contributions of the authors. I extend a warm thanks to each of them. Also, a very special thanks to my graduate assistants, Satish Thimmalapura and Pragya Acharya, who now have valuable experience in knowing what goes on behind the scenes in putting together an edited volume. Good luck in your future endeavors.

Diversity and Public Administration

1

The Multiple Dimensions of Diversity and Culture

Harvey L. White and Mitchell F. Rice

Current considerations for the provision of public services must include how to respond effectively to the principal challenges of the twenty-first century. Many of these challenges will emanate from changing demographics that are impacting the demand for and the delivery and provision of public goods and services. For instance, the U.S. Census Bureau (2000) notes that Hispanics are officially the largest minority group in the United States; African-Americans are the second. There are also increasing numbers of individuals from other nationalities who represent a mosaic of colors, languages, cultural values, and ethnic traditions. This situation will pose tremendous challenges that require the creation of a diverse and more efficient public service workforce. Some of the challenges that changing demographics will pose are discussed in the *Workforce 2000* report published by the Hudson Institute (Johnston and Packer 1987). The report indicates that there will be major changes in the workforce by the twenty-first century. For example, 84 percent of new entrants into the workforce will be women and men of color, white women, and foreign nationals (Johnston and Packer 1987). These changes will affect employee expectations about the employee-employer implied contract, the numbers of dual career and nontraditional families, and the overall diversity of the workforce.

These demographic changes suggest that public sector organizations must be prepared to develop more inclusive work cultures that have a better understanding of the many ways people are different from one another and/or different from the organizations' traditional employees. Public service organizations must give renewed (or new) attention to such defining characteristics as race, gender, age, disabil-

3

ity, sexual orientation, and religion. However, attention is also required for other diversity factors such as the college one attended, varied communication and management styles, and problem-solving approaches (Jensen and Katz 1996). Diversity has the potential of becoming the most important consideration for public service organizations in the twenty-first century. However, this consideration is not confined merely to the workforce. Diversity also includes the production and provision of public services. In other words, it is not just a question of knowing who will be the public servant(s). Other important questions will need equal consideration. Among these are: What populations will be served? What goods and services will be provided? How will these goods and services be produced? For example, due to the changing demographics in Texas, where the Hispanic population is growing quite rapidly, the state's demographer implicitly notes that in the not too distant future a disproportionately older Anglo population will be served by a public service workforce that is more and more minority (Murdock et al. 2002). The Texas demographer also points out that the state's economic future will be tied to the future socioeconomic status of the growing minority populations.

Further, other factors will help determine the answers to these questions including: (1) the increasingly ethnic, racial, and gerontological diversity of society; (2) an increasingly gender-diverse workforce; (3) the growing interdependence of the global community, which calls for greater knowledge, understanding, and appreciation of human diversity; and (4) the increasing technological diversity behind the production and provision of goods and services. As these factors suggest, public service organizations will be confronted with a multiplicity of needs and interests that will require a workforce that has a broad knowledge base and a variety of skills and talents. Addressing these needs and interests will require the application of innovative technologies and management-diversity practices if public goods and services are to be delivered efficiently. What follows is an examination of diversity factors that will influence the future of public service.

Racial Diversity: Toward a Representative Bureaucracy

Many concepts have been used to express the need for a diverse workforce in the public sector. Multiculturalism, affirmative action, and equal opportunity are the more recent. Implicit in each of these concepts is the premise that enhanced efficiency can be derived through a more diverse workforce. This premise is also an intricate part of the concept of representative democracy (see Long 1952; Van Riper 1958; Waner et al. 1963; Mosher 1968; Kranz 1976). Norton Long (1952) described the linkage between diversity and a representative democracy more than fifty years ago. According to Long, it is of critical importance that bureaucracy be both representative and democratic in composition and ethos. To be truly representative, he insists that public service must be inclusive of diverse "races, nationalities, and religions." This inclusiveness is to be achieved through a recruitment process designed to create a workforce of individuals similar to the pluralism that exists in society. The concept of a representative bureaucracy was also used by Frederick Mosher to emphasize the need for a more diverse public service. Mosher (1968, 15) argues that "representativeness concerns the origin of individuals and the degree to which, collectively, they mirror the whole society. . . . A public service, and more importantly the leadership personnel of that service, which is broadly representative of all categories of the population in these respects, may be thought of as satisfying [President] Lincoln's prescription of government by the people. . . ."

Similar to Long, Mosher views diversity as a requisite for both democracy and representative bureaucracy. Mosher (1968, 16) correctly points out that it is crucial for good policy and management decision-making as well. "Persons drawn from diverse groups . . . will bring to bear upon decisions and activities different perspectives, knowledge, values, and abilities. And the products of their interaction will very likely differ from the products were they all of a single genre." Building on the foundation laid by Long, Mosher, and others, Harry Kranz spells out the specific benefits that he believes can be achieved through a representative bureaucracy. Kranz (1976, 110–11) argues that a representative bureaucracy would lead to more democratic decision-making resulting in better decisions because it would expand the number and diversity of views brought to bear on policy-making. Kranz (112–16) also notes that representative bureaucracy improves bureaucratic operations and outputs: by insuring that the decisions and services are more responsive to the needs of agency clientele and potential consumers, particularly members of minority groups; through a more efficient use of the country's human resources; through an increase, both symbolically and actually, in the legitimacy of public service institutions; and by elevating social equity and justice to prime political values at least as important as the prevailing paradigm of "economy and efficiency" and its fellow traveler "stability."

Race is one component of the diversity that Long, Mosher, and Kranz call for. As these scholars have come to realize, Europeans, Africans, Native Americans, Asians, and other racial groups possess unique cultural norms and values that affect their decisions. Numerous studies have confirmed racially differentiated perspectives on a variety of issues and events that are diverse and salient. Differences have been found to persist in such areas as political alienation, childbearing, school choice, and the environment (Herring et al. 1991; Mohai 1990; Henig 1990; St. John and Rowe 1990; Lipset and Schneider 1983; Kahn and Mason 1987). Despite these findings, most racial groups continue to be underrepresented in public service organizations at all levels of government.

As Kim and Lewis (1994) found in their research, Asian-Americans are significantly underrepresented in state and local governments. Several studies have found that African-Americans are underrepresented at all levels of government; and their representation is severely restricted at middle and upper management levels (Murray et al. 1994; Cornwell and Kellough 1994; Kellough 1990). Meier (1975) found in his study of the federal civil service that minority representation decreases as rank (or grade) increases. As Guajardo (1996) learned in his study of the federal civil service, minority underrepresentation in federal agencies remained constant between 1982 and 1990. His conclusion was that agencies with representative workforces continued to have integrated staffs, while underrepresentative agencies continued to have workforces that were predominately white. Hence, even after nearly fifty years of efforts, which began with the 1964 Civil Rights Act, achieving racial diversity still remains one of the greatest challenges facing contemporary public service.

Diversity as Differences in Ethnic Norms and Behaviors

Ethnic differences within racial groups is an aspect of diversity that has been almost completely overlooked in an attempt to create a more representative bureaucracy. All Europeans, all Africans, all Asians, and all Hispanics are frequently considered homogeneous groups. As is becoming increasingly clear, the various European communities have distinguishing cultural and religious differences that are a source of continual conflict among them. European interethnic conflicts are found in Irish religious differences, the conflict between the Basques and Castile, and the crisis a few years ago in the former Yugoslavia. Europeans speak different languages and may be Protestant, Catholic, Jewish, or Muslim. They have various customs and social mores. As exhibited in subnational politics and employment practices in state and local government, these differences may be minimized but not abandoned when Europeans move abroad.

African-Americans can be similarly differentiated. They come from different ethnic and language groups in Africa, and have different religious beliefs. African-Americans can also be distinguished between those who are descendants of former slaves and those who are more recent arrivals from Africa and the Caribbean Islands. Each group has norms and values that affect its demand for, participation in, and perception of public service. Asians, like other groups, are a single race in U.S. statistics. However, as Kim and Lewis (1994, 286) note, "they vary widely in culture, language, and recency of immigration." A 1990 report by the General Accounting Office identifies seventeen nationalities that make up the Asian population in the United States. In 1990, nearly two-thirds of the Asian-American community was foreign-born, with one-quarter of the adults having immigrated in the past five years. As a reflection of the growing populations of minority groups, the 2000 census form saw the addition of an extended category of racial groups (some fourteen categories) and four ethnic classifications for Hispanics/Latinos for self-identification (Rosenblum and Travis 2003). Nobles (2003, 52) notes that the importance of census results is that they produce entitlements including political power, economic power, social power, and public goods.

As mentioned above, the Census Bureau sees ethnic differences among Hispanics/Latinos. Gomez (1994) points out that Hispanics are a highly heterogeneous group with major variations in terms of race, socioeconomic status, native region, and immigration status. For instance, Hispanics can be any combination of European, African, Asian, and Native American ancestry, yet be officially classified as white. In terms of religion, most are Catholic, many are Protestant, and some are Jewish. Hispanic ethnic groups also vary by nationality. They may be from one of several Caribbean Islands, Mexico, Central America, Spain, or South America. Some Mexican-American families have lived in the Southwest United States since before the arrival of the *Mayflower*. Ethnic diversity is real and should be appreciated by the public manager. As with race, it can help expand the organization's capacity to understand and address the needs of the individuals they serve.

Gender and the Public Service: The Glass Ceiling Dilemma

In the aggregate, increases in employment opportunities for women in public service seem impressive. For instance, female employees hold nearly half of all federal white-collar jobs (Naff 1994); they hold nearly 20 percent of top administrative posts in state governments (Bullard and Wright 1993); and they are nearly half of the new hires in state and local governments (Guy 1993). However, gender biases and discriminatory policies serve to limit the upward mobility of women. As Johnston and Packer report in *Workforce 2000* (1987, 105), "Despite the huge increases in the number of women in the workforce, many of the policies and institutions that cover pay, fringe benefits, time away from work, pensions, welfare, and other issues have not yet been adjusted to the new realities." The public sector is no exception. Barriers have been found between women and an equitable consideration for advancement in public service at all levels of government (Naff 1994; Guy 1993; Bullard and Wright 1993). These barriers constitute what is described as a "glass ceiling" (also referred to as "sticky floor") that relegates most women to lower management and clerical positions. As Naff points out, even though women make up nearly half of the federal civil service, women are only 18 percent of top-grade-level groups (GS/GM 13–15), and only 11 percent of the Senior Executive Service. In contrast, they hold nearly 75 percent of positions in the lowest six grades of the federal civil service.

While the glass ceiling is denying women the opportunity to hold top-level administrative positions, other gender-based workplace practices are limiting their influence in public service. Two of the more notable practices are pay distinctions across grades (compa-rable worth) and disparities within grades. The pay distinction issue emerged in 1983, when U.S. District Judge Jack E. Tanner ruled that the state of Washington had illegally discriminated against thou-sands of women by paying them 20 percent less than men doing jobs of "comparable worth." Disparities that exist within grades re-sult in women earning approximately 35 percent less than men (Fuller and Schoenberger 1991). The pay disparity created by these prac-tices results in relationships of permanent inequality and impedes women's ability to influence the design and implementation of pub-lic policy (Guy 1993).

Although giving the appearance of being representative in terms of gender, Guy (1993) points out that most public service agencies are anything but representative in their decision-making processes. She says, "Women occupy the lower rungs on the agency ladders and men occupy the upper rungs" (291). Obstacles to the advance-ment of women into management positions in the public service persist, even though research suggests that women often make bet-ter managers (White and Micheaux 1995; Frieman 1990; Grant 1988; Jago and Vroom 1982). Scholars have found that the nontraditional leadership styles women exhibit are well suited for rapidly chang-ing work situations prevalent in modern economies. As they ob-serve, the presence of these leadership styles can increase an organization's chances of surviving in an uncertain environment (Korabik 1990; Gregory 1990). Women are also believed to have management styles that are more conducive to the needs of profes-sional workers.

Professionals who are highly skilled and highly mobile expect the organizations they work for to help them meet their personal goals. Such workers also expect to be active participants in decision-making. Findings from a survey of both men and women suggest that women may be better managers for these workers (Rosener 1990). Men, in this survey, indicate the use of a series of transac-tions in their management practices, that is, rewards for services rendered or punishment for inadequate performance, in their rela-tions with subordinates. They also rely more on power that comes from their organizational position and formal authority. Generally, responses given by men suggest an inclination toward exhibiting traditional management behavior, which is characterized by extreme competitiveness, striving for achievement, and an intense drive and aggression. Such behavior is often counterproductive for both the organization and the individual. It usually includes some hostility, time urgency, impatience, and accelerated activity (Rowney and Cahoon 1990). As Friedman and Rosenman (1974, 37) note, this behavior characterizes someone "who is aggressively involved in a chronic, incessant struggle to achieve more and more in less time, and if required to do so, against the opposing effects of other things or other persons." Such behavior often leads to stress-related health problems for the individual and unhealthy tension in the organization.

In contrast to men, women managers indicate the frequent use of transformational leadership to encourage subordinates to transform their self-interest into the interest of the group through concern for a broader goal. As Judy Rosener (1990) observes, women work to make their interactions with subordinates positive for everyone involved. More specifically, women are more likely to encourage participation, share power and information, enhance other people's self-worth, and get others excited about their work. Moreover, women managers have many useful skills that can enhance management in organizations. The results of research by Korabik (1990), which focused on conflict resolution, are illustrative of how nontraditional leadership styles exhibited by women can enhance managerial effectiveness. In her study of male and female middle- to upper-level managers, masculinity was significantly related to the use of a competitive style of conflict management, whereas femininity was significantly correlated with an accommodative style. Each style can be an asset. Yet public sector organizations have failed to make effective use of the managerial skills women possess.

Taking advantage of the gender assets women managers have to offer as public managers does represent a challenge in organizations when the top leadership positions are usually held by men. However, in order for government to ensure maximum efficiency in the delivery of public goods and services, it must utilize all the resources at its disposal. As Lynwood Battle, a Procter & Gamble executive, points out, "When it gets right down to it, . . . [organizations] that are going to survive and thrive in the next century are the ones that take full advantage of their work force" (quoted in Solomon 1989, 50). Battle further observes that failure to utilize the skills and talents of women represents a waste of valuable managerial resources.

The consequences of this failure can affect both the productivity and survival of an organization. Thus, government organizations should have selfish reasons for utilizing the assets that women bring with them as managers.

The successful provision of public services in the future will be intricately linked to government's ability to develop a more inclusive work culture. This inclusive work culture must be one in which all people can contribute their full potential, unhindered by stereotypes or prejudices about their differences. It must be one in which people's differences are viewed as organizational assets, new perspectives that enhance the overall performance of the organization. Moreover, an inclusive work culture must embrace people's ideas, and their input must be sought and valued (Jensen and Katz 1996). An inclusive work culture will allow diverse people to contribute to the organizational mission in meaningful ways. When an organization has developed a work culture that values contributions from a diverse workforce, it is poised to realize new efficiencies in the provision of public services.

Gerontology as a Diversity Issue: A Graying of the Civil Service

One of the challenges to public service, which was described in the Hudson Institute's report, is that being posed by an aging workforce. The concern is that as the average worker's age climbs toward forty, the workforce may "lose its adaptability and willingness to learn." The median age of the population, which had been declining until 1970, was projected to reach thirty-six by the year 2000 (Johnston and Packer 1987). This challenge is expected to be particularly strong in the public sector, where the average worker is older than the norm. As Johnston and Packer discern, most of this aging will be the result of huge increases in the number of middle-age individuals. At the new millennium, the number of people between ages thirty-five and forty-seven was expected to have increased by 35 percent, and those forty-eight and fifty-three were projected to have increased by a staggering 67 percent. Overall population growth was expected to increase by only 15 percent during this same time (Johnston and Packer 1987). These demographics suggest that gerontological considerations will become extremely important in the production, delivery, and mix of public goods and services. As Wolf et al. (1987) found in a study of social service agencies, public organizations are faced with continuing problems and challenges created from several closely related social and demographic factors. Three factors are thought to be of particular importance relative to issues of diversity:

- An overall slowing of organizational growth in the public sector and a reduction of career opportunities for professionals in all sectors;
- More aspirants seeking middle- and senior-level positions as the baby boom generation turns forty; and
- New, and to some extent conflicting, career values that include the perception that self-fulfillment should be sought outside the job and that employment is only a means to engage in other rewarding endeavors (Wolf et al. 1987).

Although some of these factors are beyond the control of government organizations, they nevertheless directly bear upon the ability of public managers to create a more diverse workforce. In particular, the decreasing opportunities that are the result of these factors will make it difficult to help women and minorities break through the glass ceilings they face. Similarly, older, more outwardly focused workers are expected to affect managers' abilities to foster new ideas; ensure employee motivation and performance; and achieve the efficiency thought possible with a more inclusive work culture. As emerging gerontological factors take effect in the public sector, they are transforming human resource management practices and policies in civil service (Wolf et al. 1987). These factors are expected to affect the mix of public service as well.

This situation is particularly germane at the beginning of the new millennium, when the elderly population is increasing significantly and is expected to increase for some time. A rapidly expanding older population will likely make greater demands on the services that they value. These include health care and hospitals, transportation, and housing. As noted above, this age cohort's perspective is that "self-fulfillment should be sought outside the job and that employment is only a means to engage in other rewarding endeavors" (Button and Rosenbaum 1990). Consequently, this group is likely to amass less wealth and be less able to pay for the services they will need. Button and Rosenbaum (1990) assert that this in turn may translate into a greater demand for the government to provide the desired services and perhaps an unwillingness to help pay for services desired by others. Furthermore, it may also create heightened competition between the aged and other groups for government resources.

Myrtle and Wilber (1994, 245) suggest that this competition may not only exist, but that the contest may have already been won. They point out that "the variety of services and benefits available to the elderly, in particular, suggests that age-based interest groups, and those who benefit from services to the elderly, have been effective in advancing their social policy agendas. . . . The expansion of services benefiting older adults, coupled with the rise in the number of elderly . . . has resulted in the 'graying' of the federal budget." While some may disagree with the concept of an aged-based interest group that dominates American politics, there is consensus that prevailing demographics are having a significant impact on the mix of goods and services provided by government.

Technology as a Diversity Issue

The application of advanced technology in the public sector shows the potential for enhancing government efficiency and how easily disparities can be created in providing public goods and services. To be clear, technology in and of itself is not the problem. To the contrary, recent applications of technology for the delivery of public services constitute one of the crowning achievements of the civil service. Computers, facsimile equipment, voice mail, electronic commerce, the World Wide Web, video conferences and training, and digital telecommunications are all being use to provide services to citizens. These technologies are not only resulting in new efficiencies, they are also creating new mediums for the delivery of public services. Electronic banking for Social Security and other monetary transactions has become a standard service provided by the government. Sometimes referred to as electronic commerce, this service is a source of security and convenience for thousands. A similar use is made of electronic commerce for filing and processing taxes and tax refunds. Many governments use voice mail to maximize time spent actually providing services to citizens. Recent service arrangements even involve using the Internet to announce, submit, peer review, award, and administer federal grants (Kestenbaum and Straight 1996). Governments are using new technologies to allow managers and citizens access to up-to-date government information quickly and cheaply. Fax communication has replaced the mail for many types of information exchanges. Computer-to-computer links facilitate immediate exchange of data across vast geographical areas. While the application of new technologies for the provision of public services is advancing every day, there are reasons for concern.

First, many of these technological advances effectively exclude low income groups, the elderly, and other groups that lack the access and knowledge needed to use and be served with these technologies. This disparity in access to advanced technology was evidenced by research findings in the early 1990s, which revealed that only 11 percent of African-American households owned home computers and just 520,000 owned modems. In contrast, 29 percent of European-American households owned computers and 10.1 million owned modems (Carter 1996). Although by 2002 the number of African-American households having access to computers and the Internet had increased significantly, the annual income threshold for computer ownership and Internet access is around $75,000 (see Rice 2001; U.S. Dept. of Commerce 2000). Further, immediate access to a computer, fax machine, and the Internet is often a prerequisite for many advanced technologies. Basic computer literacy and the ability to navigate the Internet are also requirements. For the growing "underclass," computers are becoming luxury items that they cannot afford. Many older adults are computer illiterate. Hence, an overreliance on advanced technology can result in excluding individuals from the services they need. To avoid this exclusion, governments must employ "diverse technologies." This should include those that are "user friendly" and contain no "use costs" for citizens.

A second concern is that the application of technologies is making government less labor-intensive, which will consequently result in few new employees. If the only consideration is to enhance efficiency through the application of advanced technology, it is feared that the result will be a civil service that is overwhelmingly middle-aged, white, and male. Another concern is that computers and information technology often reduce the need for middle managers and thus make it more difficult for minorities and women to advance into upper-level positions. As Peter Drucker (1989, 20) points out, "a great many—maybe most—American companies have cut management levels by one-third or more." The Clinton-Gore administration reinvention effort in Washington, D.C. is illustrative of this reduction in middle mangers in the federal civil service. According to former vice president Al Gore's National Performance Review report, *From Red Tape to Results* (1993), which is the masterpiece for the reinvention process, the positions of more than 250,000 "supervisors, headquarters staff, personnel specialists, budget analysts, procurement specialists, accountants and auditors" in the federal government will be eliminated. Many of the middle managers will be women and minorities. Thus, women and minorities will continue to occupy the "lower rungs" of the civil service and white men the "upper rungs." Collectively, these concerns suggest that technological advances must be utilized with care. Unless they are employed in ways that enhance diversity and reduce disparities in the provision of public services, short-term gains in efficiency could be short lived. This result is likely because the organization will be unable to take advantage of efficiencies facilitated through an inclusive workforce.

Conclusion

The discussion in the opening chapter of this book has focused on diversity factors and the challenges they present to public service. Race, ethnicity, cultural differences, gender, gerontology, and technology are individually and collectively factors that affect the diversity of the public sector. They determine what types of people and what sets of skills will be required to meet the changing and complex demands of new customers, new markets, and new economic realities within the public milieu. They will help determine who will be the public servants, which goods and services will be provided, and the manner in which services are produced. Diversity factors will affect how managers manage, the location for the production of goods and services, and the mix of goods and services. Moreover, these diversity factors are likely to be the primary challenges facing the public sector in the new millennium century. Continuing research is needed concerning the aforementioned factors to more precisely determine the effects they will have on public service.

The remaining chapters in this book discuss many of the diversity factors and issues raised above in public and business organizations. As a revised edition, the chapters that have been retained have undergone some revisions. Chapters 2, 4, 5, 9, and 10 are completely new. The chapters present theory, issues, and perspectives about diversity and the workplace in both public and business organizations. It is clear that the demographic diversity changes in American society are requiring drastic alterations in the way government organizations administer and manage public service delivery systems. Jordan, Rice, and Mathews (1994, 51) observe that "the challenges these changes pose for the public sector are significant, due in part, to the delicate balance between quality, human well being, and public service policy and programming." Concurrently, however, public organizations are faced with a set of constraining factors that make it difficult to deal with diversity changes. These factors are resource limitations, cutback management, downsizing (or rightsizing), public program realignment (McBriarty 1988), and most recently, conservative policy-making in the area of civil rights.

A book focusing on diversity in public organizations must provide some attention to race, culture, and gender. After all, diversity in public organizations is much about race, culture, and gender. Rice and Arekere in chapter 2 discuss why workplace diversity is important to both business and governmental organizations. The chapter identifies "best practices" in diversity programming in business and governmental organizations and asks whether replicating best practices in diversity programming is the most appropriate strategy for other organizations. The chapter introduces the student or reader to important diversity terms, concepts, and phrases such as diversity recruitment quotient, diversity audit, diversity climate, cultural audit, and glass ceiling audit. Wooldridge, Smith-Mason and Maddox in chapter 3 discuss and call for more research on identity groups, and describe and relate organizational behavior literature to behavior differences of identity groups in a diverse workforce. The chapter's central theme is that more research is needed on how diversity is impacting the workplace to better assist managers to manage a diverse workforce.

In chapter 4, Rice points out that public organizational diversity initiatives and efforts are affected by the teaching of diversity and social equity in college/university classrooms. Why? Students in public administration programs are the future public executives, public managers, and public service delivery personnel. Rice asks the question: Is public administration education curricula relevant in a contemporary multicultural and diverse society? He goes on to discuss ways in which public administration coursework can be made more relevant to students and subsequently to public practitioners in managing diversity and promoting social equity in public service delivery. In chapter 5, Farmbry gives results from a study that utilized surveys and interviews to show that the extent to which demographic diversity trends in California have impacted public administration education in Master's of Public Administration programs at colleges and universities within California. Program directors of thirteen Master's of Public Administration programs participated in the study (from a total of twenty-four programs accredited by the National Association of Schools of Public Affairs and Administration).

Burton and Tryman in chapter 6 discuss the role of African-American public administrators in urban government bureaucracies. They are concerned with "how diversity management ethos influences administrative operations and [how] the cultural background of the emerging African-American bureaucracy influences public decisions and solutions. . . ." As Burton and Tryman suggest, the more urban government reflects the community diversity that encompasses its African-American constituency, the greater are the expectations placed on African-American leaders to function as change agents for policies and solutions to long-standing problems, which supersede the equity and diversity issues of representative government. Winn and Cory-Scruggs in chapter 7 discuss "the organization's or management's responsibilities 'to' the new entrants entering public organizations."[11] They refer to these individuals as "diversity newcomers" and note that these individuals are confronted with the challenge of assuming "the same values and behavior" necessary to fit into a homogeneous organization dominated by white males. For Winn and Cory-Scruggs, this challenge can be met by being "ethically responsible" public administrators. In this way, diversity newcomers can "respond to bureaucratic values and set higher standards than their predecessors."

Networking as a way of enhancing a minority public professional's marketability in an era of diversity is the central focus of chapter 8. Rich provides an overview of research on network behavior, discusses networking literature, points out why networking is needed by minority public professionals, distinguishes between networking and loose coupling, provides insights into the role of professional conferences in networking, explains self-command capital and networking, and argues for finding the structural hole in the organization in order to advance one's career. Last, Rich notes the many barriers to networking. In chapter 9, Green, Lewis, and Watkins point to the importance of diversity in an important policy arena—the health professions. They discuss the rationale of having diversity in the health care professions to meet the needs of medically underserved populations and solve problems associated with achieving diversity in the health professions.

In chapter 10, Bailey argues for culturally competent public administration to maximize effective service delivery that reflects the cultural influence of their clients. She notes that culturally competent practices have been adopted in social work practices, health care delivery, and psychiatric services, and cultural competency skills in public administration are required for an increasingly multicultural society. In chapter 11, Mathews, by way of an extensive literature review, develops and presents a human resources guide for increasing productivity using cultural diversity management policies and practices. Mathews captures literature written mostly in the 1990s (with some written earlier) to establish the foundation for the guide, followed by some new millennium literature. In the concluding chapter 12, written by Rice and White, achieving and maintaining diversity in public organizations is seen as requiring a comprehensive strategy involving a major transformational process. They conclude that public organizations that achieve and manage diversity well see diversity as a "business necessity" and have a growing realization of how diversity can result in a more effective way of working and interacting in the interest of organizational productivity and individual well-being and satisfaction.

As you read through each chapter, you will find concepts, terms, and phrases that are highlighted. This indicates that these concepts, terms, and phrases are closely related to diversity developments in the literature. I recommend that you familiarize yourself with these concepts, terms, and phrases. They are likely to become highly useful in the era of diversity.

References

Bullard, Angel M., and Deil S. Wright. 1993. "Circumventing the Glass Ceiling: Women Executives in American State Governments." *Public Administration Review* 53 (3): 189–202.

Button, James, and Walter Rosenbaum. 1990. "Gray Power, Gray Peril, or Gray Myth? The Political Impact of the Aging in Local Sunbelt Politics." *Social Science Quarterly* 71(1) (March): 25–38.

Carter, Rochelle. 1996. "Black Entertainment TV, Microsoft Team On Line." *USA Today,* February 2: B-1.

Cornwell, Christopher, and J. Edward Kellough. 1994. "Women, Minorities and Federal Government Agencies: Examining New Evidence from Panel Data." *Public Administration Review* 54 (3): 265–70.

Drucker, Peter. 1989. "Peter Drucker's 1990s: The Futures That Have Already Happened." *The Economist* (October 21–27): 19–20, 24.

Friedman, M. and R.H. Rosenman. 1974. *Type A Behavior and Your Heart.* New York: Knopf.

Frieman, J. 1990. "Do Women Manage Differently?" *Fortune* 122 (15): 115–18.

Fuller, Rex, and Richard Schoenberger. 1991. "The Gender Salary Gap: Do Academic Achievement, Internship Experience, and College Major Make a Difference?" *Social Science Quarterly* 72 (4) (December): 715–26.

Gómez, Maria J. 1994. "Latinos/Latinas at Work: Cultural Considerations." *Public Manager* 23 (3) (fall): 36–38.

Gore, Al, and Executive Office of the President. 1993. *From Red Tape To Results: Creating a Government that Works Better and Costs Less.* Washington, DC: U.S. Government Printing Office.

Grant, J. 1988. "Women as Managers: What They Can Offer To Organizations." *Journal of Organizational Dynamics* 16 (3): 56–63.

Gregory, A. 1990. "Are Women Different and Why Are Women Thought to be Different? Theoretical and Methodological Perspectives." *Journal of Business Ethics* 9: 257–66.

Guajardo, S.A. 1996. "Minority Employment in U.S. Federal Agencies: Continuity and Change." *Public Personnel Management* 25 (2): 199–208.

Guy, Mary E. 1993. "Three Steps Forward, Two Steps Backward: The Status of Women's Integration into Public Management." *Public Administration Review* 53 (4): 283–84.

Henig, Jeffrey R. 1990. "Choice in Public Schools: An Analysis of Transfer Requests Among Magnet Schools." *Social Science Quarterly* 71 (1) (March): 69–72.

Herring, Cedric et al. 1991. "Racially Based Changes in Political Alienation in America." *Social Science Quarterly* 72 (1) (March): 123–34.

Jago, A.G. and V.H. Vroom. 1982. "Sex Differences in the Incidence and Evaluation of Participative Leader Behavior." *Journal of Applied Psychology* 67: 776–83.

Jensen, Marjane, and Judith H. Katz. 1996. "Downsizing and Diversity: Navigating the Path Between Trauma and Opportunity." *Journal of Public Management and Policy* 2 (1) (winter): 22–31.

Johnston, William B., and Arnold H. Packer. 1987. *Workforce 2000: Work and Worker for the 21st Century.* Indianapolis: Hudson Institute.

Jordan, Kenneth A. et al. 1994. "Educating Minorities for Public Service in the Year 2000." *Public Manager* (summer): 51–56.

Kahn, Joan R., and William M. Mason. 1987. "Political Alienation, Cohort Size, and the Easterlin Hypothesis." *American Sociological Review* 53: 155–69.

Kellough, J. Edward. 1990. "Federal Agencies and Affirmative Action for Blacks and Women." *Social Science Quarterly* 71 (1) (March): 83–92.

Kestenbaum, Martin I., and Ronald L. Straight. 1996. "Paperless Grants via the Internet." *Public Administration Review* 56 (1): 114–20.

Kim, Pan Suk, and Gregory B. Lewis. 1994. "Asian-Americans in the Public Service: Success, Diversity, and Discrimination." *Public Administration Review* 54 (3): 285–90.

Korabik, K. 1990. "Androgyny and Leadership Style." *Journal of Business Ethics* 9: 283–92.

———. 1982. "Sex-Role Orientation and Leadership Style." *International Journal of Women's Studies* 5: 328–36.

Kranz, Harry, 1976. *The Participatory Bureaucracy: Women and Minorities in a More Representative Public Service.* Lexington, MA: Lexington Books.

Lipset, S.M., and William Schneider. 1983. *Confidence Gap.* New York: Free Press.

Long, Norton E. 1952. "Bureaucracy and Constitutionalism." *American Political Science Review* 46: 808–18.

McBriarty, Mark. 1988. "Toward the Year 2000: Are We Ready?" *The Bureaucrat* (summer): 8–12.

Meier, Kenneth. 1975. "Representative Bureaucracy: An Empirical Analysis." *American Political Science Review* 69: 527–42.

Moe, Ronald C. 1994. "The 'Reinventing Government' Exercise: Misinterpreting the Problem, Misjudging the Consequences." *Public Administration Review* 54 (2): 111–22.

Mohai, Paul. 1990. "Black Environmentalism." *Social Science Quarterly* 71 (4): 744–65.

Mosher, Frederick C. 1968. *Democracy and the Public Service.* 2d ed. New York: Oxford University Press.

Murdock, Steve H. et al. 2002. *The Texas Challenge in the Twenty-first Century: Implications of Population of Change for the Future of Texas.* Department of Rural Sociology, Department Technical Report 2002–1, Texas A&M University, College Station, Texas.

Murray, Sylvester, Larry D. Terry, Charles A. Washington, and Lawrence F. Keller. 1994. "The Role, Demand, and Dilemmas of Minority Public Administrators: The Herbert Thesis Revisited." *Public Administration Review* 54 (5): 409–17.

Myrtle, Robert C., and Kathleen H. Wilber. 1994. "Designing Service Delivery Systems: Lessons from the Development of Community-Based Systems of Care for the Elderly." *Public Administration Review* 54 (3): 245–52.

Naff, Katherine C. 1994. "Through the Glass: Prospects for the Advancement of Women in the Federal Civil Service." *Public Administration Review* 54 (6): 503–6.

Nobles, Melissa. 2003. "Race, Censuses and Citizenship." In *The Meaning of Difference: American Constructions of Race, Sex and Gender, Social Class and Sexual Orientation.* Karen E. Rosenblum and Toni-Michelle C. Travis, eds. Boston: McGraw Hill, 47–55.

Rice, Mitchell F. 2001. "The Digital Divide and Race in the United States." *Politics, Administration and Change* 36 (July–December): 20–31.

Rosenblum, Karen E. and Toni-Michelle Travis, eds. 2003. *The Meaning of Difference: American Constructions of Race, Sex and Gender, Social Class and Sexual Orientation*. 3d ed. Boston: McGraw Hill.

Rosener, J.B. 1990. "Ways Women Lead." *Harvard Business Review* 68 (6): 119–25.

Rowney, J.I.A., and A.R. Cahoon. 1990. "Individual and Organizational Characteristics of Women in Managerial Leadership." *Journal of Business Ethics* 9: 293–316.

Solomon, C.M. 1989. "The Corporate Response To Work Force Diversity." *Personnel Journal* 6 (8): 43–53.

St. John, Craig, and David Rowe. 1990. "Adolescent Background and Fertility Norms: Implications for Racial Differences in Early Childbearing." *Social Science Quarterly* 71 (1) (March): 152–63.

Stowers, Genie N.L. 1996. "Moving Government On-Line and Policy Analysis." *Public Administration Review* 56 (1): 121–25.

U.S. Department of Commerce, National Telecommunications and Information Administration. October 2000. *Falling Through the Net: Toward Digital Inclusion—A Report on American Access to Technology Tools*.

Van Riper, Paul P. 1958. *History of the United States Civil Service, 1789–1957*. Evanston, IL: Row, Peterson.

Waner, W.L. et al. 1963. *The American Federal Executive*. New Haven, CT: Yale University Press.

White, Harvey L., and Doris Micheaux. 1995. "Diversity as Differences in Ways of Managing: Cultivating an Appreciation for Feminine Styles of Management." *Journal of Public Management and Social Policy* 1 (1): 66–75.

Wolf, James F. et al. 1987. "Greying at the Temples: Demographics of a Public Service Occupation." *Public Administration Review* 47 (2): 190–99.

2

Workforce Diversity Initiatives and Best Practices in Business and Governmental Organizations

Developments, Approaches, and Issues

Mitchell F. Rice and Dhananjaya M. Arekere

It is no accident that business and governmental organizations in the United States are concerned about workplace diversity. The concept of workplace diversity takes into account not only race, ethnicity, and gender, but also includes other ways in which individuals are different from one another, such as age, sexual preference, and disability (Thomas 1990, 1991). *The Diversity Dictionary* (1996) defines diversity as differing cultures, languages, ethnicities, races, sexual orientations, religious sects, abilities, classes, ages, and national origins of individuals in an institution, workplace, or community. Business and governmental organizations have implemented workforce diversity initiatives to better serve their employees and external constituents while simultaneously enhancing productivity, effectiveness, and sustained competitiveness. Subsequently, a number of organizations' diversity initiatives have been identified as "best practices" and, as such, it is believed that they can be adopted or replicated in any workplace. This chapter discusses best practices, developments, approaches, and issues involving workforce diversity initiatives in business and governmental organizations. The first section discusses organizations' interest in workplace diversity and diversity programming initiatives. The second section examines the components necessary for organizations to receive best practices recognition in diversity programming. The third section addresses the potential problem of diversity and glass ceiling audits as important diagnostic tools for diversity programming initiatives. The conclusion questions whether replicating diversity best practices approaches is the most appropriate strategy because there are not yet clear and overall standards of success and practice.

Organizations' Interest in Workforce Diversity

Diversity as a Productivity and Risk Management Issue

For organizations, workplace diversity is both a productivity issue and a risk management issue. As a productivity issue, the lack of workplace diversity initiatives may adversely affect employee relations, employee attitudes, employee retention and turnover, and employee hiring (lack of employment applications from diverse groups of individuals). From a risk management perspective, inattention to diversity can negatively impact a business's bottom line, profit earnings, or in the case of the public sector, lead to clients' dissatisfaction with public service delivery organizations. Further, a lack of organizational workplace diversity can be a precursor to discrimination lawsuits. An employee's chances of winning discrimination claims in the business sector increased by nearly 30 percent over the five-year period from 1994 to 1999—from 45 percent to 72 percent, respectively (Grenseng-Pophal 2001). The median award increased by nearly $100,000 from 1996 to 1999—from $128,000 to $221,612 (Grenseng-Pophal 2001).

During the 1990s, large, well-known U.S. businesses were hit with legal settlements or class action discriminatory claims involving millions of dollars. Texaco was ordered to pay out $176 million (Church 1997; Adams 1999; Palmer 2000; Bland and Hall 2001). Texaco also agreed to establish an independent equality and tolerance task force, monitor hiring and promotions for five years, and implement an unprecedented company-wide diversity and sensitivity program (Rosin 1998). Bell Atlantic, Microsoft, Coca-Cola, and Denny's Restaurants were among other large businesses defending themselves against class-action discrimination claims (Bland and Hall 2001). Coca-Cola agreed to settle a class action discrimination claim for $192.5 million. Coca-Cola further agreed to provide $1.5 million to establish a Diversity Leadership Academy (King 2001) and to create an oversight task force of its diversity efforts (Palmer

2000; Harris 2001). In the Microsoft claim, African-American employees alleged discrimination through evaluations, being passed
over for promotions, and higher forced resignations (Bland and Hall
2001). Thus, it seems that the financial stakes relating to organizational diversity have become quite costly.

Another important reason large U.S. companies are interested
in workforce diversity is the rising spending power of minority
groups. For Fortune 500 companies, the spending power of minority groups has been estimated to be $650 billion (Sappal 2001).
Nationally, it has been estimated that Latinos spend more than $450
billion annually (Olivera 2002). In the Dallas/Fort Worth area it is
estimated Latinos spend more than $8 billion annually (Olivera
2002). One CEO of a major company makes the relationship between corporate diversity and minority economic power quite clear
by noting: "As the economic strength of the minority community
continues to climb, those that embrace corporate citizenship and
diversity within their companies, their customer base, their distribution system, their dealer network and their supply chain will
have a competitive edge over those that do not" (*Hispanic,* special
advertising section, 2000). Similarly, IBM, who conducts business
in more than 160 countries, notes that: "Our strategic imperative
says emerging markets are growing—minorities and women en-
compass a $1.3 trillion market—and we cannot afford to ignore
that" (Shum and Moss 2002, 10, 14).

As a way of emphasizing the importance of diversity in corporate
strategy, Fortune 500 companies in the United States have created
high-level positions such as director of diversity (Best Foods), manager of corporate diversity and work life planning (Ford Motor Co.),
director of work force diversity (Hewlett-Packard), director of
workforce diversity operations (IBM), and director of equal oppor-
tunity/affirmative action and global diversity (Lucent Technologies)
(see White 1998). These positions are supported by diversity leadership councils, internal diversity steering committees, diversity field
input committees, external diversity advisory boards, employee diversity action councils, and/or similar other initiatives (*Fortune* 2001).
It is estimated that some three-fourths of the largest corporations in
the United States have some form of diversity management program in place (Egan and Bendick 2001) and nearly 60 percent have
staff members dedicated to these issues (Caudron 1998).

The Federal Government's Interest in Diversity

For governmental organizations, these changing population demographics will impact who delivers public services, how public services are delivered, and to whom. As a result, it is paramount that public organizations implement diversity programs as a necessary step to be able to compete and hire the best-qualified persons in the changing workforce. By the late 1990s, federal agencies in particular had become much more aware of the need for diversity programs. Naff and Kellough (2001) identify at least 120 federal agencies that have implemented formal and informal diversity initiatives. Some federal agencies with formal diversity programming initiatives include: National Institutes of Health (Workforce Diversity Initiative); National Institute for Standards and Technology (Diversity Program Office); Bureau of Land Management (Workforce Diversity Program); Mine Safety and Health Administration (Diversity Action Plan); and Substance Abuse and Mental Health Services Administration (Diversity Programs) (see Naff and Kellough 2001). Those federal agencies with no formal diversity initiatives focus primarily on traditional equal employment opportunity concerns with some attention to diversity training and/or diversity awareness (Naff and Kellough 2001). The agencies that have formal diversity initiatives have more comprehensive diversity programming including diversity councils, diversity strategic plans, diversity training and awareness, and/or a diversity component in a supervisor/manager performance evaluation plan (Naff and Kellough 2001). The discussion below highlights the actions of several important federal agencies regarding diversity initiatives and managing diversity.

The U.S. Merit System Protection Board

In February 1993, the U.S. Merit System Protection Board (USMSPB), the federal agency statutorily responsible for ensuring that federal agencies adhere to merit principles in hiring and managing employees, convened a "symposium on diversity" in which the leadership of USMSPB and other federal officials and human resources experts were invited participants. This symposium may have been among the first of federal efforts to bring together representatives from different agencies in one forum to discuss diversity. The goal of the symposium was "to heighten awareness of what managing diversity is all about and what agencies are doing in that area" (USMSPB 1993, 5). The symposium consisted of two interactive group panel sessions. The first panel session, titled "The Challenges of Managing Diversity in the Federal Workplace," was asked to address specific questions relating to diversity. These questions were:

1. Can and should the government manage workforce diversity?
2. How does managing diversity differ from federal equal employment opportunity (EEO) and affirmative action?
3. What challenges are associated with managing a diverse workforce? (5)

The second panel session, entitled "Implementing Diversity Programs in Federal Agencies," focused on the actions agencies are taking to manage diversity and provided examples of what has worked and not worked (5). This symposium noted that diversity initiatives were being considered at the Internal Revenue Service, Environmental Protection Agency, National Aeronautics and Space Administration, and the Federal Aviation Administration (USMSPB 1993, 6–9).

Participants on these panels included: the director of Federal Human Resource Management Issues at the General Accounting Office; director of the Office of Federal Operations at the Equal Employment Opportunity Commission; director of Human Resources at the Library of Congress; director of Personnel at the Small Business Administration; director of Career Development and Training at the General Services Administration; diversity officer at the Treasury Department; manager, Human Resource Management Division, Federal Aviation Administration; Hispanic program coordinator, Environmental Protection Agency; and diversity officer, Internal Revenue Service. The following points were highlighted at the Symposium (USMSPB 1993, 6–9):

- When diversity is managed well, all workers are valued and included.
- Managing diversity improves productivity.
- Diversity alone is not enough.
- Accountability and incentives are important.
- Support and involvement must be broadened.
- Diversity programs differ from EEO and affirmative action efforts.

- Managing diversity is a process.
- There is no one way to manage diversity.

These highlighted points led to the following key conclusions at the symposium (USMSPB 1993, 9):

- Managing diversity is part of being a manager. It is not a special task to be assigned to certain managers or staff.
- Agencies should not view diversity as something they can choose to value or not; valuing diversity is related to adhering to the merit principles of Title 5 that govern civil service personnel management.
- Managing diversity is part of getting the job done efficiently; since it engenders supportive environments that promote the best use of all workers. . . . Failure to manage diversity appropriately will waste scarce resources.
- Just as there is no single approach to being a good manager, there is no single approach to managing diversity well. Each agency should develop an approach tailored to its own needs, cultures, problems, resources, missions, and external obligations.
- Achieving a diverse workforce and managing diversity are tasks that may have to overlap. An agency can not wait until it has the desired workforce diversity before it works to create a welcoming, supportive environment for all its employees.

The U.S. Department of Labor

The secretary of one of the largest federal agencies, the U.S. Department of Labor (USDOL), in 1997 established a diversity task force comprised of fourteen senior-level officials, to: "(1) assess the status of our [USDOL] efforts in achieving a diverse workforce; (2) identify issues and challenges that may arise in achieving our [USDOL] goal; and (3) present recommendations to me [the secretary] on how and what improvements are needed to achieve greater diversity and equal opportunity in DOL" (USDOL 1998, Appendix A). The task force formulated a set of recommendations that included the following (USDOL 1998, Appendix B):

- Communicate our values
  (Emphasize workplace values)

Table 2.1

USOPM's Three Stages in Building and Maintaining a Diverse Workforce

Requirements		
Stage 1 Positioning the agency	Stage 2 Designing and implement- ing a diversity program	Stage 3 Sustaining commitment
Strong top level commit- ment and support	Outreach and hiring	Monitoring results
Agency demographic and workforce profile analyses	Rewards and recognition program	Accountability procedures
Cultural or environmental assessment	A supportive work environment	Celebrating success activities
Future workforce planning analysis	Professional development and training opportunities	

Source: USOPM (2000).

- Be accountable
  (Emphasize manager performance in workplace values)
  (Emphasize a reward system for making contributions to diversity initiatives and workplace values)
- Expand growth opportunities and employee self-development
- Improve recruiting
- Include and inform

U.S. Office of Personnel Management

In June 2000 the U.S. Office of Personnel Management (USOPM) released a guide entitled *Building and Maintaining a Diverse, High Quality Workforce: A Guide for Federal Agencies* (USOPM 2000). The purpose of the guide was "to help Federal agencies develop an effective program to build and maintain a diverse, high-quality workforce" and to "provide agencies a basic blueprint of the actions they can take to build and maintain a diverse, high quality workforce . . ." (1–2). The guide emphasizes three stages in building and maintaining a diverse workforce (USOPM 2000). These three stages must become critical parts of an overall diversity programming initiative. Table 2.1 shows the three stages and the required components of each.

Table 2.2

SES Leadership Competency Differences Between Cultural Awareness and Leveraging Diversity

Old cultural awareness	New leveraging diversity
Initiates and manages cultural change within the organization to impact organizational effectiveness.	Recruits, develops, and retains a diverse high-quality workforce in an equitable manner. Leads and manages an inclusive workplace that maximizes the talents of each person to achieve sound business results.
Values cultural diversity and other individual differences in the workforce.	Respects, understands, values, and seeks out individual differences to achieve the vision and mission of the organization.
Ensures that the organization builds on these differences and that employees are treated in a fair and equitable manner.	Develops and uses measures and rewards to hold self and others accountable for achieving results that embody the pinciples of diversity.

Source: LaChance (2001); USOPM (2001).

Further, the Federal Human Resources Management Council in January 2001 issued a "Memorandum for Heads of Departments" announcing that the leadership competency for diversity has been revised from "Cultural Awareness" to "Leveraging Diversity" (LaChance 2001; USOPM 2001). According to this memorandum, the revision "stems from research that shows high performing leaders and organizations are those that view diversity as an asset and make diversity a business imperative" (LaChance 2001; USOPM 2001). The memorandum is applicable to Executive Core Qualifications under the Senior Executive Service. Table 2.2 compares the leadership competency differences between "Cultural Awareness" and "Leveraging Diversity."

Prior to the action of the Human Resources Management Council and before the release of the guidebook, USOPM in September 1999 launched the seminar "Diversity: A Business Necessity for the Millennium" (USOPM 1999). The objectives of the seminar were "to improve the quality of leadership in the federal workforce by equipping executives and managers with the skills needed to capitalize on workplace diversity" and to "enable our managers and executives to acquire the necessary skills to develop workplace diversity as an organizational advantage" (USOPM 1999). The seminar was a response to former President Clinton's "vision of creating a government for the 21st Century that looks like America" (USOPM 1999).

Other Federal Agencies

Other federal agencies visibly display on their websites their agencies' commitment to diversity by noting the offices and/or individuals responsible for diversity. For example, the U.S. Department of the Interior (USDOI) indicates contact information for all eight offices and the head office who oversee diversity efforts (USDOI n.d.). The eight offices include the Bureau of Land Management, the Bureau of Indian Affairs, U.S. Geological Survey, National Park Service, U.S. Fish and Wildlife, Office of Surface Mining, and Minerals Management Service (USDOI n.d.). The website of the National Institute of Mental Health identifies the functions and duties of the Office of Diversity and Employee Advocacy Programs (USNIMH 2000).

In retrospect, it seems that two societal conditions (minority purchasing power and changing demographics) in themselves require that businesses and governmental organizations create and maintain an inclusive and diverse workforce to respond to a changing customer base and public service clientele. Stated another way, workforce diversity is a profitable resource for business organizations and an important service delivery asset for governmental organizations. The operating assumption behind workforce diversity is: "different types of employees increase productivity and effectiveness because people with different characteristics have different attitudes, work styles, and cultural knowledge, which makes them assets to corporations [and organizations] in a changing world" (Edelman, Fuller, and Mara-Drita 2002, 1618). Miller and Katz (1995) observe that "diversity leads to greater strength [and] High-Performing Inclusive Organizations utilize diversity as a source of added value—a resource crucial to the organization's success." They continue by noting that "diversity gives a group a greater range of creativity, problem-solving, and decision-making skills, and a potential for seeing 360 degrees of the landscape" (Miller and Katz 1995).

Developments in Diversity Best Practices

Wise and Tschirhart (2000, 387) note that there exists among businesses "an underlying assumption that diversity produces positive results . . . through heightened group commitment and individual satisfaction." Wentling and Palma-Rivas (1998, 242) observe that organizations implement and manage diversity for reasons of improving productivity and maintaining competitiveness. Similarly, Bowen, Bok, and Burkhart (1999, 141) argue that "how well an enterprise works—how productive and successful it is in a highly competitive global economy—depends on whether it has the best people and people who are comfortable working across lines of race, class, religion, and background." The International Personnel Management Association and the National Association of State Personnel Executives (IPMA/NASPE) Benchmarking Committee points out that "diversity efforts in the workplace facilitate the exchange of new perspectives, improve problem solving by inviting different ideas, and create a respectful, accepting work environment, all of which makes good business sense."

Further, a report by the U.S. Department of Commerce and Vice President Al Gore's National Partnership for Reinventing Government Benchmark Study, *Best Practices in Achieving Workforce Diversity* (1999, 1), offers a similar point by noting that: Organizations that promote and achieve a diverse workplace will attract and retain quality employees and increase consumer loyalty. For public organizations, it also translates into effective delivery of essential services to communities that have diverse needs. The primary objective of the NPR study was to identify "best practices used by leading organizations to achieve workforce diversity" (3) in order for the federal civilian sector "to learn more about diversity from world-class organizations" (4). After identifying more than 600 business and governmental organizations that were recognized for their diversity efforts, the report examined the diversity practices of 65 organizations that were viewed as having "world class" exemplary programs in achieving workforce diversity. However, the report did not identify these organizations.

Relatedly, after examining findings from a 2001 survey of companies on the Fortune 1000 list, the Society for Human Resource Management (SHRM) concluded that "companies that recognize

the strategic value of human capital are the companies that succeed" (SHRM 2002a). The survey, which has been conducted for
four consecutive years, was sent to all Fortune 1000 companies
and the 200 largest privately held firms in the United States. The
respondent companies were measured in fifteen qualitative and
quantitative categories, including percent of minority new hires,
whether the company ties performance reviews and bonuses to
diversity goals, the number of minorities in leadership positions
throughout the management chain, and number of minorities among
the top fifty in salary (Chen and Hackman 2000). The survey findings from 136 respondent companies revealed that an overwhelming percentage of the survey respondents believed "that diversity
initiatives help an organization maintain a competitive advantage"
(91 percent), improves corporate culture (83 percent), leads to better
employee morale (79 percent), higher retention (76 percent), and
decreases complaints and litigation (68 percent) (SHRM 2002a).
Ironically, the number one ranked company according to the survey results for two years in a row was Advantica, the owner of
Denny's Restaurants. As noted earlier, the restaurant chain had been
besieged with discrimination claims from African-Americans in
the early 1990s (Chen and Hackman 2000; Kahn 2001). Shoney's
Restaurants, a company with a similar history of discrimination
claims, was ranked thirty-six on the 2000 survey and has been in
the top fifty in each of the preceding three years (Mehta 2000).
Other well-known companies ranked in the 2001 top ten on *Fortune* magazine's list include Fannie Mae, McDonald's, Xerox, SBC
Communications, Lucent Technologies, and BellSouth (Kahn
2001). Fannie Mae, ranked number two on the list, was the highest-
ranked company that had an African-American CEO. McDonald's,
ranked number three, was the list's top purchaser of goods from
minority businesses ("America's 50 Best Companies for Minorities," 122–23).

The Glass Ceiling Commission's 1995 fact-finding report, *Good
for Business: Making Full Use of the Nation's Human Capital,* cites
several studies which note that implementing diversity initiatives
positively affects an organization's bottom line. A finding from one
interesting study noted by the report was that the Standard & Poor's
500 companies rated in the top 100 in leveraging diversity and managing change effectively (i.e., hiring and advancement of minorities

and women; compliance with EEOC and other regulatory requirements; and reduced employee litigation) averaged more than twice
the investment returns than companies rated in the bottom 100 (Glass
Ceiling Commission 1995). The study conducted by Wright et al.
(1995, 284) reports that "the favorable market reaction to announce-
ments of corporations' winning [diversity and affirmative action]
awards may be a result of investors' realization that the corporations
might have lower costs than other companies because they have
lower absenteeism, turnover, and job dissatisfaction levels." Wright
et al. (1995, 284) go on to say "discriminatory corporations will not
have the same access to talented human resources. . . . Consequently
firms with discriminatory practices may have less talented and committed work forces, high operating costs because of high turnover,
absenteeism, and job dissatisfaction, poor reputation with their diverse customers, less creative cultures, poor problem solving, and
low adaptability." Wright et al. (1995, 284) conclude, "The prevalent organizational ethnic and gender bias should be eradicated . . .
because it does not make *economic* sense [emphasis added]. As the
climate of competition becomes more intense, no enterprise can afford the senseless practice of discrimination."

The Glass Ceiling fact-finding report (1995), which was an "environmental scan" of glass ceiling perceptions of company barriers
and initiatives in the private sector relating to women and minorities, identifies several common factors in businesses that lead to
successful glass ceiling or diversity initiatives. These factors are:

- They have CEO support.
- They are part of the strategic business plan.
- They are specific to the organization.
- They are inclusive; they do not exclude white, non-Hispanic
  men.
- They address preconceptions and stereotypes.
- They emphasize and require accountability up and down the
  line.
- They track progress.
- They are comprehensive (9).

The NPR (1999) study identified similar critical success factors to
evaluate best practices:

- Leadership and management commitment
- Employee involvement
- Strategic planning
- Sustained investment
- Diversity indicators
- Accountability, measurement, and evaluation
- Linkage to organizational goals and objectives (3).

Among the successful companies the Glass Ceiling Commission report (1995) identified as eliminating glass ceiling barriers while remaining competitive and profitable are: The Xerox Corporation, Procter & Gamble, and IBM (47–53).

State and Local Government Best Practices

In 1998 the IPMA/NASPE Benchmarking Committee conducted a survey in the areas of recruitment and selection, recruitment and retention of information technology staff, and training (Reichenberg 2001). About 350 public sector organizations responded to the survey. An important goal of the survey was to identify best practices organizations in diversity. Based on the survey findings, the Benchmarking Committee identified the states of Oklahoma, Washington, Wisconsin, and the city of St. Petersburg, Florida, as best practice organizations. The organizations had the following common diversity practices that made them best practices organizations (Reichenberg 2001):

- The development of a formal process that is contained in laws, rules, or procedures. Both human and financial resources are devoted to the program. In best practice organizations, diversity is a process that is integrated, ongoing, and measurable.
- Diversity efforts are primarily decentralized, with a central governing body outlining the requirements of the plans, and individual agencies and departments having their own plans tailored to their specific needs. This reinforces a sense of ownership and ensures that managing diversity both has top-level support and is a reality throughout the organization.
- In best practice organizations, diversity training is not limited to managers, but is extended throughout the workforce. Suc-

cessful organizations incorporate diversity into mentoring efforts, leadership training, and management-by-results programs.

- Best practice organizations utilize workforce data and demographics to compare statistics reported for the civilian labor force. . . .
- Best practice organizations have established a review committee that is responsible for establishing policies, providing technical assistance, reviewing/approving plans, and monitoring progress toward the achievement of goals.
- Effective diversity programs also link recruitment, development, and retention strategies to organizational performance. They integrate employee development processes and map career paths to see what critical skills are necessary for advancement, then communicate these skills to employees and provide training.
- Accountability for results of diversity programs is another attribute of best practice organizations. Accountability is determined through the use of metrics, surveys, focus groups, customer surveys, management and employee evaluations, and training and education evaluations. . . .

Approaches for Advancing Best Practices

Other studies suggest that organizations having widely recognized diversity programs and diversity results "will attract the best and brightest employees to a company" (see, for example, SHRM 2002b). Thus, the public's perception of which organizations are rated as having good, excellent, or outstanding diversity programs is an important intangible asset. Being listed in a guide, such as *Black Enterprise* magazine's "Best Companies for Blacks to Work" or *Fortune* magazine's "America's 50 Best Companies for Minorities" (2001), provides a company a recruiting advantage in maintaining a diverse workforce with the best and the brightest. Therefore, it is important that organizations conduct a *"diversity recruitment quotient"* (Sappal 2001), a process in which an organization's materials and environment are analyzed from a minority perspective, to determine why the organization does not receive employment applications from diverse applicants (Bland and Hall 2001). The contemporary literature on diversity management sees diversity as an organizational necessity directly linked to organizational survival (see, for example, Edelman, Fuller, and Mara-Drita 2001) because it is a profitable resource in more ways than one. Further, organizational diversity initiatives represent *"managerialized law."* That is, while diversity is not formal civil rights law, external legal ideas and rules have been infused with managerial values as a means of rationalizing and supporting diversity programming (Edelman, Fuller, and Mara-Drita 2001).

Moreover, expensive employer discrimination settlements have led to the rise of a new type of insurance called *"employee practices insurance,"* with agents who examine a business's antidiscrimination policies for weaknesses (Church 1997). To determine a business's potential insurability and premium to charge, an insurer gauges the business's vulnerability to a discriminatory suit by examining answers to the following questions:

- What is the annual rate of turnover for the past four years?
- What is the number of involuntary terminations in the past two years?
- Does the company have written procedures for termination, hiring, and discipline?
- What are the numbers of women and minorities in senior management positions? (Church 1997)

As a result, it has become necessary for organizations to conduct what is referred to as a *diversity audit* or *glass ceiling audit* and develop benchmarks to monitor and/or measure diversity progress. Some kind of comparative process must take place between baseline data and intervention strategies developed that has clear, measurable objectives. This process assesses the diversity program's strengths, weaknesses, and impacts to determine what changes in program content and delivery may be necessary. One area that must be assessed is the duration of the diversity initiative. Is it short, intermediate, or long-term? Rynes and Rosen (1995) view the length of diversity programs as vitally important. They argue that the longer the duration of the diversity program, the greater likelihood of program success (Rynes and Rosen 1995, 250). This observation is strongly supported in the literature (see, for example, Caudron 1993).

Another area that must be assessed covers the type of diversity training methodologies utilized. The training methodology literature has long stressed selecting and utilizing the appropriate methodological approach (Nemetz and Christensen 1996). For diversity training the different methodologies include psychotherapeutic (participative) sensitivity training, dissonance creation, cultural awareness, and legal awareness (Nemetz and Christensen 1996). Psychotherapeutic approaches involve participative group therapy. Sensitivity training involves sensitizing individuals to situations and feelings of discrimination. Dissonance creation uses cognitive dissonance to change attitudes. Cultural awareness discusses cultural differences, stereotypes, and unintentional slights and biases. Legal awareness involves explaining discrimination laws, activities that violate the law, and the consequences of violations (Nemetz and Christensen 1996). It is important that the diversity training methodology utilized is appropriate and fits the findings from the diversity audit, because training and education is the first step in diversity programming (Wentling and Palma-Rivas 1998). The key training evaluation questions are: Did the diversity training methodology employed accomplish what it intended to accomplish? Did the target individuals respond to the training itself? Did some change in behavior or attitude occur? The answers to these questions may dictate the survival of the overall diversity program.

A Diversity/Glass Ceiling Audit

What Is a Diversity Audit?

A diversity initiative or program should not be created and implemented in a haphazard manner, without direction and without purpose. A most important question is: What are the reasons for beginning a diversity initiative? Or, stated another way, what steps must the organization take to foster and facilitate diversity and how must this process begin? At a multistate, global enterprise a diversity audit project consisted of the following: "An audit team, diverse in its own membership, is assigned to visit each site and conduct one-on-one interviews with the employees. The team spends three or four days at each facility with about 10 percent of the employees. The interviews are set up and carried out with confidentiality. The team also reviews policies and demographics and does a walkthrough of the facility, looking for inappropriate materials, postings or graffiti that might suggest a hostile working environment. After the audit, feedback is provided to the management of the site and sent to . . . headquarters" (Grenseng-Pophal 2001).

Thomas (1999, 59) sees a diversity audit as focusing on "determining how selected groups of employees are experiencing the organization." A *diversity audit* "allows the employer to uncover hidden perceptions or confirm perceived biases before an incident of harassment or discrimination occurs" (Amalfe and Akawie n.d.). Stated another way, a diversity audit determines the prevailing diversity climate in the organization; specifically, opportunities available to women and minorities and how these opportunities are perceived. *Diversity climate* "refers to employee behaviors and attitudes that are grounded in perceptions of the organizational context related to women and minorities" (Barak, Cherin, and Berkman 1998, 83). A diversity audit should not be confused with a *cultural audit*, which systemically "examines the organization's core assumptions and their manifestations with the goal of describing both the organization's present state and foundations for it" (Thomas 1999, 5a). Although both kinds of audits are useful to an organization, conducting the incorrect audit would generate data for the wrong purpose.

An important component of a diversity audit is the use of an *employee survey* and/or *focus group* to take the pulse of the organization. The survey should include responses from various positions and ranks and from various members of both management and subordinate groups in the organization (see White 1998). The tools of the audit must be carefully tailored to the organization and devised to provide enough demographic data to pinpoint issues and problems (SHRM 2002c). The audit must be implemented in such a way as to encourage employee participation. Once data is obtained, the question becomes: To what extent is the data broken down and what actions result from the survey? The survey should focus on some or all of the following areas:

- What are the demographics of your customer/client base (e.g., age, income, gender, education, ethnicity, etc.)?
- How many languages are spoken by the customers/clients?
- In how many countries does your organization operate?
- How much does employee turnover cost your company?
- How much does your company spend annually on recruitment?
- How much have discrimination/harassment suits cost your organization in the past year (in both legal fees and settlements)?
- How frequently does intergroup conflict arise?

- Are your policies and benefits attractive to potential diverse recruits?
- Is your organization losing top talent because people do not feel valued, included, or heard?
- Do all employees feel that their talents and skills are well rewarded?
- Is there some career advancement possibility for employees and a focus on developing people internally?
- Is diversity reflected in your procurement policies and among your suppliers? (see Society for Human Resources Management 2002c)

Glass Ceiling Audit

Beginning in 1990 the U.S. Department of Labor (USDOL) launched the Glass Ceiling Review. This initiative "examines corporate processes, methodologies, practices that promote employees to the top or create barriers to upward mobility" (see American Corporate Counsel Association 1996). Companies can receive a glass ceiling audit in one of two ways: as a federal contractor or subcontractor, or if a Title VII or state civil rights action is involved. Although a glass ceiling audit is, in many ways, different from a diversity audit, it seeks very similar information and data about a company's practices and culture and the extent to which it values individuals and provides an environment that helps them succeed. Following the procedures in the Office of Contract Compliance Training Manual, USDOL will generally request enormous amounts of information relating to hiring practices, as well as organizational charts, information on compensation and bonus patterns, performance appraisals, perks, promotion rates, termination procedures, diversity initiatives, training and development, and awards programs (American Corporate Counsel Association 1996). If a company is found in compliance, it will receive a letter that indicates no deficiencies. If a company is found not in compliance, it will receive a letter pointing out deficiencies to be corrected in a specified period of time. Obviously, organizations operate most efficiently and effectively when events are consistent, routine, and predictable. Diversity and glass ceiling audits attempt to reduce or eliminate unpredictability by detecting and correcting biases and problems relating to unfair and disparate treatment of employees. Such audits result in a large base of comparative data that is instrumental in the development of a diversity monitoring system. The bottom line is that audits seek to identify and avert discrimination problems before they become detrimental to the organization. Audits of this type are not inexpensive. They are conservatively estimated to cost at least $100,000 (MacDonald 1993).

Conclusion

When embarking on diversity initiatives, many organizations turn to approaches and methods that have received "best practices" recognition. This observation leads to critically important questions. Would it be better to follow the successful practices of others, or should an organization learn from the failures of others? Or, simply put, should an organization in examining best practices look closely at the worst practices for diversity change efforts? These questions are important because the literature, while noting best practices, does not identify clear standards of best practices success. According to Thomas (1999, 59), "managers [or businesses] risk discontinuities as they bounce from one best practice to another." Despite these observations, there are clear indications of what *not* to do when establishing diversity initiatives. Frost (2001) identifies several "worst practices" for diversity change efforts. Some of these are:

- Senior leadership delegating the formation of a diversity philosophy and approach to those in staff positions.
- Focusing the change strategies and actions on the subordinate or excluded groups.
- Creating a series of activities that have no strategic link to business success will only give the appearance of true commitment.
- Beginning a corporate diversity effort focused on customers and external public relations will lead to false expectations (Frost 2001).

Further, organizations in general and governmental organizations in particular clearly need to understand and embrace diversity relative to their particular mission. Mello (1996, 434) points out that "organizations need to consider specifically the dimensions of the purpose and/or strategic objectives of the institution that make diversity important, desirable, or necessary." If the purpose of workplace diversity programming/initiatives is not carefully and clearly articulated, organizations will have no basis on which to focus their efforts. When this is the case, organizations will have difficulty operationalizing diversity. Having a clear purpose is also important because it may reduce the likelihood of short-term controversies that can cause major conflict and dysfunction in an organization. It is important then for top-level executives and managers to develop and promote what the organization expects to gain from embracing diversity. These expectations should be articulated in the context of organizational shared values and a common fate (Chatman et al. 1998). Top-level executives and managers must also demonstrate their support of diversity by their actual behavior. In other words, executive management behavior must be consistent with espoused policy statements on diversity.

Finally, diversity audits can be controversial. The audits could lead to data that may be actionable in discrimination claims. In other words, audits could reveal information about individuals in a company's workplace and show potentially liable deficiencies that could be used in an employment discrimination lawsuit (Grenseng-Pophal 2001). Because of this issue, it has been suggested that a diversity audit be carried out with the assistance of in-house or outside legal counsel. In this way the audit may be seen as protected by attorney/client privilege as long as a nonclient does not examine the data (Grenseng-Pophal 2001). The point here is that, while a business is conducting a diversity audit to assess what is needed in a diversity program, the business must also be aware of the potential for litigation resulting from an audit's findings.

References

Adams, Marc. 1999. "Fair and Square." *HR Magazine* (May): 44.

Amalfe, Christine A., and Heather L. Akawie n.d. "Diversity in the Workplace: The Benefits and Shortcomings of Internal Audits and Surveys." www.acca.com/vl/diversity/oc.html

American Corporate Counsel Association. 1996. "Glass Ceiling Audits." (May–June). www.acca.com/diversecounsel/resources/audits.html

"America's 50 Best Companies for Minorities." 2001. *Fortune* (July 9): 122–27.

Barak, Michael E. Mor et al. 1998. "Organizational and Personal Dimensions in Diversity Climate: Ethnic and Gender Differences in Employee Perceptions." *Journal of Applied Behavioral Science* 34 (1) (March): 82–104.

Bland, Timothy, and Robert D. Hall, Jr. 2001. "Do the Math." *HR Magazine* (June): 121–25.

Bowen, William G., Derek Bok, and Glenda Burkhart. 1999. "A Report Card on Diversity: Lessons for Business from Higher Education." *Harvard Business Review* (January–February): 139–49.

Caudron, Shari. 1993. "Successful Companies Realize that Diversity is a Long-Term Process, Not a Program." *Personnel Journal* 72 (4) (April): 54–55.

———. 1998. "Two Companies' Diversity Efforts Are Screened and Evaluated by the Experts." *Black Enterprise* (February). http://blackenterprise.com/pageopen.asp?source=/archive1998/09/0998–31.htm

Chatman, Jennifer A. et al. 1998. "Being Different Yet Feeling Similar: The Influence of Demographic Composition and Organizational Culture on Work Processes and Outcomes." *Administrative Science Quarterly* 43 (4) (December): 749–80.

Chen, Christine Y., and Jonathan Hackman. 2000. "Best Companies for Minorities: The Top 50." *Fortune* (July 10).

Church, George J. 1997. "On the Job: Equality Pays." *Time* (June 23): 38–39.

Diversity Dictionary. 1996. University of Maryland Diversity Database. www.inform.umd.diversity/reference

Edelman, Lauren B., Sally R. Fuller, and Iona Mara-Drita. 2001. "Diversity Rhetoric and the Managerialization of Law." *American Journal of Sociology* 106 (6) (May): 1589–641.

Egan, Mary Lou, and Marc Bendick Jr. 2001. *Workforce Diversity Initiatives of U.S. Multinational Corporations in Europe.* Washington, DC: Bendick and Egan Economic Consultants, Inc.

Frost, DeLyte D. 2001. "Diversity Worst Practices." www.acca.com/diverse counsel/resources/worstpractices.html

Glass Ceiling Commission. 1995. *Good for Business: Making Full Use of the Nation's Human Capital: A Fact-Finding Report of the Federal Glass Ceiling Commission.* Washington, DC: U.S. Government Printing Office.

Grenseng-Pophal, Lin. 2001. "A Balancing Act on Diversity Audits." *HR Magazine* (November): 87–95.

Harris, Hamil R. 2001. "Alexis Herman Heads Coca-Cola Task Force." *Black Enterprise* (July). http://blackenterprise.com/pageopen.asp/source?=/archive2001/07/0701–05.htm

Kahn, Jeremy. 2001. "Diversity Trumps the Downturn." *Fortune* (July 9): 114–18.

"Keeping Your Edge: Managing a Diverse Corporate Culture." 2001. *Fortune.* www.fortune.com

King, Angela G. 2001. "Another Major Corporation Is Forced to Pay Dearly for Discrimination Practices." *Black Enterprise* (February): 23. http://blackenterprise.com/pageopen.asp?/source=/archive2001/02/0201–01.htm

LaChance, Janice R. 2001. "Transmittal #MSG-021b and Transmittal #MSG-021c: Memorandum for Heads of Departments and Agencies," January 18, *Human Resources Management Council.* www.opm.gov/hrmc/2001/msg-021b.htm

MacDonald, H. 1993. "The Diversity of Industry." *New Republic* 2 (1) (July): 22–25.

Mehta, Stephanie N. 2000. "What Minority Employees Really Want." *Fortune* (July 10). www.fortune.com

Mello, Jeffrey. 1996. "The Strategic Management of Workplace Diversity Initiatives: Public Sector Implications." *International Journal of Public Administration* 19 (3): 425–47.

Miller, Fredrick A., and Judith H. Katz. 1995. "Cultural Diversity as a Developmental Process: The Path from Monocultural Club To Inclusive Organization." *The 1995 Annual: Volume 2, Consulting.* San Diego: Pfeiffer, 267–81.

Naff, Katherine C., and J. Edward Kellough. 2001. *A Changing Workforce: Understanding Diversity Programs in the Federal Government.* Price Waterhouse Coopers, The Business of Government (December).

Nemetz, Patricia L., and Sandra L. Christensen. 1996. "The Challenge of Cultural Diversity: Harnessing a Diversity of Views to Understand Multiculturalism." *Academy of Management Review* 21 (2) (April): 434–62.

Olivera, Mercedes. 2002. "Business Expo Testament To Latinos Clout." *Dallas Morning News*, 30A.

Palmer, Pittershawn. 2000. "Coca-Cola in a Landmark Settlement: Racial Discrimination Suits in Perspective." *Black Enterprise* (November): 28. http://blackenterprise.com/pageopen.asp?/source=/articles/11222000255.htm

Reichenberg, Neil E. 2001. Best Practices in Diversity Management. Paper presented at the United Nations Expert Group Meeting on Managing Diversity in the Civil Service. New York, May 3–4.

Rosin, Hanna. 1998. "Cultural Revolution at Texaco." *New Republic* (February 2): 5–11.

Rynes, Sara, and Benson Rosen. 1995. "A Field Survey of Factors Affecting the Adoption and Perceived Success of Diversity Training." *Personnel Psychology* 48 (2): 247–70.

Sappal, Pepi. 2001. "A Diverse Work Force Demands New Initiatives." www.careerjournal.com/hrcenter/articles/20010518–sappal.html

Shum, Mike, and Jacqueline Waites Moss. 2002. "IBM: A Case Study in Affirmative Action Best Practices." *Diversity Factor* 10 (2) (winter): 101–46.

Society for Human Resource Management. 2002a. "Impact of Diversity Initiatives on the Bottom Line. www.shrm.org/diversity

———. 2002b. "How Can the Results of Our Diversity Initiative Be Measured?" www.shrm.org/diversity

———. 2002c. "What are the Components of a Successful Diversity Initiative?" www.shrm.org/diversity

Soni, Vidu. 2000. "A Twenty-First Century for Diversity in the Public Sector: A Case Study." *Public Administration Review* 60 (5) (September–October): 395–408.

Special Advertising Section. 2000. *Hispanic* (July–August).

Thomas, R. Roosevelt, Jr. 1990. "From Affirmative Action to Affirming Diversity." *Harvard Business Review* 68 (2): 107–17.

———. 1991. *Beyond Race and Gender: Unleashing the Power of Your Total Workforce by Managing Diversity.* New York: Amacom.

———. 1999. "Diversity Management: Some Measurement Criteria." *Employment Relations Today* (winter): 49–62.

U.S. Department of Commerce and Vice President Al Gore's National Partnership for Reinventing Government Benchmarking Study. 1999. *Best Practices in Achieving Workforce Diversity.* Washington, DC.

U.S. Department of Interior. n.d. "Orientation to the U.S. Department of Interior." www.doi.gov/orientation/diversity.html

U.S. Department of Labor. 1998. *An Equal Opportunity Workplace: Recommendations of the Secretary of Labor's Diversity Task Force.* Washington, DC: USDOL.

U.S. Merit System Protection Board. 1993. *The Changing Face of the Federal Workplace: A Symposium on Diversity.* Washington, DC: U.S. Merit System Protection Board.

U.S. National Institute of Mental Health. 2000. "Office of Diversity and Employee Advocacy Programs." www.nimh.nih/odeap/index.cfm

U.S. Office of Personnel Management. 1999. "OPM News Release" (August 11). www.opm.gov/pressrel/diversity.htm

———. 2000. *Building and Maintaining a Diverse, High Quality Workforce: A Guide for Federal Agencies.* Washington, DC: USOPM, Employment Service Diversity Office.

Wentling, Rose Mary, and Nilda Palma-Rivas. 1998. "Current Status and Future Trends of Diversity Initiatives in the Workplace: Diversity Experts' Perspectives." *Human Resource Development Quarterly* 9 (3) (fall): 235–53.

White, Margaret Blackburn. 1998. "Measuring Change." *Diversity Factor* 7 (1) (fall): 2–6.

Wise, Lois Recasino and Mary Tschirhart. 2000. "Examining Empirical Evidence on Diversity Effects: How Useful Is Diversity Research for Public Sectors Managers?" *Public Administration Review* 60 (5) (September–October): 386–94.

Wright, Peter, Stephen P. Ferris, Janine S. Hiller, and Mark Kroll. 1995. "Competitiveness through Management of Diversity: Effects on Stock Price Valuation." *Academy of Management Journal* 38 (1): 272–87.

3

Increased Diversity of the Workforce

Opportunities for Research in Public and Nonprofit Organizations

Blue Wooldridge, Jacqueline Smith-Mason, and Barbara C. Maddox

Changing demographics provide an important opportunity for researchers in public administration to advance management theory and be helpful to practitioners. Jamieson and O'Mara, writing in *Managing Workforce 2000* (1991), suggest that diversity is creating unparalleled workplace challenges. Thus, research that empirically identifies and explores trends is needed to help public practitioners anticipate, understand, and appropriately address the numerous challenges of managing a diverse workforce (Lewis 1995). Yet, in a recent *Public Administration Review* article, Wise and Tschirhart (2000, 390) lamented, "Public management journals have made virtually no contribution to this body of research." They call for greater contributions from public administration scholars. This chapter answers this call by identifying key components of workforce diversity (called "identity groups") and providing current data on their magnitude; briefly reporting some organizational research that suggests significant differences between these groups as the subjects of traditional organizational research; and complementing the call for more research to provide practical information for public and not-for-profit managers. Finally, the chapter suggests areas of future research.

It is conventional wisdom that all individuals are different. However, life attitudes are not randomly distributed through the population. Members of the same "identity groups," say those having the same age, gender, race, and such, have had overlapping life experiences that may, in turn, predispose them toward more or less favorable attitudes about particular company practices and cultures (Mirvis and Kanter 1991).

As one writer on leadership has suggested, understanding the differences in coworkers assists in developing effective work teams now, but assuredly more so in the future (Fairholm 1994). Besides facilitating team relationships, leaders who effectively and appropriately consider the diverse needs and capacities of their people can expect improvement in the overall quality of life on the job (Fairholm 1994). Such understanding is vital in light of the important attributes of high-performing organizations (HPOs), which must: manage by data (Deming 1986; Cornesky, McCool, Byrnes, and Weber 1991); empower employees (Popovich 1998; Crosby 1979; Deming 1986; Juran and Gryna 1988); work through teams (Crosby 1979; Juran and Gryna 1988; Hunt 1992); provide recognition and rewards desired by employees (Lawler 2000; Vroom 1964); depend on shared values, commitment and participation (Popovich 1998; Deming 1986; Crosby 1979); and use technology appropriately (Popovich 1998; Wooldridge 1994a; Goddard 1989). As managers take these attributes into consideration, the implications of workforce demographics must be considered for a balanced approach to achieving HPOs.

Changing Diversity of the U.S. Workforce

The U.S. workforce is rapidly changing, and the Bureau of Labor Statistics, the Hudson Institute's *Workforce 2000* report, and other reports have identified several demographic changes in the U.S. workforce (Fullerton 1991; Fullerton and Toossi 2001). These changes are discussed below.

Gender Diversity

Much of the increase and diversity of the workforce can be attributed to women. For instance, current workforce participation rates of women are very different from the 1950s. "The labor force participation of women stood at 34 percent in 1950 and increased to 60 percent by 2000. The number of women in the labor force rose from 18 million in 1950 to 66 million in 2000" (Toossi 2002, 1).

Dual-Income Couples

Research shows that more than three out of four married employees have spouses or partners who are also employed, an increase from 66 to 78 percent over the past twenty years (Families and Work Institute 1997). Other findings of the institute include: 46 percent of the workforce are parents of children under the age of eighteen, and 20 percent are single parents; and 20 percent of all parents also have responsibilities for raising children and caring for elderly relatives. This is often referred to as the *sandwich generation.*

Older Workers

The U.S. population is growing older because of increased life expectancy and lower birthrates than in past decades. The graying of America is increasingly visible in the workforce. Women are a large proportion of the older working population. According to the U.S. Bureau of Labor Statistics, women represented 38 percent of all older workers in 1975 (age sixty-five and older). In comparison, women accounted for 43 percent of all older workers in 1990. Furthermore, retirement does not mean that men and women completely leave the world of work. Many may reenter and work part-time or fulfill temporary work assignments (Halachmi 1998).

Generational Differences

Yet, the diversity categories discussed above are not the only diversity issues that will be faced by public administrators. Generational differences are emerging in the workforce. Every seven seconds in America, someone turns fifty years old. According to the U.S. Bureau of Labor Statistics, 22 percent of the workforce was over fifty in 1998, but this will grow to almost 27 percent by 2008 (Quaddumi 2001). There are four generations currently in the workforce—*Matures* are about 5 percent of the workforce, *Baby Boomers* are about 45 percent, *Generation Xers* are about 40 percent, and the *Millennial Generation* about 10 percent (*Work & Family Newsbrief* 2002).

As noted earlier, some groups of individuals, because of overlapping life experiences, will react similarly to organizations' policies and procedures. When these "overlapping" life experiences are a result of the timing of their births, this phenomena is referred to as *peer personality*, a set of collective behavioral traits and attitudes that later expresses itself through a generation's life-cycle trajectory (Strauss and Howe 1991, 32). Others refer to these similarities as *age cohorts*—a group of people who share given historical or socially structured life experiences, the effects of which are relatively stable over the course of their lives and serve to distinguish one generation from another (Rosow 1978, as cited in Jurkiewicz and Brown 1998). As Halachmi (1998) points out, every age group presents managers with "age-related" problems. Zemke, Raines, and Filipczak (1999) highlight the generational composition of the workforce in their book entitled *Generations at Work: Managing the Clash of Veterans, Boomers, Xers and Nexters in Your Workplace.* The authors point out that separation by age group and function is fading away. Positions once staffed by older employees are being occupied by younger workers and vice versa. Consequently, each generation brings a different perspective to the workplace and requires human resource management practices congruent with their generational perspectives (Caudron 1997; Corley 1999; Dunn-Cane, Gonzales, and Stewart 1999; Haworth 1997; Jenning 2000; Jurkiewicz and Brown 1998).

Racial and Ethnic Minorities

Immigration and birthrates indicate that by the year 2010 about 38 percent of people under the age of eighteen in the United States will be African-American, Asian, or Hispanic-American. The 2000 census found that the Hispanic population more than doubled during the 1990s and Hispanics have passed African-Americans as the nation's largest minority group. Hispanics make up about 13 percent, African-Americans about 12.7 percent, and Asians about 4 percent of the U.S. population. The Bureau of Labor Statistics data for 1999 indicates that white males will account for only 31.6 percent of new entrants in the workforce during the twenty-first century.

Gay and Lesbian Employees

Sexual orientation has become a mainstream diversity topic for many organizations (*HR Focus* 2002; Lewis 1995). Alfred Kinsey's classic 1948 studies found that about 10 percent of American adults are homosexuals (cited in Kahan and Mulryan 1995). However, more recent research indicates that the gay and lesbian population estimate is between 4 and 7 percent (Kahan and Mulryan 1995, and Zill and Robinson 1995).

Disabled Workers

Approximately 54 million noninstitutionalized Americans have physical, intellectual, or psychiatric disabilities (the term intellectual disability is used instead of cognitive disability and mental retardation, and the term psychiatric disability is used in place of emotional disability). Of these cases, 26 million are classified as having a severe disability. Severe disabilities include Alzheimer's disease, autism, mental retardation, and long-term use of a cane, crutches, walker, or wheelchair. Historically, individuals with disabilities have not fared well in the U.S. labor force (Levitan and Taggart 1977). Census figures indicate that of the 15.6 million working-age adults (ages 16–64) with disabilities, only 34.6 percent were employed in contrast with 79.8 percent of those without disabilities. A preferential hierarchy based on disability type persists, whereby workers with physical disabilities continue to be viewed more positively than workers who have intellectual or psychiatric disabilities (see Hernandez, Keys, and Balcazar 2000).

Contingent Workers and Alternative Work Arrangements

As a result of changing demographics, nontraditional work arrangements are increasing. A survey of CEOs in Fortune 500 companies shows that 44 percent rely more on temporary, part-time, leased, and contract workers than they did five years ago, and 44 percent expect to rely more on external workers in the next five years than they do now (Fierman 1994). These workers are referred to as *contingent workers*. Based on the Bureau of Labor Statistics' definition, contingent workers are those persons who expect their jobs to end in a year or less or report their jobs as temporary. There are an estimated 5.4 million contingent workers in the United States (*Monthly Labor Review* 2001). In addition to contingent workers, the bureau refers to independent contractors, temporary workers, on-call workers, day laborers, and those employed by contract firms as workers employed in alternative work arrangements. The bureau in 2001 reported 8.6 million independent contractors (6.4 percent of total employment), 2.1 million on-call workers (1.6 percent of total employment), 1.2 million temporary help agency workers (0.9 percent of the employed), and 633,000 contract company workers (0.5 percent of total employment).

Workplace Illiteracy

At a time when international competition is increasing and technology quickly changes, workplace illiteracy is a growing problem. Although reports often differ on the extent of illiteracy because of difficulty in measuring, there is agreement that illiteracy is high, particularly among immigrants and racial and ethnic minority groups. A 1992 survey by the U.S. Department of Education's National Center for Education Statistics estimates that about 21 percent of the adult population—more than 40 million Americans over the age of sixteen—had only rudimentary reading and writing skills. In 1982 the English Language Proficiency Survey (ELPS) placed the nonliterate U.S. adult population at between 17 and 21 million; 7 million of that group was from a home where a language other than English was spoken (U.S. Department of Education 1986; National Clearinghouse on Literacy Education 1991). Other research indicates that half of the adult workforce does not read, write, or compute well enough to perform their work satisfactorily (Ford 1992). The U.S. Department of Education estimates that the functionally illiterate now account for 30 percent of the unskilled, 29 percent of the semiskilled, and 11 percent of the managerial, professional, and technical workforce. It is estimated that more than half of the 26 million new jobs that will be added to the economy during the early years of the new millennium will require some postsecondary training, and about one-third will demand a college degree (Bernardon 1989).

Current Organizational Workforce Diversity Research Findings

As long ago as 1976, Dunnett pointed out a major gap in the field of organizational psychology: the absence of coverage given to groups such as women, minorities, and the disadvantaged. In spite of recognition of the growing diversity of the workforce, this gap still exists. For example, in the matter of racial diversity, Cox and Nkomo (1990) surveyed twenty major management journals that published organization behavior research between 1964 and 1989 and found that the amount of total published research is small relative to the importance of the topic. They also found that the topics covered are not representative of the domain of organizational behavior. Amazingly, they concluded that the trend is for less rather than more research on these topics. Frideger (1992) agrees and argues that, with a very few exceptions, research in organizational behavior has generally disregarded the domestic cross-cultural and interracial implications of its theories (Wise and Tschirhart 2000). Not surprisingly, some demography researchers have emphasized the following: (1) the need for developing an understanding of the effects of racial and gender diversity in organizational content, particularly as this increasing diversity impacts individuals who are members of what have traditionally been the dominant majority group in organizations; and (2) the need for understanding the relationship between demographic attributes and process variables such as communication, conflict, influence, and decision-making (Tsui and Egan 1992).

Cox and Nkomo (1990, 420) conclude, at least in the area of racial diversity, that "in addition to a general lack of researcher attention, the development of research in this area has been hindered by research questions that are too simplistic, by an absence of theories of race effects and by the types of research designs employed." They also observe that less than 35 percent of the 140 empirical studies reviewed addressed racial groups other than African-Americans and whites, and only 33 percent of the 132 organizations studied were public organizations.

While the research is limited, it indicates that there are differences between various identity groups that will impact the workforce. Brenner, Blazini, and Greenhaus (1988), for instance, examine whether the work values of 322 white and African-American managers differed based on race and gender. The managers were asked to indicate the importance of several job characteristics: Factor I—extrinsic (respect for others, job security, income, and working conditions); Factor II—managerial activities (opportunity to take risks, work on important problems, supervise others, and develop personal contacts); Factor III—independence (working independently and determining one's own work method); and Factor IV—intrinsic (importance of task variety, feelings of accomplishment, and recognition for a job well done). The researchers conclude that both African-American female and male managers place a greater importance on extrinsic work values than do white managers. With regards to managerial activities, there is little difference between the groups. Both African-American females and males place a higher emphasis on the values of working independently than do white managers. Finally, under Factor IV—both the African-American and white females place greater importance on intrinsic work values than do male managers. Thus, these differences could have an influence on how individuals feel about their workplace cultures. Fernandez (1991) notes that over the years he has found that African-American employees are by far the most critical of corporate treatment of minorities. He points out that 87 percent of African-Americans, 57 percent of Asians, 54 percent of Hispanics, 44 percent of Native Americans, and 35 percent of whites believe that minorities have a more difficult time finding a sponsor or mentor than white employees do.

Other studies have explored racial and ethnic diversity in the realm of discrimination and resistance to diversity. A January 1994 cover story in *BusinessWeek* titled "White, Male & Worried" (Galen and Palmer 1994) describes the reaction of white, nonHispanic males in companies that are aggressively supporting diversity programs. "They're feeling frustrated, resentful, and most of all, afraid. There's a sense that, be it on the job or at home, the rules are changing faster than they can keep up" (Galen and Palmer 1994, 50). "White males are like the firstborn in the family, the ones who have had the best love of both parents and never quite forgave the second child for being born" (Kochman, as quoted in Galen and Palmer 1994, 52). This reaction has profound organizational consequences. While some authors suggest that race relations will improve as the representation of racial and ethnic groups increase in the workplace (Blau 1977; Kanter 1977), others argue that discrimination will increase as the proportion of the minority groups increases (Blalock 1957).

Hernandez's (1992) review of the organizational communication literature suggests that heterogeneous work groups have a dysfunctional impact on communication, which negatively affects creativity. This line of research contrasts with that identifying higher organizational creativity associated with greater work group diversity. Tsui, Egan, and O'Reilly (1992) do an excellent job of reviewing the available literature on this issue and point out that there is evidence that the diverse work groups are beneficial for tasks requiring creativity and judgment. They also note the research shows that homogeneous groups are more likely to be socially integrated and experience higher satisfaction and lower turnover (O'Reilly, Caldwell, and Barnett 1989; Jackson 1991). In a recent study of the interaction process and performance of culturally homogeneous and culturally diverse groups, researchers found that the homogeneous groups score higher on both process and performance effectiveness initially (Watson, Kuman, and Michaelsen 1993).

Tsui and Egan (1992) also review previous research studies that report on the reactions of the usual numerical majority (men and whites) in the presence of the usual minorities (women and nonwhites). Their review suggests that women in predominantly male jobs are treated with hostility by male coworkers, while men in predominantly female jobs experienced almost no hostility from female coworkers. Their review further indicates that in balanced settings, when neither men nor women are the numerical majority, men reported lower job-related satisfaction and self-esteem and more job-related depression. They note that research in race relations in organizations is more consistent with the hypothesis that discrimination by the majority will increase as the proportion of the minority increases, than with the view that the quality of intergroup relationships will improve with greater heterogeneity. Their own research with more than 1,700 respondents shows that for men: "Increased differences in the gender composition of the group are associated with lower levels of psychological attachment, increased absence, and a lower intent to stay [with the organization]. . . . Similarly, for whites, increasing difference from others in the work unit is related to lower attachment, while for nonwhites, being different in race has no effect on attachment to the organization" (Tsui and Egan 1992, 569). Furthermore, token women were isolated, whereas token men appeared to be socially well integrated into the female work group. "All else being equal, men in balanced settings and in settings containing a small proportion of women are significantly less satisfied than women in these settings" (Wharton and Baron 1989). Tsui and

Egan (1992) conclude that "future research should expand its focus from analyzing how women and people of color 'fit' the dominant culture to understanding the adjustment process of the dominant group to the reality of diversity and heterogeneity."

From research on gender differences, Segal (1991) finds that men and women have different management styles. The "operating style model" of men is competitive, while that of female managers is cooperative. The organizational structure for men is vertical and hierarchical, while that of women is horizontal and egalitarian. The basic objective for male managers is winning, while the female managers' basic objective is that of quality output. The problem-solving approach of men is rational and objective and for the female manager intuitive and subjective. It is true that most managers possess a combination of both male and female managerial characteristics. However, in a study that compared perceptions about male and female managers who used either an authoritarian or participative leadership style, managers were viewed more positively when they used a leadership style that was typical of and consistent with their gender (Griffin 1992). The study further indicates that more participants said that they would not like to work for an authoritarian female manager. Women managers, however, have found that using the "command-and-control" style of managing others is not the only way to be effective and successful. They are drawing on the skills and attitudes they have developed from their shared experiences as women, not by adopting the style and habits that men have found successful (Rosener 1990). Other research also indicates that men and women have different learning styles that need to be taken into consideration when developing job training (Chanlin 1999).

As noted elsewhere in this chapter, Hispanics are the fastest-growing ethnic group and have surpassed African-Americans to become the largest ethnic group in the United States. However, very limited research has been conducted to understand the experiences of Hispanics in the workplace (Knouse, Rosenfeld, and Culbertson 1992). Among the few studies identified in our literature review, Rubaii-Barrett, Beck, and Lillibridge 1991) investigate the differences between Hispanic (predominantly Mexican-American) and Anglo employees of a local government agency in terms of their attitude toward the work environment and job satisfaction. Table 3.1 summarizes their findings.

Further, very little research on Hispanic women who work outside

Table 3.1

Satisfaction with Job Attributes for Hispanics and Anglo Employees

Job attributes	Satisfaction
Employees	
Satisfaction with personnel policies	Hispanics more satisfied
Satisfaction with supervision	Hispanics less satisfied
Satisfaction with job tasks	Hispanics less satisfied
Satisfaction with work rewards	Hispanics less satisfied
Satisfaction with coworkers	Hispanics less satisfied
Satisfaction with employee competence	Hispanics less satisfied
Satisfaction with promotion, pay, employee motivation, participatory management, stress levels, and overall satisfaction with the job	No difference in satisfaction
Supervisors	
Satisfaction with personnel policies	Hispanics more satisfied
Satisfaction with employee competence	Hispanics more satisfied
Satisfaction with participatory management	Hispanics more satisfied
Satisfaction with supervision, job tasks, work rewards, coworkers, promotion, pay, employee motivation, stress levels, overall satisfaction with the job	No difference in satisfaction
Managers	
Satisfaction with personnel policies	Hispanics more satisfied
Satisfaction with employee competence	Hispanics less satisfied
Satisfaction with supervision, job tasks, participatory management, work rewards, coworkers, promotion, pay, employee motivation, stress levels, overall satisfaction with the job	No difference in satisfaction

Source: Derived from Rubaii-Barrett, Beck, and Lillibridge (1991).

the home has been conducted. Previous research focused on their domestic workforce participation. Thus very little is known about Hispanic women in managerial and professional jobs (Sisneros 1993). Due to their positions, these women may serve as community leaders and important role models for young Hispanic women. Because of the visible and demanding nature of their jobs, the challenges they face in majority work settings and their break from traditional female roles, Hispanic women professionals are subjected to multiple sources of stress at home and in the workplace (Amaro, Russo, and Johnson 1987). To complicate matters, research indicates that Hispanics are not a homogeneous group, and there are important differences between Hispanic subgroups depending upon level of education, socio-economic status, and other factors (Arbona 1990).

Although high levels of education and socioeconomic status suggest that Asian-Americans have succeeded in American society, leading them to often be referred to as the *model minority*, they frequently face a glass ceiling and discrimination (Cheng 1997). In their summary of organization-related research on Asian-Americans, Sue and Wagner (1973) report that, in general, Asian-American males exhibit less need for dominance, aggressiveness, exhibitionism, autonomy, and heterosexuality, whereas Asian-American females are more deferent, nurturing, and achievement-oriented than their white counterparts. Historically, Americans have directed both positive and negative attitudes toward the Asian population.

Other Identity Group Characteristics Requiring Further Research

As the workforce grows more diverse, there is a need to conduct a wider breadth of research beyond class, gender, race, and ethnicity. For instance, Yuker (1988) reports on a study where adults worked at tasks given to them by a research assistant who was either disabled or nondisabled, and either likable or obnoxious. It was expected that people would be more willing to help the disabled research assistant than the nondisabled one when both were likable, but less willing to help the disabled person as compared with the latter when they were equally obnoxious. Contrary to the theoretical expectations, subjects in the positive/pleasant condition were three times as willing to help the nondisabled research assistant as they were to help the disabled research assistant. In the negative/obnoxious condition they were just as strongly biased in the opposite direction—that is, in the direction of giving relatively more help to the research assistant with the disability. Yuker (1988) concludes that nondisabled people tend to (1) insist that the disabled person is suffering, even when there is no evidence of suffering, or (2) devaluate the unfortunate person's behavior because she ought to suffer and does not. The implications of this experiment are that some people become angry and annoyed with the disabled because they violate their beliefs about how people with disabilities are supposed to behave. Furthermore, due to myths about the disabled, many employers are not taking advantage of this increasing talent pool (*HR Focus* 2003). Other research that contributes to meeting the challenges of twenty-first century public managers also includes studies on cognitive style diversity and its effects on organizational communication as well as its effects on the ability of different people to work together and achieve consensus (Cox and Beale 1997). For example, some exciting and interesting recent research shows that matching e-mail correspondents on one important cognitive style, called *perceptual modality preferences*, can increase rapport in written electronic mail communication and thus improve communication effectiveness (Crook and Booth 1997).

In employment as well as other aspects of life, gay men and lesbians are in a classic double-bind. It is very stressful and demeaning to remain closeted; that is, to hide an essential aspect of one's identity. However, it can also be stressful and dangerous to come out of the closet, particularly if there are no civil rights protections to employment on the basis of sexual orientation (Hixson 1992). Levine and Leonard (1984) surveyed 203 women to explore in-depth the factors affecting employment discrimination against lesbians. To shield themselves from possible discrimination, most women in the study reported that they stayed closeted; only 23 percent informed most or all work associates. Seventy-seven percent were partially or totally closeted on the job; 29 percent told some friends, 21 percent told only close friends, and 27 percent told no one at all. Such caution appears justified. In the same article the authors find that "thirty-one percent of the lesbians surveyed anticipated employment discrimination because of sexual orientation, and 13 percent had actually experienced it; 8 percent of the women had lost or had almost lost their jobs because they were lesbians. The only comparable estimates for gay men reveal that 29 percent of all gay male workers have had their careers negatively influenced by their sexual orientation" (Levine and Leonard 1984). Such anxiety makes gay and lesbian employees less productive. Brian McNaught (quoted in Stewart 1991) says, "My basic premise is that homophobia takes a toll on the ability of 10 percent of the workforce to produce."

Implications for Future Research

The following implications for public managers are summarized from Sawyer (1993). The overwhelming research on sexual orientation issues in the workplace indicates that the biggest area of concern is discrimination. The manager is responsible for assuring a climate that is accepting of all workers. Research indicates that gay men and lesbians experience higher job satisfaction when they are able to come out of the closet. They are more likely to do this when they do not fear discrimination or negative social consequences. Public managers must be sensitive to diverse lifestyles, to allow friends or partners to replace spouses at business and social functions, and let it be known that jokes and negative remarks about any lifestyle are not acceptable in the workplace. Gay men and lesbian women highly value their careers and management needs to respond by providing opportunities for advancement and career planning. Every effort should be made to break the "glass ceiling" that is experienced by gays and lesbians, as well as other identity groups. Training of all employees in issues of sexual preference must become a major element of all organizational human development efforts. For example, in West Hollywood, California's new employee orientation classes, nondiscrimination is one of the topics for discussion. Included in these classes is treatment of the subject of sexual orientation (Edgerly 1992). Findings from other research suggest that exposure to and interaction with homosexuals results in self-reported reduction in discomfort with homosexuals (Lance 1987).

This type of research on organizational-related attributes of the members of a diverse workforce can be thought of as the first step toward managing and valuing diversity (Thomas 1991). Moreover, not all demographic characteristics are equal. Cummings, Zhou, and Oldham (1993) suggest that those highly visible demographic characteristics such as gender and race produce more negative relationships than those less visible demographics such as job tenure or religion. Research is needed to determine under what organizational and societal situations different demographic characteristics become salient. Research is also needed on how an organization creates a situation where the functional instead of the dysfunctional consequences of workforce diversity are manifested. One suggestion is to look at the organizational culture. Chatman et al. (1993) conclude that in organizations that are characterized by the collective dimension of Hofstede's Individualistic-Collective dimension of culture (Hofstede 1980), heterogeneous work groups performed better in terms of creativity, having beneficial conflict, degree of interaction and participation, and timeliness of task completion. In individual-istic organizations such groups did not perform as well as homoge-neous work groups. Cox, Lobel, and McLeod (1991) examined the differences between minorities and whites in levels of individualism and collectivism and concluded that European cultures tend be more individualistic, whereas people from Asian, African, and Hispanic cultures tend be more collective. Research that identifies the charac-teristics of team assignments leading to the functional rather than the dysfunctional consequences of team diversity is important in contemporary workforces (Watson, Kuman and Michaelsen 1993). Hernandez (1992) reports that one characteristic of organizations that maximize the potential of their diverse workforce is the pres-ence of effective "Valuing Diversity" programs. Such programs in the private sector are described in Jackson (1992) and Thomas (1991). An excellent description of a methodology for establishing "Valu-ing Diversity" efforts can be found in Thomas's *Beyond Race and Gender*, a must reading for today's public managers.

Summary and Conclusion

After reviewing this literature, Wooldridge, Smith-Mason, and Clark Maddox (1993), in their paper entitled "Changing Demographics of the Work Force: Implications for Research in Human Resource Man-agement," identified at least twenty areas of organization behavior where further research to detect significant identity group differ-ences is required. Some of these areas include:

- Organizational design—do any of the identity groups react sig-nificantly different to degrees of centralization/decentralization, specialization, formalization, span of control, organization size, and/or work unit size? (Steers 1978)
- Cognitive styles—implications for organizational communica-tion, training, and development efforts
- Basic Personnel/Human Resource Management (P/HRM) func-tions—these include elements such as effectiveness of recruit-ment strategies and performance appraisal methods
- Barriers to effective organizational performance; strategies for effective organizational development and growth; determinant of upward mobility; effectiveness of various incentives in moti-

vating desired behavior; training needs and the selection of train-
ing strategies; occupational safety and health issues
- Organizational communication
- Causes of organizational conflict and effective conflict resolu-
tion strategies
- Magnitude of organizational influence; modes of exerting or-
ganizational influence
- Relationship to types of organizational culture
- Types and manifestation of organizational creativity
- Causes of and reaction to organizational stress
- Determinants of job satisfaction and job commitment and the
relationship between these organizational elements
- The effects of organizational stress on job satisfaction and job
performance
- Work values and attitudes such as involvement, loyalty, inten-
tions to leave, cynicism, and compatibility with technology.

Understanding the challenges and opportunities that diversity brings
is critical to twenty-first century public managers. Human resource
management practices deemed effective in a homogeneous workforce are showing signs of not being as effective in a highly diverse
workforce. Human resource professionals surveyed for the Hudson
Institute's *Workforce 2000* report indicate three major concerns about
the increasingly diverse workforce: (1) hiring and managing diverse
groups, (2) creating family-friendly policies to meet the needs of
the increasing number of women in the workforce, and (3) the possibility of labor force shortages. Consequently, there is a need for
consistent and ongoing research in organizational behavior. Scholars of public administration must recognize these changes and their
implications for public sector management. One size does not "fit
all." As pointed out by Cox and Nkomo (1990), the effect of race on
work-related variables has been rare and the research results have
often been mixed. Furthermore, Adler (1983) argues that researchers have limited their research efforts to differences between identity groups, but similarities should also be explored. Consequently,
we have a unique opportunity to offer insights and perspectives on
changing demographics in the public sector and how to effectively
administer services to an increasingly diverse population at all levels of government.

References

Adler, N.J. 1983. "Cross-Cultural Management Research: The Ostrich and the Trend." *Academy of Management Review* 8 (2): 226–32.

Amaro, Hortensia, Nancy Russo, and Julie Johnson. 1987. "Family and Work Predictors of Psychological Well-Being Among Hispanic Women Professionals." *Psychology of Women Quarterly* 12 (11): 505–21.

American Federation of Labor-Congress of Industrial Organizations–Executive Paywatch. www.aflcio.org/paywatch/ceopay.htm.

American Federation of Labor–Congress of Industrial Organizations–Fact Sheet. www.aflcio.org/women/wwfacts.htm

Arbona, Consuelo. 1990. "Career Counseling Research and Hispanics: A Review of the Literature." *Counseling Psychologist* 18 (2): 300–24.

Bernardon, N.L. 1989. "Let's Erase Illiteracy from the Workplace." *Personnel* 66 (1): 29–33.

Blalock, Hubert M., Jr. 1957. "Percent Nonwhite and Discrimination in the South." *American Sociological Review* 22: 677–82.

Blau, Peter M. 1977. *Inequality and Heterogeneity.* New York: Free Press.

Brenner, O.C., A.P. Blazini, and J.H. Greenhaus. 1988. "An Examination of Race and Sex Differences in Managerial Work Values." *Journal of Vocational Behavior* 32 (3): 336–44.

Caudron, S. 1997. "Can Generation Xers be Trained?" *Training and Development* 51 (3): 20–25.

Center for Individual Rights. 2002. "HUD and EEOC Sued over Reverse Discrimination." Press release, August 8.

Chanlin, L. 1999. "Gender Differences and the Need for Visual Control." *International Journal of Instructional Media* 26 (13): 329–33.

Chatman, Jennifer A. et al. 1993. The Influence of Team Diversity and Organizational Culture on Decision Making Processes and Outcomes. Paper presented at the Annual Meeting of the Academy of Management, Atlanta.

Cheng, Cliff. 1997. "Are Asian American Employees a Model Minority or Just a Minority?" *Journal of Applied Behavioral Sciences* 33 (3): 277–91.

Corley, T. 1999. "Becoming an Employer of Choice for Generation X: The Elements of the Deal." *Journal of Career Planning and Employment:* 21–26.

Cornesky, R. et al. 1991. "Implementing Total Quality." *Management in Higher Education.* New York: Magna Press.

Cox, Taylor H., and Ruby L. Beale. 1997. *Developing Competency to Manage Diversity: Readings, Cases, and Activities.* San Francisco: Berrett-Koehler.

Cox, Taylor H. et al. 1991. "Effects of Ethnic Group Cultural Differences on Cooperative and Competitive Behavior on a Group Task." *Academy of Management Journal* 34 (4): 827–47.

Cox, Taylor, and Shelia Nkomo. 1990. "Invisible Men and Women: A Status Report on Race as a Variable in Organizational Behavior Research." *Journal of Organizational Behavior* 11 (6): 419–31.

Crook, Connie W., and Rosemary Booth. 1997. "Building Rapport in Electronic Mail Using Accommodation Theory." *SAM Advanced Management Journal* 2 (1): 4–10.

Crosby, P.B. 1979. *Quality Is Free: The Art of Making Quality Certain.* New York: Mentor.

Cummings, Anne et al. 1993. Demographic Differences and Employee Work Outcomes: Effects of Multiple Comparative Groups. Paper presented at the Annual Meeting of the Academy of Management, Atlanta.

Deming, W.E. 1986. *Out of Crisis.* Boston: MIT Center for Advanced Engineering Study.

Dunn-Cane, K.M. et al. 1999. "Managing the New Generation." *AORN Journal* 69 (15): 930.

Dunnett, Marvin D., ed. 1976. *Handbook of Industrial and Organizational Psychology.* Chicago: Rand McNally.

Edgerly, Robert. 1992. Diversity in the Public Workplace: Integrating Employee Sexual Orientation into a City's Multi-Cultural Mix. Paper presented at the Annual Conference of the American Society for Public Administration, Chicago.

Fairholm, Gilbert W. 1994. "Leading Diverse Followers." *Journal of Leadership Studies* 1 (4): 82–93.

Families and Work Institute. 1997. *The 1997 National Study of the Changing Workforce, Executive Summary.* New York: Families and Work Institute.

Fernandez, John. 1991. *Managing a Diverse Work Force.* Lexington, MA: Lexington Books.

Fierman, Jaclyn. 1994. "The Contingency Work Force: Increasing Use of Freelance Workers, Just-In-Time Employees, Temporary Executives and Other Kinds of Alternatives to Full-Time, Permanent Workers." *Fortune* (January 24) 129 (2): 30.

Ford, D. 1992. "Toward a More Literate Workforce." *Training and Development* 46 (11): 52–55.

Frideger, Marcia A. 1992. The Effect of Accent on Hiring Decisions: Human Resource Implications. Paper presented at the Academy of Management Meeting, Las Vegas.

Fullerton, Howard N., Jr. 1991. "Labor Force Projections: The Baby Boom Moves On." *Monthly Labor Review* 114: 31–44.

Fullerton, Howard N. Jr., and Mitra Toossi. 2001. "Labor Force Projections To 2010: Steady Growth and Changing Composition." *Monthly Labor Review* 124 (11): 21–38.

Galen, Michele, and Therese Palmer. 1994. "White, Male and Worried." *Business Week* (January 31): 50–55.

Goddard, Robert. 1989. "Workforce 2000." *Personnel Journal* 68 (2): 64–71.

Griffin, Betsy Q. March. 1992. Perceptions of Managers: Effects of Leadership Style and Gender. Paper presented at the Annual Meeting of the Southeastern Psychological Association.

Halachmi, A. 1998. "Dealing with Employees over Fifty." *Public Productivity and Management Review* 22 (1): 6–14.

Haworth, J.G. 1997. "The Misrepresentation of Generation X." *About Campus* 2 (4): 10–15.

Hernandez, Brigida et al. 2000. "Employer Attitudes Toward Workers with Disabilities and Their ADA Employment Rights: A Literature Review." *Journal of Rehabilitation* 66 (14): 4.

Hernandez, Edward. 1992. The Unclear Role of Workplace Diversity on Group Level Creativity. Paper presented at the Academy of Management Meeting, Las Vegas.

Hixson, Emma. 1992. Employee Sexual Preference: A Lesson in Managing Diversity. Paper presented at the annual conference of the American Society for Public Administration, Chicago.

Hofstede, Geert. 1980. *Culture's Consequences: International Differences in Work Related Values.* Beverly Hills, CA: Sage.

HR Focus. 2002. "Sexual Orientation: The Latest Diversity Challenge." 79 (16): 3–4.

———. 2003. "Advantages and Opportunities in Hiring Disabled Workers." 80 (16): 11.

Hunt, V.D. 1992. *Quality in America: How to Implement a Competitive Quality Program.* Homewood, IL: Business One Irwin.

Jackson, Susan E. 1991. "Team Composition in Organizational Settings: Issues in Managing an Increasingly Diverse Workforce." In S. Worchel et al. eds. *Group Process and Productivity.* Beverly Hills, CA: Sage, 138–73.

Jackson, Susan E. et al. 1992. *Diversity in the Workplace: Human Resources Initiatives.* New York: Guilford Press.

Jamieson, David, and Julie O'Mara. 1991. *Managing Workforce 2000: Gaining the Diversity Advantage.* San Francisco: Jossey-Bass.

Jenning, A.T. 2000. "Hiring Generation X." *Journal of Accountancy* 189 (12): 55.

Juran, J.M. and F.M. Gryna, eds. 1988. *Quality Control Handbook.* New York: McGraw-Hill.

Jurkiewicz, C.L., and R.G. Brown. 1998. "GenXers vs Boomers vs Matures: Generational Comparisons of Public Employee Motivation." *Review of Public Personnel Administration* 180: 37.

Kahan, H., and D. Mulryan. 1995. "Out of the Closet (the gay market)." *American Demographics* 17 (5): 40–46.

Kanter, Rosabeth M. 1977. *Men and Women of the Corporation.* New York: Basic Books.

Knouse, Stephen B. et al. eds. 1992. *Hispanics in the Workplace.* Newbury Park, CA: Sage.

Lance, Larry M. 1987. "The Effects of Interaction with Gay Persons on Attitudes Towards Homosexuality." *Human Relations* 40 (6): 329–36.

Lawler, Edward E. III. 2000. *Rewarding Excellence: Pay Strategies for the New Economy.* San Francisco: Jossey-Bass.

Lee, Chris. 1992. "Miracle Cures." *Training* 29: 8.

Lester, Rick A., and Donald Caudill. 1987. "The Handicapped Worker: Seven Myths." *Training and Development Journal* 41 (8): 50–51.

Levine, Martin P., and Robin Leonard. 1984. "Discrimination Against Lesbians in the Work Force." *Signs* 9 (4): 700–10.

Levitan, Sam, and Robert Taggart. 1977. *Jobs for the Disabled.* Baltimore: Johns Hopkins University Press.

Lewis, Gregory. 1995. "Gays and the Workplace." *Public Administration Review* 55 (2): 201–3.

Losyk, B. 1997. "How to Manage an X'er." *The Futurist* 31 (2): 39–44.

Mirvis, Phillip H., and Donald L. Kanter. 1991. "Beyond Demography: A Psychographic Profile of the Workforce." *Human Resource Management* 30 (1): 45–68.

O'Reilly, Charles A. et al. 1989. "Work Groups Demography, Social Integration, and Turnover." *Administrative Science Quarterly* 34 (1): 21–37.

Popovich, M.G. 1998. *Creating High-Performance Government Organizations.* San Francisco: Jossey-Bass.

Porter, Rebecca. 2000. "Contingent Workers: Trailing Behind." *Trial* 36 (10): 12.

Quaddumi, T. 2001. "Matures' Age 55 to 69, Differ from Baby Boomers in Workforce Issues." *Houston Business Journal* 32 (22) (October 12): 36.

Rosener, Judy B. 1990. "Ways Women Lead." *Harvard Business Review* 68 (6): 119–25.

Rubaii-Barrett, Nadia et al. 1991. "Minorities in the Majority: Implications for Managing Cultural Diversity." *Public Personnel Management* 22: 503–21.

Sawyer, Mary F. 1993. Workforce 2000: Sexual Orientation. Paper presented in partial fulfillment of course requirements for PAD 691, Special Topics: Workforce 2000: Creating Effective Organizations for the 21st Century. Department of Public Administration, Virginia Commonwealth University. Spring Semester.

Segal, Jonathan A. 1991. "Women on the Verge of . . . Equality." *HR Magazine* 36 (6): 117–23.

Sisneros, Antonio. 1993. "Hispanics in the Public Service in the Late Twentieth Century." *Public Administration Review* 52 (1): 1–7.

Steers, Richard M. 1978. *Organizational Effectiveness: A Behavioral View.* Santa Monica, CA: Goodyear.

Stewart, Thomas. 1991. "Gay in Corporate America." *Fortune* 124 (42) (December 16): 6–8.

Strauss, W., and N. Howe. 1991. *Generations: The History of America's Future, 1584–2069.* New York: William Morrow and Co.

Sue, S., and N.N. Wagner. 1973. *Asian Americans: Psychological Perspectives.* Palo Alto, CA: Science and Behavior Books.

Thomas, R. Roosevelt, Jr. 1991. *Beyond Race and Gender: Unleashing the Power of Your Total Workforce by Managing Diversity.* New York: Amacom.

Toossi, Mitra. 2002. "A Century of Change: The U.S. Labor Force, 1950–2050." *Monthly Labor Review* 125 (15): 15–28.

Tsui, Anne S. et al. 1992. "Being Different: Relational Demography and Organizational Attachment." *Administrative Science Quarterly* 37: 549–79.

Tsui, Anne, S., and Terri D. Egan. 1992. Communication and Conflict: The Impact of Ethnic and Gender Diversity in Management Teams. Paper presented at the Academy of Management Meeting, Las Vegas.

U.S. Bureau of Labor Statistics. 1999. *Employment Characteristics of Families in 1999.* http://stats.bls.gov/newsrel.htm

U.S. Department of Education. 1986. National Center for Education Statistics. http://www.nces.ed.gov/naal/resources/92results.asp

Vroom, V. 1964. *Work and Motivation.* New York: Wiley.

Watson, Warren E. et al. 1993. "Cultural Diversity's Impact on Interaction Process and Performance: Comparing Homogeneous and Diverse Task Groups." *Academy of Management Journal* 36 (3): 590–602.

Wharton, Amy S., and James N. Baron. 1989. Satisfaction? The Psychological Impact on Gender Segregation on Women at Work. Paper presented at the Annual Meeting of the American Sociological Association.

Wiant, C.J. 1999. "Are You Listening To Your Employees?" *Journal of Environmental Health* 62 (3): 51.

Wise, Lois R., and Mary Tschirhart. 2000. "Examining Empirical Evidence on Diversity Effects: How Useful Is Diversity Research for Public Sector Managers?" *Public Administration Review* 60 (5): 386–94.

Wooldridge, Blue et al. 1993. Changing Demographics of the Workforce: Implications for Research in Human Resource Management. Paper presented at the Annual National Conference of the American Society for Public Administration, San Francisco.

Wooldridge, B. 1994a. "Changing Demographics in the Work Force: Implications for the Use of Technology in Public Organizations." *Public Productivity and Management Review* 17 (4): 371–86.

——— 1994b. "Increasing the Effectiveness of University and College Instruction: Integrating the Results of Learning Style Results into Course Design and Delivery." In Sims, R.R., and S.J. Sims, eds., *The Importance of Learning Styles: Implications for Learning, Course Design, and Education*, Westport, CT: Greenwood Publishing.

Work and Family Newsbrief. 2002. "Generations Strive to Communicate: As Older Workers Stay Longer on the Job and Corporate Hierarchies Flatten, There Are Now Four Generations Struggling to Work Together" (2) July: 7.

Yuker, Harold E. 1988. *Attitudes Towards Persons with Disabilities.* New York: Springer.

Zemke, Ron et al. 1999. *Generations at Work: Managing in the Clash of Veterans, Boomers, Xers, and Nexters in Your Workplace.* New York: Amacom.

Zill, N., and J. Robinson. 1995. "The Generation X Difference." *American Demographics* 17 (4): 24–31.

4

Teaching Public Administration Education in the Postmodern Era

Connecting Organizational Culture to Diversity to Social Equity

Mitchell F. Rice

Public administration operates in a postmodern period, a period viewed by Cunningham and Weschler (2002) when traditional methods, processes, and teachings are not compatible with current constructs and realities. The orthodox (bureaucratic) public administration in both theory and practice must give way to a new model of public administration and policy in the postmodern era (Fox and Miller 1995). The postmodern era in the United States consists of diverse population groups led by rapidly increasing numbers of Hispanics and Latinos (any race), Asian-Americans, African-Americans, and other racial groups (see U.S. Census 2000). Therefore, teaching public administration education in postmodern times requires the inclusion of important topics such as diversity and social equity in curricula and courses to facilitate students' knowledge and learning about different cultures, ethnicities, and racial groups and to better prepare them to both manage and work in public organizations and deliver equitable public services in a contemporary multicultural society.

Why is the inclusion of these topics (diversity and social equity) important in the public administration education of future public administrators, managers, and public service delivery personnel? First, in contemporary society, how well government organizations implement and manage diversity will impact how productive and successful they are in meeting their missions, and determine how well they are able to attract the best and the brightest people who are comfortable working with others who are different and at ease when delivering services across lines of race, class, religion, and background. Second, if social equity involves "fairness" and "different equalities" of outcomes (Frederickson 1990, 2002) in public service delivery and public policy implementation, then a more basic focus in curricula and courses in public administration education has to examine who works in public organizations, how well are they managed, who receives public services, and to what extent in a diverse, multicultural society.

Does a public organization's culture have an impact on how well the organization meets and responds to the challenges of diversity and social equity? In other words, is there a connection between a public organization's culture, its ability to promote and manage diversity among its workforce, and its interest or lack of interest in social equity in service delivery outcomes? *Social equity in public service delivery emphasizes the following four tenets.* First, public administrators should not be value-neutral. Orthodox (bureaucratic) public administration requires that citizens or clients be treated the same regardless of need(s) (Fox and Miller 1995). Second, public administrators are morally obligated to provide more and better services to those who need them most (Frederickson 1990; Pops and Pavlak 1991). Third, public administrators should be "evaluated on how well [they] manage to enhance fairness, justice and equity in the outcomes of governance processes" (Rutledge 2002). Fourth, social equity takes four criteria into account: procedural fairness, access, quality, and outcomes (Svara and Brunet 2003). The National Academy of Public Administration's Standing Panel on Social Equity (2000, 2–3) defines *social equity* as *"The fair, just and equitable management of all institutions serving the public directly or by contract, and the fair, just and equitable distribution of public services, and the implementation of public policy, and the commitment to promote fairness, justice, and equity in the formation of public policy."*

The connection between organizational culture, social equity, and diversity takes into account that public organizations and public administrators, managers, and public service delivery personnel can profoundly impact how well they manage and deliver services equitably to all groups in society. If a public organization's culture promotes and maintains a diverse workforce that is well managed and has proactive diversity strategies in place, will this contribute to a public organization's consideration of social equity in service delivery outcomes? An operating assumption behind diversity in public organizations is: different types of employees increase productivity and organizational effectiveness because individuals with different characteristics have different work styles and cultural knowledge that make them valuable assets to public organizations in a changing society and world (Edelman, Fuller, and Mara-Drita 2001, 1618). Miller and Katz (1995) note that diversity gives an organization a greater range of creativity, problem-solving, and decision-making skills and a potential for seeing 360 degrees of the landscape. The point here is that a proactive organizational diversity strategy operating in a supportive organizational culture can be a vital social equity asset in public service delivery outcomes.

Therefore, it would seem an argument can be made that an important issue closely related to organizational culture and social equity in public service delivery outcomes is the teaching of diversity/diversity management in public administration education. This chapter addresses this observation in two ways. First, the chapter provides an overview of the cultural environment of public organizations and offers some elements of a social equity organizational culture. Second, the chapter presents a perspective on teaching diversity in public administration education, including a focus on social class, and distinctions between affirmative action, multiculturalism, and diversity. The premise of the chapter is that social equity in public service delivery decision-making and outcomes can best be achieved if public administrators, public managers, and public service delivery personnel have a clear understanding and appreciation of diversity and diversity management that is built into the organization's culture. If organizational culture is seen as having a connection to diversity within a public organization, it may impact how well the organization advances social equity in the service delivery process. It is expected that the discussion that follows may generate considerable debate and controversy in the teaching of public administration education among both public administration scholars and practitioners.

The Cultural Environment of Public Organizations: An Overview

Traditionally, the cultural environment of public organizations has not been positively associated with social equity or diversity. Promoting social equity in public service delivery outcomes involves citizen input and participation, neither of which a public organization has a strong interest in pursuing and operationalizing (see King, Feltey, and Susel 1998 and Peters 1999). Perhaps one explanation is that the bureaucratic culture of an organization reflects those who run and control it. Generally, public organizations in the United States are controlled by individuals of Western European descent who have adopted a specific process in regard to "the way things are done." The literature has identified this specific process as a culture of conformity (Feldman 1985), a culture of technical rationality (Adams and Ingersoll 1990), a culture of control (Ban 1995), and a culture of process (Deal and Kennedy 1982). Claver et al. (1999, 456) argue that "it is possible to analyze how to improve working habits and the service delivery results" of a public organization by examining its culture.

Culture in an organizational context is "a set of values, symbols and rituals shared by members of an organization," describing the way duties and responsibilities are carried out internally together with how the organization relates to its customers (or clients) and the environment (Claver et al. 1999, 456). These values, symbols, and rituals are both formal and informal or written and unwritten and, as Howard (1994) notes, reflect a largely middle-class standard of rules and behavior. Developing and promoting principles, standards, and behavior that could be adapted to differing socioeconomic circumstances of public service delivery clients is not compatible with this view of culture. *Culture in public organizations determines how employees are treated and how the public service delivery process is rationalized. In other words, the culture of a public organization determines its public service orientation and public service delivery outcomes.* As new employees join a public organization's workforce, they are expected to conform to the prevailing organizational culture. Traditional bureaucratic culture is internally centered and oriented and has the following features (Claver et al. 1999, 456):

- The management style is authoritarian, and there is a high degree of control.
- There is little communication, and management is usually univocal and top-down in style.

- Individuals search for stability, have limited scope for initiative, and are oriented to obeying orders.
- The decision-making process is repetitive and centralized.
- There is reluctance to start innovative processes.
- There are high degrees of conformity.

A *citizen-oriented culture* in a public organization is more externally focused and has the following orientation (Stewart and Clarke 1987, 459):

- The tasks and activities that are carried out . . . are solely aimed at usefully serving the citizens.
- The organization will be judged according to the quality of the service given with the resources available.
- The service offered will be a shared value provided that it is shared by all members of the organization.
- A high-quality service is sought.
- Quality in service requires a real approach to the citizen.

Claver et al. (1999, 459) add to these features:

- The citizens have a primary role in the scale of shared values.
- There is frequent contact with citizens.
- Problems that arise in public service are thoroughly analyzed.
- Prompt service is sought by all members of a section or department of public administration.

These features when combined together would seem to add some elements of a social equity perspective to public service delivery in comparison to the features of a public organization with a traditional bureaucratic culture where internal processes, proper hierarchical protocol, verticality, and formality are emphasized. A social equity orientation perspective would require that a public organization have responsibility to all clients or customers, not just majoritarian preferences (Vigoda 2002). A responsive public organization "must be reactive, sympathetic, sensitive and capable of feeling" its clients' needs and opinions (Vigoda 2002, 529). Responsiveness also denotes fairness in service delivery, accuracy in service delivery, and speed in service delivery. Traditional public administration education has not fully stressed the external responsibility of the public organization. This observation is expanded below.

Traditional Public Administration Education

Course work in public administration education consists of many of the following subjects: public personnel management/human resources management; public management; public budgeting; organizational theory and behavior; research methods/qualitative analysis; policy analysis; and ethics. The National Association of Schools of Public Affairs and Administration (NASPAA 2003, 11) requires that university public administration programs seeking accreditation offer course work that fits into three "common curriculum components": The Management of Public Service Organizations, The Application of Quantitative and Qualitative Techniques of Analysis, and Understanding of the Public Policy and Organizational Environment. The overall objective of this course work is to cover such topics as: the origin and development of public administration as a field of study and academic inquiry; how to prepare a budget; decentralization, devolution, and bureaucracy; the public policy process; personnel/human resources functions and processes; distinction between public administration and business administration; political and legal institutions affecting public management; economic and social institutions and processes; and the principles of public management—efficiency, effectiveness, and economy in the public sector. There is no in-depth course work focusing on diversity and social equity. The closest topics that can be associated with diversity and social equity are the issues of representative bureaucracy and affirmative action. Public administration literature covers these topics quite extensively, yet, as will be discussed later, these concepts are different from diversity/diversity management.

Traditional course work in public administration sees the influence of cultural differences in organizations as something that is invisible, illegitimate, and negative (Adler 1991) and inconsistent with the values of efficiency, effectiveness, economy, and good management, and the practices of control, standardization, neutrality, and impersonality. If these values and practices continue to receive primary consideration in the classroom, are professors of public administration teaching courses that are necessary and relevant? Are professors preparing aspiring students for public service to work in a multicultural and diverse society? If professors continue to teach the *Weberian model of bureaucracy* and all of the characteristics that have come to be associated with it, are professors continuing to promote a bureaucratic culture that is rigid and that does not emphasize innovation and change? If so, are professors teaching that those who work in a bureaucratic culture have routines and habits that lead to safety and conformity, and that any modification of these routines and habits will create a state of anxiety and discomfort on the part of the public organization administrators, managers, and service delivery personnel? Golembiewski and Vigoda (2000) maintain public bureaucracies have a vertical flow of orders and reports, accountability to highly ranked officers, fear of sanctions and restrictions, and sometimes even a lack of sufficient accountability dynamics. Therefore, traditional curricula and course work in public administration are well suited to transmitting well-defined facts and theories, particularly to academically inclined, well-schooled student audiences. Yet, this kind of teaching and course work may not be particularly suited to educating a broader and more diverse group of future public administration decision-makers and service delivery personnel.

Instead, professors should provide students with the perspective that a public organization can be transformed to a culture of responsibility, a culture of innovation, and a culture of cost awareness. In other words, an organization's culture can be transformed from a culture of conformity and status quo stressing procedures and conformity to a culture of performance (Keston 1992) with a social equity subculture. *A social equity subculture stresses responsibility to clients who require more public services, innovative public service delivery strategies and techniques, and more focus on cost awareness of programs and services as opposed to a focus on budgeted costs.* Students, as future public administrators, public managers, and public service delivery personnel, must be taught that traditional bureaucratic culture can be modified or changed to reflect a citizen-oriented or social equity–oriented service delivery culture. Claver et al. (1999) offer a cultural diagnosis methodology consisting of the following process: (1) making a diagnosis of the present culture; (2) explaining the need for modifications; (3) defining the

values desired; (4) involving management; (5) making collabora-
tors aware of these new needs; (6) changing the symbols; (7) changing training programs to incorporate the new values; and (8)
periodically revising the values. This methodological approach, sometimes known as a *cultural audit,* examines the organization's core
assumptions and their manifestations as a way of describing its present
state and the reasons for it (Thomas 1999).

In a related way, Denhardt (2001, 507) raises the question: "Do
[professors] seek to educate [public administration] students with
respect to theory or to practice?" The question begs discussion because pre-service students and in-service students bring to the classroom different mind-sets shaped by their educational and social class
backgrounds, and/or life experiences. Mind-sets may also be different for students from different cultures, ethnicities, and races for the
same reasons. Students from different cultures, ethnicities, and races,
in many instances, may be seeking a public administration education to sincerely carry out the adage "to make a difference in the
quality of life" for individuals within their specific cultures,
ethnicities, and races. This point has some support in the literature.
For example, findings by Meier and Stewart (1992), Hindera (1993),
and Meier, Wrinkle, and Polinard (1999) note that the increased presence of minority groups in public agencies favors and enhances
public services for minority group recipients. Yet, professors of public
administration prepare and teach from their own frames of reference. While professors would like not to think so, teaching is not a
neutral activity. Students are influenced by a professor's answers to
their questions, what professors lecture to them, and the textbooks,
articles, and readings professors assign to them.

At the risk of raising the ire of many of my faculty colleagues, the
teaching of diversity and social equity may be problematic if a
professor's culture, background, race, and social and life experiences are very different from the students they are teaching. There
are very few faculty of color in traditional majority universities' public
administration education programs and even fewer in nationally well-
recognized programs. Research points out that faculty are generally
from higher socioeconomic status backgrounds (Oldfield and Conant
2001; Boatsman and Antony 1995), and, as a result, in the university classroom, prospective policy options or alternative social pos-
sibilities maybe overlooked (Lipsitz 1997), not examined, or not

discussed. This may be one reason why public administration education course work continues with a strong theoretical and functional orientation that has little or no focus on diversity and social equity issues. Further, as Cunningham and Weschler (2002, 106) and Faerman (2000) note, professors teach theories and practices that maintain and perpetuate stable organization systems. Of course, professors teach what they were taught in their own academic preparation, and professors teaching pedagogy do not take into consideration how students are different or their different learning styles. Further, many professors seldom teach nor do they firmly grasp organizations that may operate in unstable environments. This is to say that the issues of diversity and social equity can create and promote instability and uncertainty in organizational operating procedures and missions and disrupt the status quo (Bond and Pyle 1998).

Further, regardless of whether professors are teaching public administration students to be staff practitioners or line-manager practitioners, the issues of diversity and social equity are important in the areas of responsibilities for both types of public practitioners. On the one hand, Cunningham and Weschler (2002, 105) note that staffers' responsibilities revolve around: "(1) planning and implementing research projects; (2) carrying out statistical analysis; (3) formulating policy options; and (4) creating and refining financial, personnel and information systems." Staffers work in a multicultural environment and must possess diversity and social equity knowledge and understanding. Staffers can also incorporate social equity analysis into research projects and statistical analyses. In this way, their work can be passed on to superiors.

On the other hand, a line-manager practitioner's responsibilities include: "(1) deciding among policy options; (2) implementing policy; (3) negotiating with stakeholders; (4) motivating subordinates; and (5) anticipating impending changes in the organization's environment" (Cunningham and Weschler 2002, 105). Line managers are more directly related to the public organization's service delivery process, and their responsibilities involve both leadership of subordinates and leadership with stakeholders. Line-manager practitioners must handle social relationships, deal with emotionally challenged situations, supervise multicultural personnel, and seek win-win solutions to complex problems. Therefore, line-manager practitioners' understanding of diversity may impact their subordinates' views of social equity in the service delivery process. There-fore, the teaching of social equity and diversity would seem to be a required necessary competency for students in public administra-tion programs. The next section describes how the author teaches diversity as a way of enhancing a social equity understanding on the part of students.

Teaching Diversity as a Way of Advancing Social Equity

The first issue in teaching a class on diversity and public organiza-tions in a diversity and social equity context is to identify the pri-mary objectives of the class. In my graduate class "Diversity, Public Policy and Public Administration," the primary objectives are: (1) to prepare students who have career aspirations in the public sector to meet the diversity and multicultural challenges in society they will face as future public administrators, public managers, and public service delivery personnel; (2) to enhance students' knowledge, understanding, and appreciation of cultural diversity; (3) to provide the cultural competencies needed to interact successfully in a rap-idly demographically changing society; and (4) to provide a per-spective on the issue of social class as a component for understanding cultural diversity. While the importance of race and gender has been acknowledged in public administration and public policy implemen-tation, the role of social class has not (Oldfield, n.d.). Although there is considerable literature about how social class affects most facets of life and living in American society, public administration educa-tion seldom stresses social class as an important area of study and inquiry. According to Loewen (1995, 197–98), social class is prob-ably the single most important variable in society. From womb to tomb, it correlates with almost all other characteristics of individuals that we can measure.

In my class, students are required to complete two field assign-ments. One assignment requires an interview (from a set of ques-tions provided by me) with a public administration executive or administrator (city manager, police chief, fire chief, personnel ad-ministrator, etc.) to obtain their views on how diversity is affecting the work environment and public service delivery. This assignment gives students the opportunity to meet and talk directly with a pub-lic administrator, public executive, or department head. An indirect outcome of this interview assignment is that students are sometimes asked to submit a job application to the organization. The other assignment consists of attending a public policy-making body meeting to observe firsthand interactions between policy-makers and public administrators and the extent of the diversity of both policy-makers and public administrators and whether and how this diversity plays out in an interactive policy-making process. Both of these field assignments provide students with a closer connection to their public administration education. Further, many students have never met or spoken with a public administrator, public executive, or department head about the profession or attended a public body policy-making meeting and observed politics and administration interaction. This is especially the case for pre-service students until their internship experiences. These assignments fill this void.

With regard to affirmative action, multiculturalism, and diversity, the class maintains that the concepts have different meanings and operational procedures leading to different quantitative, qualitative, and behavioral outcomes. The different outcomes result from different implementation strategies and approaches. Tables 4.1 and 4.2 define key terms and show the differences between affirmative action, multiculturalism, and managing diversity. Unlike affirmative action and multiculturalism, managing diversity is a pragmatic, synergistic strategy driving productivity, service delivery; organizational competitiveness and social equity (see Rice 2001). The course also discusses the differences in organizational culture between a contemporary monocultural, affirmative action, and multicultural organization (see Table 4.3 on p. 80).

Among the important learning outcomes in the class are: (1) hiring diverse personnel is simply not an end in itself, nor is a diversity edict from top leadership; (2) implementing public policy initiatives requires an understanding of the diverse constituencies served by the organization; (3) public organizations are synergistic organizations (Adler 1991) that seek to maximize the advantages of diversity while minimizing its disadvantages; (4) diversity strategies should be preceded by a cultural audit and/or diversity audit and what they consist of to provide a comparative analysis for measuring diversity progress; (5) social class and socioeconomic status are important elements necessary for learning about and understanding diversity; and (6) there are several types of diversity train-

Table 4.1

Diversity Glossary

Cultural audit:	Examines a public organization's values, symbols, rules, and routines, which maintain its purpose and existence to uncover counterproductive activities and barriers that may adversely impact its public service mission and service delivery process.
Diversity:	Refers to a broad range of differences among employees, including race, gender, age, ethnicity, physical abilities, sexual orientation, education, and so on.
Diversity audit:	Allows the employer to uncover how selected groups of employees are experiencing the organization and to reveal hidden perceptions or confirm perceived biases before an incident of harassment or discrimination occurs.
Diversity climate:	Refers to employee behaviors and attitudes that are grounded in perceptions of the organizational context related to women and minorities.
Diversity quotient	A process in which an organization's materials and environment are analyzed from a minority perspective to determine why the organization does not receive employment applications from diverse applicants.
Managing diversity:	Refers to the effective utilization of the diversity of the workforce to accomplish organizational goals.
Monoculturalism:	Refers to the values, customs, and dominance of one culture over another.
Multiculturalism/ Valuing diversity:	Refers to "the process of recognizing, understanding and appreciating cultures other than one's own," and to a change in perspective in regard to the diversity of individual workers in an organization; the change is from regarding differences as a disadvantage to seeing them as an important asset in an organization.

Source: Derived from Auman and Myers (1996), Thomas (1999), and Rice (2001).

ing methodologies to draw on based on findings from a cultural audit and/or diversity audit (Rice 2002). These are two separate and distinct audits seeking different information. A *cultural audit* attempts to examine the public organization's values, symbols, rules, and routines, which maintain its purpose and existence to uncover counterproductive activities and barriers that may adversely impact its public service mission and service delivery process. A *diversity audit* seeks to uncover how selected groups of employees

Table 4.2

Comparing Affirmative Action, Multiculturalism, and Managing Diversity

Affirmative action	Multiculturalism (valuing differences)	Managing diversity
Focus. Fairness and equality.	*Focus.* Learning and effectiveness of cultural differences.	*Focus.* Integrating diversity for organizational productivity and effectiveness.
Quantitative. Emphasis is on achieving equality of opportunity in the work environment through the changing of organizational demographics. Progress is monitored by statistical reports and analysis. (Descriptive data)	*Qualitative.* Emphasis is on the appreciation of differences and creation of an environment in which everyone feels valued and accepted. Progress is monitored by organizational surveys focused on attitudes and perceptions.	*Behavioral.* Emphasis is on building specific skills and creating policies that get the best from every employee. Efforts are monitored by progress toward achieving goals and objectives.
Legally driven. Written plans and statistical goals for specific groups are utilized. Reports are mandated by EEO laws and consent decrees. Demographic characteristics are most important.	*Ethically driven.* Moral and ethical imperatives drive this culture change.	*Strategically driven.* Behaviors and policies are seen as contributing to organizational goals and objectives, such as profit and productivity, and are tied to rewards and results.
Remedial. Specific target groups benefit as past wrongs are remedied. Previously excluded groups have an advantage.	*Idealistic.* Everyone benefits. Everyone feels valued and accepted in an inclusive environment.	*Pragmatic.* The organization benefits; morale, profits, and productivity increase.

Assimilation model. Model assumes that groups brought into system will adapt to existing organizational norms. Employees' apparent differences do not count.

Opens doors. Efforts affect hiring and promotion decisions in the organization.

Resistance. Resistance is due to perceived limits to autonomy in decision-making and perceived fears of reverse discrimination.

Diversity model. Model assumes that groups will retain their own characteristics and shape the organization as well as be shaped by it.

Opens attitudes, minds, and the culture. Efforts affect attitudes of employees.

Resistance. Resistance is due to a fear of change, discomfort with differences, and a desire to return to the "good old days."

Synergy model. Model assumes that diverse groups will create new ways of working together effectively in a pluralistic environment.

Opens the system. Efforts affect managerial practices and policies.

Resistance. Resistance is due to denial of demographic realities, of the need for alternative approaches, and of the benefits of change. It also arises from the difficulty of learning new skills, altering existing systems, and finding the time to work toward synergetic solutions.

Source: Derived from Rice (2001) and Riccucci (2002).

Table 4.3

Contemporary Organizational Cultures

The Monocultural Organization
*   Domination of one group over another.
*   Seeks to establish and maintain superiority.
*   Exclusionary hiring and membership practices.

The Affirmative Action Organization
*   Committed to actively recruiting and hiring underrepresented or formerly discriminated individuals.
*   All individuals in the organization are encouraged to behave in a nonoppressive way.
*   All members of the organization still conform to norms and practices of dominant group.
*   Targets change at the individual level.
*   Focus on hiring numbers and assimilation.

The Multicultural Organization
*   Reflects contributions and interests of diverse cultural and social groups in mission, operations, etc.
*   Diverse cultural and social groups play an influential role in all levels of the organization.
*   Supports efforts to expand diversity and multiculturalism.

Source: Derived from Miller and Katz (1995).

---

are experiencing the organization and the prevailing diversity climate in the organization (Rice 2002).

A second issue in teaching diversity in public administration education in a social equity context is: What texts are available for student use? Only a few textbooks discuss diversity and social equity in a public sector context. The literature on diversity in public administration, although somewhat developed, includes only a few available texts. I put together the first volume, which you are now reading, in 1996. Other works are those by Mathews (1999), Broadnax (2000), Riccucci (2002), and Naff (2001). Scholarly articles and other publications focusing on diversity/diversity management are more plentiful and are assigned as complementary reading materials. Examples of complementary reading materials are Thomas (1999), Soni (2000), the U.S. Office of Personnel Management (2000), Naff and Kellough (2001), and Seldon and Seldon (2001). Considering social equity, Svara and Brunet (2003) argue that social equity is a "blind spot" in the seven most widely used texts in the field. They conducted a content analysis of these works and found that only one text defined social equity and only two texts gave attention to the historical aspects of social equity in the field. A majority of the texts provide coverage on the issues of due process, discrimination, sexual harassment, equal employment opportunity/affirmative action, and representativeness. None of the texts covered cultural competencies, equity measures, and ethics.

A third issue in teaching diversity in a social equity context is the need to have a diverse, multicultural student body in the classroom. This is obviously important for at least two reasons. First, a diverse, multicultural classroom provides a learning environment for emphasizing that cultural differences do indeed exist. Second, a diverse, multicultural classroom lends itself to counterarguments made by students of color (see Nemeth 1986; Darling-Hammond, French, and Garcia-Lopez 2002), affecting the number of alternative scenarios in case studies, experiential activities, and other exercises (Watson, Kumor, and Michaelsen 1993; Darling-Hammond, French, and Garcia-Lopez 2002). These observations are consistent with the diversity literature in higher education which notes the many advantages of diversity on university campuses and in classrooms (see, for example, Bowen and Bok 1998; Association of American Colleges and Universities 1997). A fourth issue in teaching diversity in a social equity context is the need to bring the issues associated with social class into the public administration education classroom. While students are aware of life outcomes and distinctions among different groups, they are less aware of the underlying causes of these outcomes and distinctions and why they continually persist. Yet, public administration literature is mostly devoid of discussion on social class and equity (Oldfield, n.d.).

Conclusion

In the postmodern era, it would seem that in order for social equity in service delivery to be a primary concern of public organizations, these organizations must first get their own house in order in regard to diversity. The culture of a public organization has to incorporate diversity within both its mission and management practices. A strong focus on diversity inside a public organization may posture it to move from a bureaucratic culture toward a more citizen-oriented/ social equity culture. This movement requires a shift and adjustment to three new subcultures: a culture of responsibility, a culture of innovation, and a culture of cost awareness (Claver 1999). Adopting this typology of culture leads to what Claver (1999) calls a "culture of performance with a social equity subculture." In this cultural environment, decision-making takes on a certain degree of innovation, improvisation, and risk (Keston 1992). Surely, social equity considerations on the part of a public organization would best occur in this kind of cultural environment. One way to ascertain this type of culture in a public organization is to conduct a *culture diagnosis*. The purpose here is to not only identify the particular culture that is present and its operating values but also the extent to which it is shared by members. The objective of the cultural diagnosis is to determine whether a negative bureaucratic culture exists that inhibits effective public service delivery and considerations of social equity. Also, a diversity audit can be administered to determine hidden perceptions or confirm biases about certain groups of individuals who are both employees and service delivery recipients.

Public administration education programs need to incorporate into their curricula and courses in a very substantive way the topics of diversity and social equity and social class to be relevant to contemporary students. Perhaps one way to achieve this is for public administration education to structure (or restructure) its learning developmental sequence to include not only cognitive development and linguistics or interactive development but also a strong focus on psychosocial development (Denhardt 2001). The knowledge attained in the psychosocial development sequence focuses on "action" skills of intrapersonal improvement that would seem to lend itself to the promotion and consideration of social equity in public service delivery. Denhardt argues (2001, 530) that "one's intrapersonal skills are those capabilities that provide psychological and moral grounding for our actions." As a result, with the psychosocial development sequence, future public administrators should be more adept in acting morally, responsibly, effectively, independently, and equitably (see also Powell 2001). Further, teaching diversity in a social equity context needs to occur in a diverse, multicultural classroom setting. Students learn not only from the professor but also from their peers in the classroom. Moreover, if social equity involves "fairness" and "different equalities" in public service outcomes, issues associated with social class (e.g., income, wealth, and education) must also receive considerable attention in public administration education. Finally, incorporating diversity and social class into public administration curricula may lead to future generations of public administrators who are able "to develop the quantitative tools, indicators and benchmarks to define objectives and measure progress in pursuit of social equity" (Rutledge 2002) in public service delivery outcomes.

References

Adams, Guy B., and Virginia M. Ingersoll. 1990. "Culture, Technical Rationality, and Organizational Culture." *American Review of Public Administration* 20 (4): 285–303.

Adler, Nancy J. 1991. *International Dimensions of Organizational Behavior.* Boston: PSW-Kent.

Association of American Colleges and Universities. 1997. *Diversity Works: The Emerging Picture of How Students Benefit.* Washington, DC: Association of American Colleges and Universities.

Auman, Rick, and Gina Myers. 1996. "Why Is Diversity Becoming a Four Letter Word?" In Mitchell F. Rice, ed., *Diversity and Public Organizations.* Dubuque, IA: Kendall Hunt Publishing.

Ban, C. 1995. *How Do Public Managers Manage? Bureaucratic Constraints, Organizational Culture, and the Potential for Reform.* San Francisco: Jossey-Bass.

Boatsman, K.C., and Jim Antony. 1995. Faculty Equity: Class Origin, Race and Gender in the American Professoriate. Paper presented at the Annual Conference of the American Educational Research Association.

Bond, Meg A., and Jean L. Pyle. 1998. "Diversity Dilemmas at Work." *Journal of Management Inquiry* 7 (3): (September) 252–69.

Bowen, William G., and Derek Bok. 1998. *The Shape of the River: Long Term Consequences of Considering Race in College and University Admission.* Princeton: Princeton University Press.

Broadnax, Walter D. 2000. *Diversity and Affirmative Action in Public Service.* Boulder, CO: Westview Press.

Claver, Enrique et al. 1999. "Public Administration: From Bureaucratic Culture to Citizen-Oriented Culture." *International Journal of Public Sector Management* 12 (6): 445–64.

Cunningham, Robert, and Louis Weschler. 2002. "Theory and Public Administration Student/Practitioner." *Public Administration Review* 62 (1): 103–11.

Darling-Hammond, Linda, J. French, and S.P. Garcia-Lopez. 2002. *Learning to Teach for Social Justice.* New York: Teachers College Press.

Deal, Terrence E., and Allan A. Kennedy. 1982. *Corporate Cultures.* Reading, MA: Addison-Wesley.

Denhardt, Robert B. 2001. "The Big Questions of Public Administration Education." *Public Administration Review* 61 (5): 526–34.

Edelmann, Lauren B., Sally R. Fuller, and Iona Mara-Drita. 2001. "Diversity

Rhetoric and the Marginalization of Law," *American Journal of Sociology* 106 (6) (May): 1589–641.

Faerman, Sue. 2000. Using Service Learning to Prepare Professionals for the Early 21st Century. Paper presented at the Annual Meeting of the National Association of Schools of Public Administration and Affairs.

Feldman, S.P. 1985. "Culture and Conformity: An Essay on Individual Adaptation in Centralized Bureaucracy." *Human Relations* 38 (4): 341–56.

Fox, Charles J., and Hugh T. Miller. 1995. *Postmodern Public Administration: Toward Discourse.* Thousand Oaks, CA: Sage.

Frederickson, H. George. 1990. "Public Administration and Social Equity." *Public Administration and Review* (March/April): 228–36.

———. 2002. "Is Social Equity Class Warfare?" *PA Times* 25 (9) (September): 3.

Golembiewski, Robert T., and Eran Vigoda. 2000. "Organizational Innovation and Science of Craft of Management." In M.A. Rahim, R.T. Golembiewski, and K.D. Mackenzie, eds. *Current Topics in Management.* Greenwich, CT: JAI Press.

Green, Richard T. 2002. "Common Law, Equity and American Public Administration." *American Review of Public Administration* 32 (3): 263–94.

Hindera, John J. 1993. "Representative Bureaucracy: Further Evidence of Active Representation in EEOC District Offices." *Journal of Public Administration Research and Theory* 3: 415–29.

Keston, J.B. 1992. "Dimensions of Excellence: Changing Organizational Culture." *Public Manager* 23 (3): 17–20.

King, Cheryl, Kathryn M. Feltey, and Bridget O. Susel. 1998. "The Question of Participation: Toward Authentic Public Participation in Public Administration." *Public Administration Review* 58 (4): 317–26.

Lipsitz, George. 1997. "Class and Consciousness: Teaching About Social Class in Public Universities." In Amitava Kumar, ed., *Class Issues.* New York: New York University Press, 9–21.

Loewen, J.W. 1995. *Lies My Teacher Told Me.* New York: New Press.

Mathews, Audrey L. 1999. *The Sum of the Differences: Diversity and Public Organization.* New York: McGraw-Hill.

Meier, Kenneth J., and Joseph Stewart. 1992. "The Impact of Representative Bureaucracies: Educational Systems and Public Policies." *American Review of Public Administration* 22: 157–71.

Meier, Kenneth J., R.D. Wrinkle, and J.L. Polinard. 1999. "Representative Bureaucracy and Distributional Equity: Addressing the Hard Questions." *Journal of Politics* 61: 1025–39.

Miller, Frederick A., and Judith H. Katz. 1995. "Cultural Diversity as a Developmental Process: The Path from a Monocultural Club To Inclusive Organization." *The 1995 Annual Volume 2, Consulting.* San Diego: Pfeiffer and Co., 267–81.

Naff, Katherine C. 2001. *To Look Like America: Dismantling Barriers for Women and Minorities in Government.* Boulder, CO: Westview Press.

Naff, Katherine C., and J. Edward Kellough. 2001. *A Changing Workforce: Diversity Programs in the Federal Government.* Washington, DC: Price Waterhouse Coopers.

National Academy of Public Administration. 2000. *Standing Panel on Social Equity Issue Paper and Work Plan* (October).

National Association of Schools of Public Affairs and Administration. 2003. *General Instructions for the Self-Study Report: National Association of Schools of Public Affairs and Administration.* Washington, DC.

Nemeth, C.J. 1986. "Differential Contributions of Majority and Minority Influence." *Psychological Review* 93: 23–32.

Oldfield, Kenneth. n.d. Social Class and Public Administration: A Closed Question Opens. Unpublished manuscript.

Oldfield, Kenneth, and Richard F. Conant. 2001. "Professors, Social Class and Affirmative Action: A Pilot Study." *Journal of Public Affairs Education* 7 (July): 171–85.

Peters, B. Guy. 1999. *American Public Policy: Promise and Performance.* New York: Seven Bridges.

Pops, G.M., and T.J. Pavlak. 1991. *The Case for Justice.* San Francisco: Jossey-Bass.

Powell, R. 2001. *Straight Talk: Growing as Multicultural Educators.* New York: Peter Lang.

Riccucci, Norma M. 2002. *Managing Diversity in Public Sector Workforces.* Boulder, CO: Westview Press.

Rice, Mitchell F., ed. 1996. *Diversity and Public Organizations: Theory, Issues and Perspectives.* Dubuque, IA: Kendall Hunt Publishing.

———. 2001. "The Need for Teaching Diversity and Representativeness in University Public Administration Education and Professional Public Service Training Programmes in Sub-Saharan Africa." In *Managing Diversity in the Civil Service.* Amsterdam, Netherlands: IOS Press, 99–110.

———. 2002. Diversity Initiatives and Best Practices in Organizations: Developments, Approaches and Issues. Paper presented at the International Conference of the Academy of Business Administration, Warsaw, Poland.

Rutledge, Philip. 2002. "Some Unfinished Business in Public Administration." Donald C. Stone Guest Lecture presented at the National Conference of the American Society for Public Administration, Phoenix, Arizona, March 26. www.Napawash.org/about_academy/rutledge_lecture.html

Seldon, Sally Coleman, and Frank Seldon. 2001. "Rethinking Diversity in Public Organizations for the 21st Century." *Administration and Society* 33 (3): 303–29.

Soni, Vidu. 2000. "A Twenty-First Century for Diversity in the Public Sector." *Public Administration Review* 60 (5): 395–408.

Stewart, J., and M. Clarke. 1987. "The Public Service Orientation: Issues and Dilemmas." *Public Administration Review* 65 (3): 161–77.

Svara, James, and James Brunet. 2003. Filling in the Skeletal Pillar: Addressing Social Equity in Introductory Courses in Public Administration. A paper presented at the National Academy of Public Administration "Social Equity Symposium."

Thomas, R. Roosevelt, Jr. 1999. "Diversity Management: Some Measurement Criteria." *Employment Relations Today* (winter): 49–62.

U.S. Census Bureau. 2000. *Statistical Abstract of the United States.* Washington, DC: Government Printing Office.

U.S. Office of Personnel Management. 2000. *Building and Maintaining a Diverse, High Quality Workforce: A Guide for Federal Agencies.* Washington, DC: USOPM, Employment Service Diversity Office.

Vigoda, Eran. 2002. "From Responsiveness to Collaboration: Governance, Citizens, and the Next Generation of Public Administration." *Public Administration Review* 62 (5) (September/October): 527–40.

Watson, W.E., K. Kumar, and L.K. Michaelsen. 1993. "Cultural Diversity's Impact on Interaction Process and Performance: Comparing Homogeneous and Diverse Task Groups." *Academy of Management Journal* 36: 590–602.

5

Diversity in Public Administration Education

A View from California

Kyle Farmbry

Recent census data indicate that the United States is rapidly becoming an increasingly diverse nation. According to census figures, the total number of racial minorities within the United States currently comprises some 28 percent of the population. It is estimated that within the next sixty years there will be no single racial majority group. Linked to these projections are a number of policy discussions of what this increasing diversity will mean for public service professions. From matters of shifting policy debates due to shifting constituencies to new considerations of how services are delivered, matters of diversity raise a number of issues for those working with and for public organizations. Some states such as Hawaii, California, Texas, and New Mexico have reached a point where in many of their counties, there is no such thing as a majority group. Other states such as New York and Florida will soon reach this demographic threshold of there not being one majority racial or ethnic group. As a result, public officials in many of these states are already engaged in discussions on what exactly a diverse constituency means in terms of service delivery and representation by public sector agencies. As those preparing future public servants, professors teaching courses in public administration are positioned to shape how future administrators will work with the public sector challenges and opportunities brought about by increasing diversity at both state and national levels. These demographic realities underscore the importance of several discussions that occurred at the 1999 National Association of Schools of Public Affairs and Administration (NASPAA) Annual Conference in

Miami and the coinciding report provided to the NASPAA membership and executive council in May 2000 (NASPAA 2000) on diversity
as it relates to university academic programs in public administration
and affairs.

This chapter examines some of the implications of diversity trends
for public administration educators in California as the state under-
goes a change in the makeup of its population. California's demographic shift has brought with it a number of challenges in ensuring
adequate service delivery and administrative representation in what
is a changing multiracial, multiethnic, and multilingual landscape.
These challenges coupled with political initiatives in recent years
have ultimately sought to limit service provisions to some members
of local communities while other initiatives have called into question various race and gender-based policies in such important areas
as public contracting, admission into public universities, and other
areas in the public domain. The chapter begins with a general profile of the demographic trends related to diversity in California. It
continues by presenting findings related to diversity trends in California public administration programs based on a survey of directors of university public administration programs in the state. The
chapter concludes with a series of recommendations on how public
administration educators might ultimately make the best use of the
opportunities of diversity in preparing future administrators based
on reflections from some of California's experiences.

Diversity in California: Demographic Shifts, Challenges, and Opportunities

California has experienced a major shift in recent years in the racial
and ethnic composition of its residents. A recent analysis of the state's
demographic trends by the Public Policy Institute of California (PPIC)
shows the changing makeup of the population between the early
1970s and latter 1990s (Reyes 2001). While nearly 80 percent of
the state's residents in 1970 were white non-Hispanics, by 1998 that
percentage had dropped to 52 percent. The PPIC analysis also notes
that in 1998, Hispanics accounted for 30 percent of the state's population, Asian-Americans accounted for 11 percent, and African-
Americans accounted for 7 percent (vii). Adding to PPIC's estimates,
Maharidge (1996) projects that between 1998 and 2000 the white

population is expected to decrease to less than 50 percent of the state's total population. Concomitant with the state's population changes have been a number of public discussions regarding the meaning of this diversity, the politics of inclusion, and the impact of public sector challenges related to an increasingly diversifying population base. Prior to the early 1970s, discussions of diversity in the state were largely framed in the context of reacting to the urban riots and social equity programs of the late 1960s.

In recent years various social and political agendas coupled with the demographic impact of increasing waves of immigration have added to the complexity of how matters of diversity are viewed and responded to in the state. In 1994, Californians passed Proposition 187, which was designed to restrict the ability of most illegal immigrants to access state social services. Two years later voters passed Proposition 209, which sought to eliminate preferential programs based on gender and ethnicity in California's public employment, college admissions, and government contract programs. In 1998 voters passed Proposition 227, which required the elimination of most established public school bilingual education programs. Finally, in the fall of 2001, a Race Privacy Initiative was introduced to California's attorney general with the goal of eliminating the racial classification of any individuals in public records. Proponents were successful in adding the Race Privacy Initiative as a voters' referendum on the October 2003 special election ballot. Administrative systems have had to adjust to new rules and regulations stemming from various propositions while at the same time recognizing that there are a number of new groups of people composing their basic constituencies. Service delivery has been enacted in a context of new cultural realities, and in some cases the makeup of the labor pool from which public organizations can draw has changed.

Methodology

To explore how public administration programs in California are responding to the state's increasing diversity, the list of NASPAA-accredited universities offering Masters in Public Administration (MPA) programs was examined to identify what schools offer MPA programs in the state (see Table 5.1). E-mails with a set of questions relating to diversity in public administration education in their schools

were sent to California-based MPA directors during the summer of
2001. The Appendix (see p. 102) lists the questions that the MPA
directors were asked to respond to. Of the twenty-four program directors who were sent e-mails in the survey, only six initially responded. Due to the low response rate, follow-up phone calls were
made in the middle of September in an attempt to increase the response rate. Six additional people were interviewed by phone. One
final program director was interviewed at the 2001 NASPAA conference. Therefore, a total of thirteen responded out of the twenty-
four MPA directors contacted—a response rate of 54 percent.

Individuals contacted by e-mail or phone were asked to comment
on the diversity of their programs from several perspectives. First,
they were asked about any changes in their programs in terms of
student and faculty composition, course offerings, recruitment strategies, and classroom-based discussions that, in their opinion, resulted from some of the recently reported demographic changes.
They were also asked to comment on any changes in their programs
that may have surfaced following passage of the recent propositions
pertaining to diversity, especially Propositions 209 or 187. Finally,
they were asked if their programs had any explicit statement on
diversity. In addition to conducting the e-mail and phone interviews,
census data for the counties where the MPA programs are located
were collected to check for any demographic changes between 1990
and 2000. It was anticipated that MPA programmatic factors and
composition of students and faculty might result from changes in
the population of the counties in which the programs were located.

It should be noted that in addition to only a 54 percent rate of
response (in e-mail and phone surveys), two items complicated some
of the data collection. First, MPA programs in California are pres-
ently experiencing a turnover of professors due to retirement. As a
result, many new professors in different disciplines, including public administration, are being hired, bringing with them different social frameworks for diversity than those who started in these
university positions twenty or thirty years ago. The trend of recent
hires has brought about a number of challenges in terms of institutional memory. Two of the interviewees indicated that they were
relatively new to their institutions and thus could not comfortably
comment on changes in diversity in their universities over the years.
Second, because of the youth of public administration as a disci-

Table 5.1

Schools Offering Masters in Public Administration Programs and Their Counties in California

County	School
Alameda	California State University, Hayward
Butte	California State University, Chico
Fresno	California State University, Fresno
Kern	California State University, Bakersfield
Los Angeles	California State Polytechnic University, Pomona
	California State University, Dominguez Hills
	California State University, Long Beach
	California State University, Los Angeles
	California State University, Northridge
	University of California, Los Angeles
	University of LaVerne
	University of Southern California, Los Angeles
Monterey	Monterey Institute of International Studies
	Naval Postgraduate School
Orange	California State University, Fullerton
Sacramento	California State University, Sacramento
	University of Southern California, Sacramento Center
San Bernardino	California State University, San Bernardino
Santa Clara	San Jose State University
San Diego	National University
	San Diego State University
San Francisco	Golden Gate University
	San Francisco State University
Stanislaus	California State University, Stanislaus

Source: National Association of Schools of Public Affairs and Administration (2002).

pline, some of the programs surveyed are relatively new. Thus, in some cases the programs have not been in existence long enough for the survey respondent or interviewee to be able to comfortably comment on what changes have occurred over the past five to ten years resulting from diversity. One program director, for example, noted that her program came into existence in the mid 1990s and thus was not able to respond to some of the diversity-related propositions. Despite some of the challenges noted, responses from interviews were categorized to provide a framework for examining the impact of changes within MPA programs as well as the impact of diversity within the past several years. These responses from California educators are helpful in framing some of the diversity implications for public administration educators in other states.

Table 5.2

Changes in Percentage of County Population by Race, 1990–2000

County	White/nonminority			African-American			Hispanic/Latino (any race)		
	1990	2000	Chg.	1990	2000	Chg.	1990	2000	Chg.
Alameda	59.5	48.8	−18.1	17.92	14.9	−16.7	14.2	18.97	33.5
Butte	90.7	84.5	−6.8	1.30	1.4	6.9	7.5	10.5	40.6
Fresno	63.3	54.3	−14.3	5.01	5.3	5.8	35.4	43.99	24.0
Kern	69.6	61.6	−11.5	5.54	6.0	8.5	27.9	38.4	37.3
Los Angeles	56.8	48.7	−14.2	11.2	9.8	−12.7	37.8	44.6	17.9
Monterey	63.8	55.9	−12.4	6.4	3.7	−41.7	33.6	46.8	39.2
Orange	78.6	64.8	−17.5	1.8	1.7	−5.4	23.4	30.8	31.3
Sacramento	75.1	64.0	−14.8	9.3	9.9	6.7	11.7	16.0	37.2
San Bernardino	73.0	58.9	−19.3	8.1	9.1	12.1	26.7	39.2	46.7
Santa Clara	68.9	53.8	−21.9	3.7	2.8	−25.3	21.0	23.9	14.1
San Diego	74.9	66.5	−11.2	6.4	5.7	−10.0	20.4	26.7	30.5
San Francisco	53.6	49.7	−7.3	10.9	7.8	−28.6	13.9	14.1	1.3
Stanislaus	80.2	69.3	−13.6	1.7	2.6	48.1	21.8	31.7	45.4

Source: U.S. Bureau of the Census (2000) and Statistical Abstract of the United States (1991).

Findings and Implications for Public Administration Programs

One of the main objectives in this study is to examine the impact of the state's diversity upon public administration education programs. To obtain a better picture of diversity within the state, county-level census data identifying demographics and changes in the demographics between 1990 and 2000 in the counties where public administration programs are located were collected. These data are presented in Table 5.2. Statewide, these data suggest that much of the state has experienced a major demographic shift in the population reflecting a decrease in the white/nonminority population over the past decade and an increase in the size of many ethnic and racial minority populations. Specifically, in terms of ethnic and racial minority populations, data indicate that each of the thirteen counties has seen a percentage increase in the Hispanic population during the same time period. Seven of the thirteen counties have seen a decrease in the African-American population. Three of the thirteen counties have seen an increase in the percentage of the

Asian/Pacific Islander			Native American			Other		
1990	2000	Chg.	1990	2000	Chg.	1990	2000	Chg.
15.0	21.1	40.0	0.70	0.63	−8.9	6.8	8.9	31.96
2.8	3.5	22.2	1.8	1.9	6.9·	3.4	4.8	42.7
8.5	8.2	−4.6	1.1	1.6	50.0	22.0	25.9	17.7
3.0	3.5	15.4	1.3	1.5	16.9	20.5	23.2	13.4
10.8	12.2	13.6	0.5	0.81	57.5	20.7	23.5	13.6
7.8	6.5	−17.4	0.8	1.0	23.3	21.1	27.8	32.1
10.3	13.9	34.5	0.5	0.7	38.6	8.8	14.8	68.3
9.2	11.6	25.6	1.2	1.1	−5.8	5.1	7.5	46.0
4.2	4.9	19.6	0.9	1.2	23.2	13.8	20.8	51.0
17.5	25.9	48.4	0.6	0.7	8.9	9.24	12.1	31.2
7.9	9.4	17.9	0.8	0.9	7.7	9.9	12.8	29.1
29.1	31.3	7.6	0.5	0.45	−6.74	5.9	6.5	9.7
5.2	4.6	−12.1	1.1	0.34	−68.6	11.7	16.8	43.3

Asian/Pacific Islander population. Four of the thirteen counties have seen a decrease in the Native American population. Data reported in Table 5.2 show that in ten of the counties where public administration programs are located, the largest racial/ethnic minority group in 2000 consists of Hispanics/Latinos. In the three other counties, Asian/Pacific Islanders make up the largest ethnic/racial minority group. Asian/Pacific Islanders comprise the second-largest racial/ethnic minority group in seven of the ten counties where Hispanics/Latinos make up the largest ethnic/racial group. African-Americans make up the second-largest ethnic/racial minority group in the remaining three counties.

While some of the MPA directors interviewed noted that diversity was an issue, others noted that, to a degree, diversity is not as much of an issue in California as in other states with one or two ethnic or racial minority groups in the population. One interviewee reflected on her experiences teaching in a largely racially homogeneous community before arriving at her current university. She noted that while in her previous community she felt that tensions resulting from differences between people were much greater than in her current relatively heterogeneous community. "Because we have a greater variety in terms of races and ethnic groups, and a larger population in each of those groups," she observed, "public discussions on race and ethnicity are not as adversarial as I saw in my previous community."

The findings related to county-level diversity provide a foundation for program directors to raise questions on how population demographic changes are seen at a local level where different MPA programs are located. The survey data demonstrate that diversity is not solely an issue to be examined from a remote statewide position: diversity is a phenomenon that can be examined at a local level where schools are located.

Student and Faculty Recruitment

One question underlying this study was the impact on MPA programs by Proposition 209, particularly relating to declines or increases in admission. Only one of the respondent program directors noted any impact of Proposition 209 on the makeup of the student body in their program. This program director noted a decline in minority students in the fall of 1998, which had a 13 percent rate of nonwhites in the entering class. This number was a dramatic decrease from the 1997 entering class, which had 45 percent nonwhites, and the 1996 entering class that had 39 percent nonwhites. The program director went on to add, however, that greater recruiting outreach efforts within the parameters established by Proposition 209 were able to help drive a minority student enrollment for the fall 1999 entering class to 44 percent and for the fall 2000 class to 53 percent of the students. Another director noted that, in anticipation of Proposition 209, his university made a decision to extend its general outreach efforts into a variety of communities and agencies that would ultimately help ensure a diverse candidate pool. More aggressive and wide-reaching recruitment efforts, in his opinion, translated in ensuring a diverse candidate pool despite any possible impact from Proposition 209. Two program directors noted that because their programs draw upon mid-career students who work in public agencies, ultimately they were able to draw upon the diversity of the agencies from which they recruit. They observed a relationship between recruiting from a diverse pool of in-service candidates and increasing diversity in their programs.

On matters of faculty recruitment, respondents noted that there has been some difficulty in recruiting and retaining a teaching faculty that is representative of the state's diversity. This challenge particularly surfaced in two themes of conversation. The first theme was among schools in the California State University's system, consisting of sixteen of the twenty-four schools listed in Table 5.1. These schools, by state law, are more focused on teaching than the more research-driven schools in the University of California system. They also tend to attract fewer research dollars and less private support than many of the University of California schools and private universities in the state. As a result, some of the schools in the California State University system expressed a challenge of offering competitive teaching loads and salaries capable of attracting a diverse population of faculty applicants, particularly when compared with the offerings of University of California schools and private institutions.

One program director observed that, of the traditional minority groups, the candidate pool for African-Americans, while still much smaller than the nonminority white population, appeared larger than for other groups. Thus, the second theme focused on the small pool of candidates for teaching positions, particularly among Hispanic, Asian, and Native American populations in the field of public administration. Another program director used the lack of what she saw as a small candidate pool for increased diversity in hiring to call for public administration doctoral granting programs to increase the diversity of the doctoral candidate pool that she might hire from in the future.

Courses

Some disagreement was expressed on the issue of how to address matters of diversity in courses. On one hand, some program directors argued that diversity matters should be integrated into core courses in MPA programs. Three of the program directors feel this means integration beyond courses such as public personnel management, where one argued that much of the diversity that is in the core curriculum tends to surface. On the other hand, other program directors feel that there should be courses offered that specifically address matters of diversity. Nine of the thirteen program directors observed that they do have courses that specifically deal with diversity; however, some of the courses are offered infrequently. The majority of the program directors interviewed or surveyed indicated that their programs attempt to integrate matters of diversity into many of the required courses. One suggestion that surfaced in one interview was to expand course elements to ensure that while the state's population continues to diversify, the experiences of as many groups as possible are reflected in public administration curricula. One director noted that while he could find the experiences of African-Americans in public administration teaching material, he found it difficult to find material reflecting Hispanic and Filipino communities, which he argued reflected the cultural backgrounds of many of his students. Thus, one continuing challenge for educators creating classroom material is in ensuring that material used in classes is reflective of the communities of students, particularly when those communities have members of a number of different groups.

Role of Diversity Statements

Only one of the MPA program directors interviewed or surveyed noted that her program had its own explicit statements of diversity. Most program directors indicated that they adopted their university-wide statements of diversity to frame their overall approaches to diversity issues within their programs. While several of the directors noted the importance of diversity statements in framing their programs' underlying goals and principles, some noted a hesitance in the post–Proposition 209 era concerning explicitly framing diversity goals at a program level. Several of the directors noted that university statements on diversity provided an opportunity to have a larger entity to respond to any legal ramifications related to implementing diversity initiatives. The strength of these statements, one program director noted, is dependent on how much upper-level administrators are willing to support them. In one case, an MPA director noted that in her university, there was little effort by the central administration to implement and support various programs, although there is an explicit statement on diversity. Another program director noted that the president and provost felt the university had an important role in community interaction and fully implemented diversity initiatives to achieve this interaction. As a result, this director had support in launching a number of diversity efforts and was able to indirectly leverage this support into additional resources for the program. "Our President and Dean realize that our state is changing," noted another director, "and can articulate in words and actions how such changes impact our campus, and will support and reward us as we support their agenda on making the most out of this change."

Recommendations from California's Experiences

The trends in California raise a number of issues worth exploring at greater length by public administration educators. These issues reflect the increasing complexity of thinking about matters of diversity and are shaped by the fact that California schools currently have several opportunities to examine how they choose to address diversity within their programs. There are increasing percentages of people of different ethnic and racial background in the state. There is an increase in faculty retirement-based turnover in existing programs. Finally, because California has already passed a demographic threshold that other states will soon follow, its lessons on managing the challenges and opportunities of increasing population diversity are being looked upon by policy-makers in other regions of the country. California's experiences, for both practitioners and those preparing practitioners, can provide a reference point for strategies to be implemented in other regions as they experience the challenges and opportunities of increased diversity. The following recommendations are drawn from reflections upon California's experiences with a hope that they might be applied both within the state and in other communities undergoing major demographic transformations.

Recommendation 1. *Develop Clear Articulation of the Value of Diversity within Public Administration Programs*

Increasingly, agencies in the public sector are implementing their own agency-level diversity initiatives. Naff and Kellough's (2001) examination of diversity programs in federal government agencies finds that 120 of 137 federal agencies that responded to a 1999 National Partnership for Reinventing Government survey on diversity initiatives indicated that their departments had undertaken some form of diversity initiative. This finding clearly suggests that there is some degree of value that federal agencies place on diversity matters. Naff and Kellough's work also found, however, that the undercurrents for some of the work of these various agencies has been undergoing a period of rejustification, from diversity being considered from the perspective of affirmative action and equal employment opportunity programs to "managing diversity" initiatives. The development of much of this new thinking from federal agencies (as well as state and local agencies) leads to questions regarding the implications for programs that are preparing future practitioners. If there is government investment in ensuring that the public workplace is able to incorporate matters of diversity, then programs working to prepare practitioners should have some focus on preparing students to work on similar issues. Increasingly, one of the challenges that face public administration programs will be to articulate clearly what the value is to any diversity propositions.

Public administration programs should be able to clearly articulate the rationale for any internal approach to diversity within their program. When they were articulated, the propositions of the schools examined were based on several frameworks. First, there was a desire expressed in several cases for programs to reflect the makeup of the communities in which they are situated. If classrooms can better reflect these communities, the students will be more able to interact in many of these diverse communities as administrators. Second, employer demands for what they might look for in the makeup of job candidates is an element to a proposition. Eight of the program directors interviewed noted that employers who recruit their students have articulated a desire to hire candidates that will help better enable their agencies to reflect and relate to the constituencies in the counties at large. This has greatly helped shift the tone on diversity in at least two of the MPA programs. Third are general student benefits from diversity efforts. In the past several years there have been accounts of how students at both the graduate and undergraduate level benefited from some integration of factors related to diversity within their curricula.

Astin (1993a, 1993b) notes that students across ethnic and racial groups have indicated that learning about different perspectives has been perceived as a positive element of their educational experience. One of Light's (1999) findings in his study of educational experiences of MPA and public policy program graduates was that many of them desired to see even more matters of diversity integrated into the curriculum. Finally, Villalpando (1994) notes that a commitment to diversity by an institution has an impact on student satisfaction of their university experiences regardless of student backgrounds. Fourth are issues of programmatic competitiveness. Programs are attempting to attract candidates from an increasingly diverse pool of students, many of whom recognize the demands that they will face in being able to interact in increasingly diverse communities. Programmatic demonstration of a commitment to preparing students to work in such an environment is perceived as an added value to the development of various programs. If students perceive that there is a benefit in their training when programs implement components that focus on diversity, then the programs will be better positioned to attract a pool of students interested in participating in these types of programs.

Recommendation 2. *Leverage Support of University Statements on Diversity*

The MPA directors interviewed have at the minimum a university-wide statement on diversity that they can use as an articulated mission on diversity issues. These statements articulate the value that the university places on factors of diversity. The public administration programs, for the most part, follow the university lead in implementing initiatives and programs related to some of these matters of diversity. This helps programs generate university support for additional initiatives to support a university-wide agenda on ensuring diversity.

At the maximum, some programs noted having used such statements to leverage additional resources for programs. At the minimum, such university policies could serve to address any legal concerns that might arise to challenge program-level approaches, which is a concern in the post–Proposition 209 era. At the department level, the question surfaces regarding how university diversity statements might impact procedures. In the majority of interviews, program directors indicated that university statements were used at the departmental level to justify any procedures that might be implemented. One possibility that departments might explore is how to utilize campus (and departmental) diversity statements to facilitate a reflective process for students and faculty on how the statements are implemented at a departmental level.

Recommendation 3. *Open Dialogue on Integration of Diversity within the Curriculum*

The directors noted the varying degrees to which strategies for integrating issues of diversity in the curriculum are explored in detail in programs. Some of the directors noted that they were engaged in developing means for implementing courses on diversity. However, most noted that they tend to integrate diversity-related content into core courses rather than developing courses that individually address matters of diversity. The question of integration of diversity versus specifically designed diversity courses is worthy of exploration both at a departmental level and a field-wide level. Several program directors suggested that they would lean toward matters of program integration instead of having stand-alone courses. Whether as part of stand-alone courses or as part of courses where matters of diversity are integrated into class curriculum is the question of how diversity impacts the communities where students will be serving as administrators. This includes exploring policies related to diversity by encouraging students to be able to ask the implications of a diversifying climate and to explore responses for the climate. Such a discussion in California, for example, would focus on how the demographics shape the question of how administrators should examine issues of diversity. Are there, for example, strategies that administrators might implement to help organizations better reflect the changes that make up the communities?

For such dialogue on educational strategies to be as effective as possible, it should include discussion beyond merely exploring curriculum issues, but also include matters surrounding issues of pedagogy. Such a dialogue should include student exploration of what changing demographics mean for the field of public administration. In California the demographic shifts present an opportunity to frame a student-inquiry-based discussion examining changes of meaning in factors of representation resulting from changing demographics. Discussions with directors, however, suggest that many programs have yet to move into inquiry-based discussions with students on matters of diversity and the impact in the field.

Conclusion

It has been a decade since the 1993 revision of NASPAA's diversity guidelines. It has also been nearly five years since NASPAA's report on diversity that stemmed out of its 1999 conference. During that time the demographic realities of many states have been brought to light by the release of 2000 census data that confirmed what demographers had been noting for some time, that many cities and states are becoming far more diverse in their ethnic and racial make up than previously thought.

In the next several years, other states are projected to pass the demographic threshold that California has passed in the makeup of its population. Administrators will face questions of what exactly that change in population means in terms of administrative representation, service delivery, and administrative responses to changing constituencies of voters. Educators of public administrators will also face a number of challenges in terms of identifying what some of these changes mean. This chapter has attempted to present the environment through which some of these questions are being explored in the state of California.

The chapter has presented three sets of recommendations drawn from reflections on California's experiences: (1) using value propositions on diversity to leverage discussions; (2) leveraging support from university-wide statements on diversity; and (3) opening dialogue on how to leverage widespread discussions of diversity curriculum integration. These recommendations represent only a starting point for reflection on how those preparing future administrators might explore matters of diversity. California's experiences, like those of a handful of other states, are at this point still unique in the demographic realities and as a result the management of trends in diversity. With the demographic makeup of the nation at large changing at such a rapid pace, the dialogue on how public administrators and the educators of public administrators respond to the opportunities and challenges of diversity is critical to the ability of communities to respond to the changes that many of them face in terms of their general makeup. California's experiences demonstrate that there is ample room for dialogue on the opportunities and challenges increasing diversity brings into the worlds of the public administration practitioner and educator.

Appendix. *Diversity in Public Administration Program Questionnaire*

1. Does your program have courses in which issues of diversity are incorporated into the curriculum? If so, please list the course names.

2. U.S. Census data indicate that California has become an increasingly diverse state in recent years. How has this demographic shift impacted your program in terms of:
   a.   student composition?
   b.   faculty composition?
   c.   curriculum?
   d.   placement of students following program completion?
   e.   in-class discussions?
   f.   other areas? (please identify them)

3. Has there been any impact from Proposition 209 or other public referenda upon your program in terms of (note: if other referenda, please identify them):
   a.   student composition?
   b.   faculty composition?
   c.   curriculum?
   d.   placement of students following program completion?
   e.   in-class discussions?
   f.   other areas? (please identify them)

4. Does your program have an explicit statement on diversity? If so, what type of impact do you feel this has on your program?

References

Astin, A.W. 1993a. "Diversity and Multiculturalism on Campus: How Are Students Affected?" *Change* 25 (2): 44–49.
———. 1993b. *What Matters in College? Four Critical Years Revisited.* San Francisco: Jossey-Bass.
Light, Paul. 1999. *The New Public Service.* Washington, DC: Brookings Institution.
Maharidge, Dale. 1996. *The Coming White Minority: California's Eruptions and the Nation's Future.* New York: Vintage Books.

Naff, Katherine C., and J. Edward Kellough. 2001. *A Changing Workforce: Understanding Diversity Programs in the Federal Government.* Arlington, VA: Price Waterhouse Coopers Endowment for the Business of Government.

National Association of Schools of Public Affairs and Administration. 2000. *Diversity Report.* Washington, DC: National Association of Schools of Public Affairs and Administration. www.naspaa.org

Reyes, Belinds. 2001. *A Portrait of Race and Ethnicity in California: The Social and Economic Well-Being of Racial and Ethnic Groups.* San Francisco: Public Policy Institute of San Francisco.

U.S. Bureau of the Census. 1991. *Statistical Abstract of the United States.* 111th ed. Washington, DC: Government Printing Office.

U.S. Bureau of the Census. 2000. U.S. Department of Commerce, *Census 2000.* www.census.gov

Villalpando, O. 1994. Comparing the Effects of Multiculturalism and Diversity on Minority and White Students' Satisfaction with College. Paper presented at the Annual Meeting of the Association for the Study of Higher Education, Tucson, Arizona, November.

6

Public Service in America's Urban Areas

Why the Bar in Perception and Practice Remains Higher for African-American Public Managers

Otha Burton, Jr. and Mfanya Donald Tryman

In 1985 the city of Jackson, Mississippi, changed its form of government from a three-member at-large elected commission to a strong mayor–council governmental structure, with part-time council members elected from seven wards. With this change came a more representative body of elected and administrative officials that reflected the racial makeup of the community. In 1990, Jackson had a 55 percent African American population. However, *Census 2000* indicates that this once capital of the Southern Confederacy is 71 percent African-American in population (U.S. Census Bureau 2000).

The public sector electoral and bureaucratic representational accomplishments for African-Americans in Jackson, Mississippi, must be considered significant, particularly when comparing this to the racially discriminatory history of the state. In 1996 the city elected its first African-American mayor, Harvey Johnson Jr. He was reelected with a 60 percent margin of support in the general election in 2001. Mayor Johnson appointed, and the city council (five of whose seven members are African-American) confirmed the appointments of African-Americans as the chief administrative officer (first to hold this position) and seven out of nine department directors, including the police chief, the fire chief, the director of personnel, the director of administration, the director of human and cultural services, the director of planning and development, and the city attorney.

The first six years in office for Mayor Johnson and his administration posed many challenges, which included creating opportunities for downtown and neighborhood revitalization; positioning the city to compete regionally and locally as an economic and cultural centerpiece; confronting unparalleled expectations by citizens of all races and income levels to quickly improve age-old deficiencies in services; reducing a ten-year high crime rate and overhauling a neglected police department; addressing the suburban–central city regional image wars, which all too often have been played out negatively as white citizens moved out by the thousands over the last twenty years; and developing for the citizens and the local bureaucracy that serves them a positive sense of direction, hope, and accomplishment in dealing with the many tasks associated with making Jackson a truly great community (Johnson 2003).

The city of Jackson is only experiencing what other major cities in America have experienced and are confronting as compositions in race and income change dramatically. There are high performance expectations for African-American public managers in these urban areas from their own race and the community in general. Urban America has become the principal domain of ethnic and racial groups, particularly African-Americans. African-American public managers, therefore, find themselves challenged by these groups to identify, develop, and implement better solutions to the urban problems and conditions they face each day.

This chapter will examine how the diversity management ethos and the cultural background and expectations of race of the emerging African-American urban bureaucracy influence urban public decisions and solutions. There are key qualities African-American leaders in the public sector must possess. In this regard, the basic hypotheses of this chapter are that (1) the more the urban government bureaucracy reflects the diversity within the community that encompasses its African-American constituency, the greater the expectations placed on African-American public leaders to function as change agents for policies and solutions to long-standing problems, and (2) these expectations supersede equity and diversity issues of representative government.

Looking at the Numbers

U.S. Census data for 1990 reflected the ever-expanding urban population of America. Although the metropolitan to nonmetropolitan

Table 6.1

1970–90 Metropolitan to Nonmetropolitan Population Change

Metropolitan area populations	Nonmetropolitan area populations
1970: 156,085,000 (76.8%)	1970: 47,217,000 (23.2%)
1980: 172,602,000	1980: 53,940,000
1990: 189,413,000 (71.1%)	1990: 56,390,000 (22.9%)

Source: U.S. Census Statistical Abstract of the United States (1990).

Table 6.2

1990 White and African-American Populations

White	African-American
1990: 210,247,000 (84.1%)	1990: 31,026,000 (12.4%)

Source: U.S. Census Statistical Abstract of the United States (1991).

percentage differential declined slightly from 1970 by 5.4 percent, the total population figure for the former increased by approximately 33,000,000 (see Table 6.1). The white population of America in 1990 was 210,247,000 (84 percent), and the African-American population accounted for 31,026,000 (12 percent) (see Table 6.2). In 1990, African-Americans represented the largest minority group in the country. The 1990 Census indicated that in addition to African-Americans, Hispanics, Asians and Pacific Islanders, and Native Americans had high concentrations in the major metropolitan areas of the nation. In 1990–91 there were 51 metropolitan areas where population figures of African-Americans ranged from 101,000 to 3,289,000. The African-American percentage of the total metropolitan statistical area (MSA) populations ranged from 4.8 percent in the Seattle-Tacoma, Washington, MSA to 42.5 percent in the Jackson, Mississippi, MSA (U.S. Census 1991, 32). Also, the top seventy MSA regions of the nation, with populations ranging from 530,000 to 18,087,000, reflected sizable concentrations of African-Americans as residents (U.S. Census 1991, 33).

Census 2000 offers similar information about the dynamics occurring in America's urban areas. In the year 2000 the total American population was 281,400,000. African-Americans, however, are no longer the largest minority group. They have been replaced by

Table 6.3

Ten Cities of 100,000 or More Population with Highest Percentage of African-American Population

Gary, Indiana	84.0
Detroit, Michigan	81.6
Birmingham, Alabama	73.5
Jackson, Mississippi	70.6
New Orleans, Louisiana	67.3
Baltimore, Maryland	64.3
Atlanta, Georgia	61.4
Memphis, Tennessee	61.4
Washington, D.C.	60.0
Richmond, Virginia	57.2

Source: U.S. Census (2000).

the Hispanic population. The African-American population contin-ued to grow to the point where it did account for 34,658,000 people, or 12.9 percent of the overall population (*Census 2000a*). About 60 percent of all African-Americans reside in ten states. According to *Census 2000*, six out of ten African-Americans live in the following states: New York, California, Texas, Florida, Georgia, Illinois, North Carolina, Maryland, Michigan, and Louisiana. At least 2 million African-Americans live in the states of New York, California, Texas, Florida, and Georgia. Over 1 million African-Americans live in ten Southern states that include Texas, Florida, Georgia, North Caro-lina, Maryland, Louisiana, Virginia, South Carolina, Alabama, and Mississippi (*Census 2000a*).

According to *Census 2000*, the ten largest American cities having African-American populations are New York, Los Angeles, Chicago, Houston, Philadelphia, Phoenix, San Diego, Dallas, San Antonio, and Detroit (U.S. Census Bureau 2000). However, the ten urban cities rep-resenting 100,000 or more in population with the highest percentage of African-Americans are: Gary, Indiana (84 percent); Detroit, Michi-gan (81.6 percent); Birmingham, Alabama (73.5 percent); Jackson, Mississippi (70.6 percent); New Orleans, Louisiana (67.3 percent); Bal-timore, Maryland (64.3 percent); Atlanta, Georgia (61.4 percent); Mem-phis, Tennessee (61.4 percent); Washington, D.C. (60.0 percent); and Richmond, Virginia (57.2 percent) (see Table 6.3) (*Census 2000a*).

The metropolitan areas composition in *Census 2000* also pro-vides some interesting dynamics. Across the country, 28.9 percent

Table 6.4

2000 Census Data Metropolitan and Nonmetropolitan Residence

Areas	Total population	African-Americans
Metro central cities	81,527,000 (28.9%)	18,546,000 (51.1%)
Metro outside of central cities	147,894,000 (52.4%)	12,977,000 (36%)
Nonmetropolitan areas	52,661,000 (18.4%)	4,499,000 (12.5%)

Source: U.S. Census (2000).

of the American population lives within metropolitan area central cities and another 52.4 percent live in metropolitan areas, but not central cities. Nonmetropolitan area residences account for 18.4 percent of the population. However, for African-Americans, 51.1 percent live in metropolitan area central cities while only 36 percent reside in metropolitan areas outside of central cities. Another 12.5 percent live in nonmetropolitan areas (see Table 6.4) (*Census 2000b*).

The significance of these data is in the apparent revelation that certain environs in the American society, that is, central city urban areas, have continued to develop as enclaves for people of color. Considerable research has been conducted on the involvement and impact of African-American political/electoral gains in the twentieth century at the federal, state, and local governmental levels. Although the civil rights movement, federal laws, and congressional mandates created an agenda for social and political incorporation, such change and empowerment began to materialize only when African-Americans exercised their strength in numbers in the political process and at the ballot box. Engstrom and McDonald (1981) indicate that as the number of underrepresented groups increases in size, they make demands on the structure and responsiveness of the urban government. As their population grows to around 10 percent of the community, a political agenda is formulated. However, when the size of the minority population reaches 15 percent of a city's constituent base, their political agenda is exercised (1981, 352).

Some research on social and political participation of people of color suggests that when socioeconomic status is factored out of the analysis, a greater degree of influence on society can be documented. Antunes and Gaitz (1975, 1115) argue that, "When social class is controlled, the social and political participation of groups which are targets of discrimination will be greater than that of the dominant groups." Browning, Marshall, and Tabb (1986) further document the significant role that size contributes to influencing political participation and community control for people of color in their study of ten California cities. Their research suggests that "More than for any other government program, the definition of responsiveness for minority employment in city government is linked to minority population. Population parity rates of percent minority employment in city population is not the only possible standard but is the one against which minority employment is typically evaluated" (1986, 171). Thus, in looking at the numbers within metropolitan and, in particular, central cities, the assumption can be made that people of color are gaining government-positive responses in numerous urban areas due in part to their increased population. The major metropolitan areas surely reflect this form of bargaining power, where sizable populations of color are present. Multifaceted demands generated through bargaining, political participation, and the social incorporation of community groups are urban realities for public managers and local government decision-makers. Fainstein and Fainstein (1976, 922) suggest that participation in the policy-making process by groups formally deprived of such activity will increase as decentralization and new linkage structures occur. The urban bureaucracy, and particularly African-American leadership within the bureaucracy that reflects the growing presence of constituencies of color, must be cognizant of the representative and policy-service demands to which they are expected to address effectively. The magnitude of such issues will be relative to the size of the community of color.

The Responsibilities of African-American Bureaucrats

Selden (1997) notes that the concept of representative bureaucracy is supported by many twentieth-century scholars. This view holds that "bureaucratic power to mold public policy can be made more responsive to public interests if the personnel in the bureaucracy reflect the public served, in characteristics such as race, ethnicity, and gender" (Selden 1997, 4). The policy-making process thus promotes input and equity, and participation in the implementation of programs and activities. A representative bureaucracy is one of the ever-emerging responsibilities African-American mayors and bureaucrats must confront in the urban setting. Expectations of African-American constituents in regard to their own who are in charge of government create what is called a "hope index" that can be satisfied only through deliverable performance and service (Black mayors land leadership 1994, 7A). Henderson (1978, 79) maintains that "because of their geographical and social proximity to black urban communities, what black administrators do for and with black communities is as essential as how many of them are employed by urban bureaucracies."

Representation within government has long been a goal of the African-American community. As a concept, representativeness has general as well as distinct implications. Rehfuss (1989) suggests that in a general sense, representative bureaucracy links the government with citizens by assuring that the bureaucracy reflects the dichotomy of group, occupations, and class interests that in turn produce representative policies. He further distinguishes representativeness by passive and active type qualities. The former implies that "representation is largely demographic, a sociological 'standing for' groups and interests in society. Further, it represents symbolic commitment to equal access to power" (454). Concerning the latter, Rehfuss holds that "it implies behavior on behalf of members of groups to which individuals belong" (454).

Krislov and Rosenbloom (1981, 65) develop a treatise of representational bureaucracy. As a functional operation, they maintain that it: "expands membership to stress diversity in policy making as well as the desirability of the bureaucracy being able to sell its program to diverse groups in society. By increasing the range of those who function within the bureaucracy, we increase both the infusion of ideas into bureaucracy and the dissemination of decisions to the outside world." Due to the growing political power of African-Americans in the late 1960s, 1970s, and 1980s, urban government employment in bureaucracy also increased among them (minorities). Eisinger (1973, 391) shows a direct relationship in this regard that is attributed to: (1) an expanding public sector acceptance of people of color; (2) an initial lack of emphasis on educational characteristics for prestigious jobs; (3) a growing and enlightened population of color; and (4) the number of mayors of color and other elected officials who stressed affirmative action.

A recent study by Murray et al. (1994) updated significant findings resulting from a 1974 *Public Administration Review* symposium on people of color in public administration written by Adam W. Herbert (now president of the University of Indiana, Bloomington). The initial findings of the symposium were captured by Herbert in what has become recognized as a critical study of how minority public servants are viewed in their role of governing in America's democratic political system. Herbert (1974, 409–11) concludes that:

1. Governmental role expectations of minority administrators do not necessarily coincide with the minority administrators' own perceptions, goals, or expectations; unresponsive public policies put minority administrators in extremely tenuous positions vis-à-vis the agency, themselves, and the community of which they are a part;
2. Frequently the minority administrator is put into *flak-catching* positions without having the capacity to make meaningful decisions, but is expected to accept the responsibilities of program failures and "keep the natives calm";
3. Advancement within the governmental system is generally a function of adherence to established organizational norms; one of these norms historically has been that one need not be concerned about the needs or priorities of minority communities;
4. Informal pay and promotional quotas still seem to exist for minority administrators; moreover, it is assumed that they can fill only certain types of positions, usually related to social service delivery or to communications with other minority group members;
5. Minority communities sometimes expect much more of the minority administrator than he or she can provide; and in most cases demand a far faster response to their demands than these administrators have developed the capacity to deliver; and
6. Agencies seem to search for the "super" minority administrator, and even then they are frequently hired as "show pieces."

In reexamining the applicability of the symposium findings of conditions facing African-American administrators, Murray and his colleagues surveyed members of the Conference of Minority Public Administrators, whose members held upper-level management positions in federal agencies (Murray 1994). The researchers held the premise that as administrators of color assumed higher levels of responsibility, they were equally challenged with "decisions about reconciling personal, group, community, and organizational demands." Results from the survey indicated that these managers are generally facing this dilemma by adhering to advocacy roles for constituents of color on one hand while also attending to their own professional, organizational, and policy demands within the bureaucracy on the other hand (416). In light of this, the study's concluding summation is that there is "a growing presence of minority administrators at all levels within the federal government who believe in advocacy roles on behalf of minorities' communities yet meet organizational demands while developing personally and professionally."

While the above discussion seems promising in terms of bureaucratic representation for African-Americans, the condition of urban America and the African-American population in it suggests that there is no room to measure, in an inclusive sense, individual gains of bureaucrats and their "accomplishments." Jones (1981, 96) writing more than twenty years ago, condemns the fact that two-thirds of the African-American population still suffers from discrimination. Desperately needed, Jones maintains, are "policies and programs that will improve their living condition and enhance the life chances of their children." The unyielding focus of African-Americans in the bureaucracy must, therefore, be to ensure that achieving equal opportunity remains the goal for the constituents they serve. Jones adequately justifies this point when asserting that "There is an enormous gap between publicly mandated goals of equal access to employment, housing, health care, education, income, and justice, and their actual attainment" (97–98). The African-American constituency expects an advocacy role of its members within the bureaucracy. African-American administrators, Henderson (1978, 79) maintains, "reveal a greater inclination to advocate the goals of the organization external to bureaucracy, both in terms of civic/community and professional advocacy" (98).

Mandates for Participation, Commitment, and Change

Dahrendorf (1973, 198) suggests that "Liberal democracy can become effective only in a society in which: (1) equal citizenship rights have been generalized; (2) conflicts are recognized and regulated rationally in all institutional orders; (3) elites reflect the color and diversity of social interests; and (4) public virtues are the value orientation of the people." Proponents of democracy and a bureaucracy that helps ensure its effectiveness become magnified in the culturally diverse urban communities. Dahrendorf's comments are used to open the last section of this chapter because of their relative significance to the challenge of managing urban communities. Bureaucracies in general are concerned with promoting cost effectiveness and efficiency.

Constituents want fairness and equity from their government. Warren (1986, 244) suggests that in the context of managing urban service delivery systems, equity and efficiency are not in conflict. He writes that "equity and efficiency are complementary rather than conflicting criteria in the provision of public services. This is necessarily tied to a second assumption that costs—monetary, psychological, and physical—absorbed by citizens in the acquisition and consumption of public services must be accounted for in measuring the efficiency of their provision." Other than for the obvious discussion of equity and efficiency principles here, the matter is presented to also underscore the complexity of the current urban community. Federal urban assistance has diminished and in some cases been discontinued; the out-migration of jobs and middle-income taxpayers has stifled the economic base; mostly lower-income people of color, the disadvantaged, and the aged have become the principal inhabitants of urban core cities; maintenance of the urban infrastructure is outdated and underfunded, with replacement costs high; the social ills of society as evidenced in crime, drugs, and welfare dependency are alarming; and suburban communities have developed to the extent where they now challenge the urban core as the new centerpieces of growth and progress. Warren (1986, 246) comments further that service delivery problems in the urban community are often detrimental to those populations disadvantaged by society. Especially during times of fiscal austerity, public officials react to increased service acquisition and consumption, costs that are regressive toward economically marginal groups.

Another dimension of the urban situation, though more salient in midsize cities, concerns changes that decentralize the structure of local government. Lineberry and Fowler (1972, 304) indicate that reform efforts to decentralize commission and mayor-council forms

of government should create multiple access points for groups attempting to influence decision-makers and basically strengthen group
participation. While Lineberry and Fowler's argument may have some
merit for groups of color still trying to maximize their vote and impact the political participation process, such reform efforts may place
them in competition with each other and dilute their emphasis through
collective bargaining. With the exception of enhancing political representation in the local government structure, other reform efforts to
decentralize government should follow. This effort may include: (1)
some assessment of how real remedies of global urban issues can be
universally approached and funded; and (2) the understanding that
expressed support for socialization and empowerment by urban constituents will be occurring at varying stages for different groups.
Also supporting caution in adapting reform decentralization efforts,
Fainstein and Fainstein (1976, 922) conclude that:

> While they have created more flexibility and more responsiveness, as
> well as new neighborhood leaders and new bureaucracies whose social
> backgrounds more closely resemble those of their clients, they have not
> produced basic changes in the distribution of social benefits. Nor have
> they really had much effect on the dominant position of central bureau-
> cratic authorities and unions of service providers.

Conclusion

As discussed above, this is the state of urban existence that African-
American leadership in local bureaucracies must manage. Admit-
tedly, effective solutions to America's urban problems will require a
focused national agenda with intergovernmental linkages incorporating federal, state, and local governments. However, urban bureaucracies must be able to address the complexity of urban issues,
have sensitivity in their dispensation, and provide the continuity of
service responses that their constituents need and expect. Particularly for the expanding number of African-Americans in urban bureaucracies, they must employ additional management attributes
encompassing participation, commitment, and change-agent status.
It will not be enough to simply diversify the municipal workforce
and construct internal human resource mechanisms that promote
career development, job satisfaction, motivation, and a generally
vague productivity ethos. The predicament of the urban environ-

ment, the historical circumstances that influence their call to public service and an obligation to responsiveness and change for people of color and the disadvantaged population, must be salient to African-American administrators and public servants in general.

Representative democracy and diversity management responsibilities for African-American leaders and managers in urban bureaucracies carry with them the enormous task of recreating these environs as productive centerpieces for the constituents they represent. These constituents are the cultural base from which they originate and who look with hope that as new administrators, certain urban problems of an institutional nature toward people of color can be better addressed. Karnig and McClain (1988, 153) also draw upon the earlier work by Herbert (1974) to offer key managerial skills that are important for minority administrators. These include the following:

1. An ability to operate effectively in conflict situations.
2. A familiarity with group dynamics.
3. An understanding of the feelings, demands, frustrations, and hopes of those citizens with whom he/she works.
4. An ability to work in very tenuous, highly uncertain work situations where clear-cut solutions are difficult to define and environmental conditions are constantly changing.
5. An ability to assume responsibility for all that goes along with making political decisions, and in a sense share the policy-making function with elected officials.

W.E.B. DuBois in his famous essay "The Talented Tenth," foresaw the enormous responsibility that would rest upon African-Americans in helping to effectively resolve some of the nation's institutional problems in race relations. He wrote this visionary piece at the dawn of the twentieth century, as he warned America that the "color line" would be its ultimate test for democracy. He also encouraged his own people by proclaiming that "The Negro race, like all races, is going to be saved by its exceptional men." While Dr. DuBois's challenge crosses all segments of society, it is indeed applicable to the democratization of government itself within the complex urban communities. These environs are the battlefronts of American democracy in the twenty-first century. Congruent with the significance of these urban communities is the call to the expanding number of African-Americans in urban bureaucracies to be effective managers. As they perform to represent all of their urban constituents, they must also ensure that equal opportunity is achieved in policies and programs that resolve long-standing problems confronting African-Americans in the community.

References

Antunes, George, and Charles M. Gaitz. 1975. "Ethnicity and Participation: A Study of Mexican Americans, Blacks, and Whites." *American Journal of Sociology* 88 (5) (March): 1192–211.

"Black Mayors Laud Leadership, Discuss Constituents Heightened Expectations." 1994. *Clarion Ledger* (May): 7A.

Browning, Rufus, Dale Rogers Marshall, and David H. Tabb. 1986. *Protest Is Not Enough.* Los Angeles: University of California Press.

Census 2000 Reports on African Americans. 2001. http://usgovinfo.about.com/library/weekly/aa081701a.htm

Dahrendorf, Ralf. 1973. "Society and Democracy in Germany." *Black Men, White Cities.* London: University Press.

DuBois, W.E.B. 1970. "The Talented Tenth." In H.J. Storing, ed. *What Country Have I?* New York: St. Martin's.

Eisinger, Peter. 1973. "Black Employment in Municipal Jobs: The Impact of Black Political Power." *American Political Science Review* 76 (2) (June): 390–401.

Engstrom, Richard L. and Michael D. McDonald. 1981. "The Election of Blacks To City Councils: Clarifying the Impact of Electoral Arrangements of the Seats/Population Relationship." *American Political Science Review* 75 (2) (June): 344–54.

Fainstein, Norman I., and Susan S. Fainstein. 1976. "The Future of Community Control." *American Political Science Review* 70 (3): 905–23.

Henderson, Lenneal. 1978. "Administration Advocacy and Black Urban Administrators." *Annuals of the American Academy of Political and Social Science* 439: 68–79.

Johnson, Harvey Jr. 2003. Mayor of Jackson, Mississippi. *State of the City Address*, August 26.

Jones, Faustine C. 1981. "External Crosscurrents and Internal Diversity: An Assessment of Black Progress, 1960–1980." *Daedalus* 110 (2) (spring): 71–101.

Karnig, Albert K., and Paula D. McClain. 1988. *Urban Minority Administrators: Politics, Policy, and Style.* New York: Greenwood.

Krislow, Samuel, and David Rosenbloom. 1991. *Representative Bureaucracy and the American Political System.* New York: Praeger.

Lineberry, Robert, and Edmund P. Fowler. 1972. "Reformism and Public Policies in American Cities." In David R. Morgan and Samuel A. Kirpatrick, eds. *Urban Political Analysis.* New York: Free Press.

Lipsky, Michael. 1980. *Street Level Bureaucracy.* New York: Russell Sage Foundation.

Murray, Sylvester et al. 1994. "The Role Demands and Dilemmas of Minority Public Administrators: The Herbert Thesis Revisited." *Public Administration Review* 54 (5): 409–17.

Ott, J. Steven. 1989. *Classic Readings in Organizational Behavior.* Belmont, CA: Wadsworth.

Redwood, Anthony. 1970. "Human Resource Management in the 1990s." *Business Horizons* 33: 1–10.

Rehfuss, John A. 1989. "A Representative Bureaucracy? Women and Minority Executives in California Career Service." *Public Administration Review* 46 (5): 454–60.

Selden, Sally Coleman. 1997. *The Promise of Representative Bureaucracy.* Armonk, NY: M.E. Sharpe.

Shafritz, Jay M. et al. 1992. *Personnel Management in Government.* New York: Marcel Dekker.

Thompson, Frank J. 1978. "Civil Servants and the Deprived: Socio-Political and Occupational Explanations of Attitudes Towards Minority Hiring." *American Journal of Political Science* 22 (2) (May): 325–47.

U.S. Census Bureau. 1990. *Statistical Abstract of the United States.* 110th ed. Washington, DC: Government Printing Office.

———. 1991. *Statistical Abstract of the United States.* 111th ed. Washington, DC: Government Printing Office.

———. 2000a. *The Black Population 2000.* Washington, DC: Government Printing Office.

———. 2000b. "Population by Metropolitan and Nonmetropolitan Residence, Sex, Race and Hispanic Origin, Current Population Survey." www.census.gov/population/socdemo/race/black/ppl-164

Warren, Robert. 1986. "Equity and Efficiency in Urban Service Delivery: A Consumption and Participation Costs Approach." Mark S. Rosentraub, ed. *Urban Policy Problems.* New York: Praeger.

7

Diversity Newcomers and the Challenge of Balancing Organizational Expectations

Assuming Ethical Responsibility

Mylon Winn and Floydette C. Cory-Scruggs

There have been significant changes, primarily for public organizations, since our initial discussions of *"Diversity Newcomers"* (Scruggs and Winn 1996) in this book's first edition. These changes have occurred because of advanced perspectives about intervention mechanisms (i.e., affirmative action) and issues of access. Other changes affecting diversity include advances in technology and globalization (Easley 2001). Our initial argument, however, is unchanged. We contend there are particular challenges faced by diversity newcomers because of two roles that they bring to public sector organizations, namely, the roles of change agent and public servant. Further, it is our argument that this perspective is a relatively silent one in the literature that needs to become an active part of the discussion about diversity. We used the term diversity newcomers in our 1996 writing and will continue to do so in this chapter. We are still defining diversity newcomers *as individuals whose characteristics include, but certainly are not limited to, race, ethnicity, gender, and sexual orientation.*

In the original chapter we examined the diversity literature as it was then constituted, paying close attention to dominant themes from both the public and private sectors. The pivotal issues on both sides of the diversity debate have been what is diversity and what difference does it make. In this chapter we continue our discussion, starting with a summary of previous diversity discussions. The chapter introduces additional current themes, and then, separately, relates our perspective to the experiences of diversity newcomers and to the challenge of balancing organizational expectations.

Context and Summary of Previous Work: Concepts and Applications

Our initial approach was primarily anticipatory in nature, as was much of the scholarly and popular literature in 1996 and earlier. This anticipatory posture was driven primarily by the work of Johnston and Packer (1987) in a seminal study that projected both demographic trends (race and ethnicity) and their impact upon the workforce into the twenty-first century. Marlene Fine notes three reasons for these projected changes in race and ethnicity: "(1) different fertility rates; (2) net immigration; and (3) age distribution" (1995, 11). Census data demonstrate the impact of some of these changing demographics, particularly race (Gibson and Lennon 1999).

A percentage comparison of race in the United States in the first and last decades of the twentieth century reveals significant changes over time in the composition of the population, as shown in Table 7.1. While the facts speak for themselves, a few comparisons are noteworthy. For example, in 1990 there are two distinguishing points. One is immigration, as construed by "foreign born," within certain categories of the total population. This immigration impact is particularly pronounced for Asian and Pacific Islanders (63.1 percent); yet, their total population is smallest compared to that of other racial groups listed. On the other hand, the number of people who are classified as Hispanic contribute significantly to the diversity of the American population. Moreover, of these Hispanics, 35.8 percent are foreign-born. The other significance of this racial diversity in the last decade of the twentieth century is more easily seen in comparison with the first decade, the 1900s. Except for the first racial category, white, there have been consistent increases in the immigration of persons of varied national origin into the United States. Only in the white category over the span of the century has there been a decrease in the number of foreign-born persons. At the beginning of the twentieth century the impact of net migration is evident (see Table 7.1). In 1900 almost 14 percent of the total population

Table 7.1

Race and Hispanic Origin of the Population by Nativity, 1900 and 1990

	Total	White	Races other than White					Hispanic origin (of any race)	White, not of Hispanic origin
			Total	Black	American Indian, Eskimo, Aleut	Asian and Pacific Islander	Other race		
1900									
Total	75,994,575	66,809,196	9,185,379	8,833,994	237,196	114,189	(X)	(NA)	(NA)
Native	65,653,299	56,595,375	9,057,920	8,813,658	234,983	9,279	(X)	(NA)	(NA)
Foreign-born	10,341,276	10,213,817	127,459	20,336	2,213	104,910	(X)	(NA)	(NA)
Percent	13.6	15.3	1.4	0.2	0.9	91.9	(X)	(NA)	(NA)
1990									
Total	248,709,873	199,827,064	48,882,809	29,930,524	2,015,143	7,226,986	9,710,156	21,900,089	188,404,773
Native	228,942,557	189,804,252	39,138,305	28,475,230	1,968,224	2,668,242	6,026,609	14,058,439	182,257,430
Foreign-born	19,767,316	10,022,812	9,744,504	1,455,294	46,919	4,558,744	3,683,547	7,841,650	6,167,343
Percent	7.9	5.0	19.9	4.9	2.3	63.1	37.9	35.8	3.3

Source: Derived from Gibson and Lennon (1999).

was foreign-born, most of whom are found in the white category. Again, with the exception of the high numbers of Asian and Pacific Islanders (91.9 percent), the presence of other races was either unnoticed (not applicable) or uncounted (not available). The pattern of immigration has changed the United States from a country of predominately white (European) immigrants to a more diverse nation.

Employment data is one area where change in racial composition is most evident. Table 7.2 shows patterns in individual characteristics, most notably, age, gender, minority group, and disability. Specifically, in Table 7.2 we see a steady aging of the workforce as well as a general increase in the employment of women and minorities. Of the minority groups depicted, employment growth has been most consistent among individuals of Hispanic and Asian/Pacific Islander origins. These data do not, however, inform us of the level at which people of color are located within the federal government; they inform only about their presence and ethnicity. This pattern may or may not reflect some of the trends that Johnston and Packer (1987) anticipated.

Peters (1995) makes some important comments about patterns of ethnic representation in public bureaucracies. Among them, Peters states, "educational and other social barriers may have to be overcome before legal efforts towards greater ethnic representativeness have the intended effects." When minorities and women are hired in organizations they frequently feel that they are cut off from promotion by a glass ceiling; "the organization may be glad to have them as employees but not as top managers" (123). Peters addresses two of the recurring themes in the earlier diversity literature. One theme is "access." Peters (1995) describes other barriers that may mitigate intended legal effects that can determine access or the lack of access to public organizations. The other recurring theme that Peters also identifies is the consequence of having diverse organizations. What difference does improving diversity make in a given public organization and to the diversity newcomers? In other words, does allowing diversity newcomers' access matter substantively to organizations? What kind of change takes place? The conceptual model, which depicts the nature of the diversity-impact relationships, is shown in Figure 7.1 (see p. 124), Conceptual Model of Diversity Impacts. The model represents much of our earlier and current discussions and that of the literature regarding workforce diversity and its implications for public organizations.

Table 7.2

Trend in Federal Civilian Employment, 1991–2001: Individual Characteristics (in percent)

	1991	1992	1993	1994	1995	1996	1997	1998	1999	2000	2001
Average age*	42.5	43.0	43.8	44.1	44.3	44.8	45.2	45.6	45.9	46.3	46.5
Gender											
Men	56.0	57.0	56.0	56.0	56.0	56.0	56.0	56.0	55.0	55.0	55.0
Women	44.0	46.0	44.0	44.0	44.0	44.0	44.0	44.0	45.0	45.0	45.0
Race and national origin											
Total minorities	27.7	27.9	28.2	28.5	28.9	29.1	29.4	29.7	30.0	30.4	30.6
Black	16.8	16.7	16.7	16.7	16.8	16.7	16.7	16.7	17.0	17.1	17.1
Hispanic	5.4	5.5	5.6	5.7	5.9	6.1	6.2	6.4	6.5	6.6	6.7
Asian/Pacific Islander	3.6	3.8	3.9	4.1	4.2	4.3	4.4	4.5	4.4	4.5	4.6
American Indian/Alaska Native	1.9	1.9	2.0	2.0	2.0	2.0	2.1	2.1	2.1	2.2	2.2
Disabled	7.0	7.0	7.0	7.0	7.0	7.0	7.0	7.0	7.0	7.0	7.0

Source: Monthly Report of Federal Civilian Employment (SF 113-A): Office of Workforce Information, Office of Personnel Management.
*Full-time permanent employees.

The Conceptual Model of Diversity Impacts (Figure 7.1) consists of three major components. Component 1, diverse population, is an external change catalyst that impacts organizations' internal environments (Scruggs and Winn 1996). This component is one of the many external forces impinging upon organizations. The first two boxes of the model (see Figure 7.1), as described by the earlier work of Johnston and Packard (1987), convey the initial impact of creating a diverse organization. Theoretically, as the population changes, so does the workforce. Thus, just using race as an example, as the population becomes more racially diverse, the same diversity should be reflected over time in the population of available workers that organizations may hire as employees. Availability of potential employees is just one of two issues that are the focus of our discussion; the other is the experience that diversity newcomers have once they enter organizations. We presume that the impact of diverse individuals, either quantitatively or qualitatively, has the potential to change public organizations. Similarly, Johnston and Packer (1987) argue that race, gender, age, and ethnicity can bring about change in organizations. Hence, Component 1 of the model, Diversity, is a composite of the relationship between the diversity of the population and diversity possible for the workplace.

Component 2 is labeled Newcomer Access to Organizations. The focus here is on positioning newcomers to enter into organizations. This component briefly examines the approach organizations can take regarding allowing diversity newcomers to enter their organizational environment and gain access to the internal environment and culture as workers. The access approach generally available to organizations is either voluntary or legally motivated. Finally, Component 3 is labeled Consequence of Newcomer Access. This portion of the model simply raises questions about the difference that diversity makes. The difference can be either symbolic or substantive in its consequences. We suggest that if the diversity newcomers fail to act ethically, in light of their dual roles of change agent and public servant, their presence is symbolic. With a presence that is symbolic rather than substantive, they ultimately meld into the organization and reinforce the status quo. Conversely, we believe that their presence is substantive when they have a positive impact on an organization's culture and daily operation.

In Figure 7.1 the conceptual model shows that there is some over-

124

Figure 7.1   **Conceptual Model of Diversity Impacts**

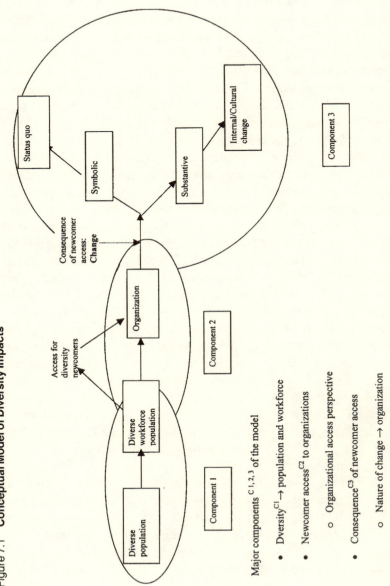

Major components [C 1, 2, 3] of the model

- Diversity[C1] → population and workforce
- Newcomer access[C2] to organizations
  - o Organizational access perspective
- Consequence[C3] of newcomer access
  - o Nature of change → organization
  - o Nature of change → newcomer

lap between Components 1 and 2. This is due to the nature of the relationship between projections of greater diversity in the workforce and the potential impact of that diversity on a given organization. It is the presence of an increasingly diverse society and the potential impact of this diversity upon the available labor pool for all organizations that ties these two components together. Once the definitional and conceptual issues are addressed, the logical question becomes what organizations do about diversity, regardless of its breadth of definition.

The Impact of Diversity: A Reflection About Earlier Work

A tacit part of Component 1 is the difficulty of defining diversity. Would a definition of diversity focus on identifying traditional categories of race, ethnicity, and gender? Hughes (1992, 26) suggests prudence regarding the penchant for categorizing groups, noting that "the need to identify the individual's cultural perspective must be balanced against the instinct of drawing conclusions about the individual based upon his or her racial background." The concern is to avoid reverting to stereotyping and division. However, a few years later, for some practitioners in the public sector, the historical foundation and legal context of race, ethnicity, and gender were significant.

Carrell and Mann's (1995) survey findings of public sector human resource practitioners note that there is division about whether diversity is more than "existing EEO/AA policies, raising serious questions about the real meaning of the term" (1995, 103). Noting that workforce diversity is neither legally nor commonly defined, Carrell and Mann also attempt to identify consensus regarding eight general diversity characteristics. Most consensuses were associated with race, followed by gender (1995, 108). There are scholars who argue for the greatest inclusion of difference, from attitudinal and personal differences (Dominguez 1992, 16) to job function and parental status (Leach et al. 1995, 3). Griggs echoes (1995, 6) the expansive approach, cautioning that limiting the definition of diversity "to differences of gender, race, and constitutionally protected differences, is to ignore much of the diversity that we bring to the workplace. Furthermore, such a limited view serves to polarize tensions around the discussion of differences."

The Current Issues via Component Three

Component 3 is initiated when organizations voluntarily diversify. The voluntary approach, often associated with the private sector, encompasses two dominant themes within the workforce diversity literature. They are "valuing diversity" and "managing diversity." The organizational focus in the literature is on strategies, challenges, and opportunities associated with workforce diversity that enhance organizations. Kendall (1995, 79) argues that differences should be valued in the workplace, and that valuing these differences creates a welcoming environment for workers: in a "work environment in which people are appreciated for who they are . . . for their difference as well as their similarities," there is a valuing of diversity. This view contrasts with the bureaucratic, more legalistic paradigm, which seeks to modify or possibly overlook individual differences for the sake of inclusion and homogeneity within the organization. Thus, when organizations value diversity, newcomers should find that their differences are assets.

In recognizing and valuing differences, organizations place much of the emphasis on relationships or interactions at the individual, group, and organizational levels (Fine 1995; Griggs 1995; Thomas 1995). Over time, the organization and its employees will change through the interactions and relationships at each of the levels—individual, group, and organizational. However, organizational change must be facilitated. Employees must be enabled to understand and accept differences in others in an organizational context. A true commitment to diversity and open communication becomes important to relational success within and across the organization. Yet, there are some concerns as to the truth and reality of our ability to value differences. It has been said that "much of the diversity literature is characterized by an upbeat naiveté that averts its eyes from the rampant conflicts and ruptures that are endemic to a changing and diverse workplace" (Prasad and Mills 1997, 5).

But are there other qualitative gains from the valuing of diversity besides interpersonal results? Organizational decision-making and problem-solving should also benefit from a more diversified workplace. Some researchers express a view that problem-solving and decision-making are enhanced through diversity rather than homogeneity in organizations, particularly when given proper leadership (Cox 1993; Carnevale and Stone 1995). When this happens, differences are no longer a source of ostracism, but are enhanced. Second, acceptance and appreciation of differences among employees are individually and organizationally accepted. Third, organizations will undergo a qualitative change in relations, interactions, and decisional capacities.

The managing diversity perspective suggests that change in the culture of an organization is a desirable outcome. Process becomes an important tool in ensuring this kind of change. Advocates contend that change is used to enhance differences that benefit organizations (Jamieson and O'Mara 1991; Loden and Rosener 1991; Cox 1993). This process includes examining systemic issues faced by organizations in response to changing demographical patterns in the workforce. R. Roosevelt Thomas (1991, 10) states "[managing] diversity is a comprehensive managerial process for developing an environment that works well for all employees." Further managing diversity "includes improvement of relationships among people who are different, but recognizes that changes in organizational culture and systems may also be required to create an environment that enables all employees" (Thomas 1991, 20). In this view, managing diversity becomes a performance issue.

Consequence of Newcomer Access

Organizational change is the final component of the model; it depicts major themes, particularly in the current literature. The questions here are grounded in assessing the difference that the diverse newcomer makes as defined by the organization and the newcomer. This difference presumes a change of some sort within the organization. Ultimately, this organizational change can be of two basic types, symbolic or substantive (Allison 1999, Minors 1996). With symbolic change, there may be an increased aging or gendering of a given organization, but the culture of the organization does not change. The status quo is reinforced. Diversity newcomers' behaviors reflect those values that are primary in the organization and its culture (Allison 1999, Minors 1996). The physical appearance of employees may have changed, but there is no substantive change that reflects an organizational culture receptive to diverse ideas.

Hence, diversity is nothing more than a veneer of inclusion. On the other hand, when there is a substantive acceptance of diversity new-comers, an organization changes its culture, which may mean that its core logic is altered. This kind of change is much more than simple "access" to organizations. Theoretically, it conveys to em-ployees that they can expect to develop their potential that is then used to enhance their organization's performance. This develop-ment assumes that diversity newcomers would have access to posi-tions that offer opportunities to professionally develop, that increased responsibilities are a realistic possibility and advancement is depen-dent on performance. The scholarly focus on creating more diverse organizations that are culturally competent (Friedman and Davidson 2001; Prasad and Mills 1997; Minors 1996; Weech-Maldonado, et al. 2002) and the discussion of perspectives of diversity newcomers (Allison 1999) are all strengths of the literature. We argue that the literature falls specifically short when it comes to examining exter-nal issues that organizations cannot ignore.

Current Issues and Themes

The new millennium begins with significant changes regarding di-versity intervention mechanisms (i.e., affirmative action) and issues of access. Earlier, the public sector was in a decisional mode regard-ing which intervention mechanism to choose, affirmative action or managing diversity, to increase minority and female access to edu-cational and employment opportunities. Recently a pronounced anti–affirmative action movement has emerged. Opponents of affirmative action promoted limiting race and gender preferences in popular initiatives in California (Proposition 209) and Washington (Initia-tive 200). Florida governor Jeb Bush has initiated a similar trend of excluding race and ethnicity as educational access factors in his *One Florida* plan. One Florida guarantees university admission to the top 20 percent of Florida high school graduates as a substitute for admission that relies on affirmative action (see www. one florida.org/myflorida/government/governorinitiatives/one_florida/education.html).

On the legal front, the *Hopwood* decision, (*Hopwood v. Texas,* Fifth Circuit 1996) negated the use of race, even as one of many factors, in the University of Texas Law School admissions decision.

Most recently the U.S. Supreme Court in 2003 made a major ruling about affirmative action. In *Grutter v. Bollinger et al.* (288 F.3d 732), the University of Michigan's Law School case, the Court held that the "Law School's narrowly tailored use of race in admissions decisions served a compelling governmental interest and therefore is not prohibited by the Equal Protection Clause, Title VI, or § 1981" (see http://supct.law.cornell.edu/supct/html/02–241.ZS.html: 2). However, in the companion case, *Gratz et al. v. Bollinger et al.* the High Court found that the University of Michigan's use of race in admitting freshmen, pursuant to achieving diversity, violated the Equal Protection Clause, and also Title VI and § 1981 (see http://supct.law.cor nell.edu/supct/html/02–516.ZS.html: 4). Thus, the legal impact was to narrow the application of affirmative action.

The Changing Diversity Discussion

Among researchers, the emphasis has changed from defining diversity to determining effectiveness by examining the individual and organizational impacts of diversity. Inquiry, broadly casted, includes questions of how diversity has affected the individuals in the organization; how effective organizations have managed diversity; and the nature and success of interventions used to ensure the goals of diversity management. Questions about effectiveness and success are part of the continuing discussion about diversity.

What is the impact of diversity upon the members of an organization? Certainly, a major goal of valuing and managing diversity is to have a positive and productive diverse workforce. Research shows that different groups (e.g., race and gender) have different attitudes toward diversity and diversity initiatives. Other research shows that members are affected differently by diversity and related initiatives (Soni 2000; Tsui 1992). Further, measures to address discrimination, such as diversity training, can generate "second-order conflicts" that often appear below the surface with their own dynamics and backlash (Friedman and Davidson 2001). Thus it is necessary to understand factors that either contribute to or inhibit a positive and cohesive diverse work environment. Allison (1999) notes that some of the factors that inhibit a positive working environment include resentment and stereotyping of those who are different. Kirby and Richard (2000),

drawing upon previous researchers' findings, indicate that benefi-
ciaries of diversity policies can also suffer from poor self-esteem if
they perceive their organizational presence and status to be contingent upon their diversity-based characteristics rather than their qualifications. Any of the above factors can inhibit productivity, flexibility,
and teamwork. What is very clear is that unless the cultures of organizations are changed to make them consonant with diversity initiatives, organizations and their members can and do suffer (Allison
1999; Easley 2001). Thus, Easley (2001) calls for an assessment of
organizational cultures to enable a more positive environment for
diversity initiatives and management.

How effective have organizations been in managing diversity?
Results appear to be mixed. For example, in Allison's (1999) limited study of women and minorities in parks and recreation,
interviewees noted that despite some gains, there are organizational barriers and merely symbolic approaches to a full commitment to diversity. Bendick et al. (2001) cite organizations that have
been relatively successful in their quests for organizational change
through diversity management, and with comprehensive diversity
training interventions, based upon organizational development-
based benchmarks. Soni (2000) argues that there is resistance toward and skepticism regarding diversity management tools. Easley
(2001) argues that the kind of organizational change necessary to
ensure the successful outcomes of a more diverse workforce must
be found not just in modified attitudes, but also within the cultural
recesses of organizations.

Organizational failure to manage differences is a problem. Soni's
(2000) study of a regional office of a federal agency highlights the
importance acknowledging and managing differences. If differences
remain unacknowledged, diversity becomes a unique dilemma that
is external to an organization's culture. In turn, diversity newcomers
are not central to the operation of organizations. Worse, they experience difficulty developing effective positional power. The effect is
that their performance is more likely to be questioned, scrutinized,
and even dismissed. These are major disadvantages that hamper the
ability of organizations to make diversity part of their logic that is
used to create and justify organizational culture. Hence, the focus is
not limited to acknowledging difference, but making sure that we
have valid means for understanding and evaluating differences.

The Challenge of Balancing Organizational Expectations

New challenges and opportunities for the diverse public administrator are emerging. Two challenges can influence public administrators who are charged with understanding differences in organizations. These are bureaucratic and ethical. The public administrator is seen as being challenged because at times the underlying values of bureaucracy and ethics often conflict. In addition to setting forth these challenges, we present an approach for balancing these challenges. In so doing, we believe that we can further enhance the notion of stewardship through diversity.

Bureaucratic Values: The First Challenge

The environment that administrators enter as they join organizations to create diversity is governed by a commitment to bureaucratic values: efficiency, efficacy, expertise, loyalty, and accountability. These are established values that public administrators use to judge conduct and performance. As administrators enter an organization, they are socialized to accept the prevailing bureaucratic values. Minority administrators experience this expectation in the form of role determinants. Adam Herbert (1974, 556–63) discusses several role determinants that he believes influence minority administrators' perception of their responsibility to their employing agency. Two of Herbert's role determinants most relevant to the discussion here are *system demands* and *colleague pressure.* System demands refer to organizational performance expectations that are manipulated through various rewards and sanctions. One objective is to get administrators to follow orders without questioning their validity. A second objective is to get minority administrators to conform to organizational standards of acceptable behavior. Herbert suggests that minority administrators who fail to satisfy these role determinants are eliminated from organizations.

The second role determinant, colleague pressure, involves judging whether a worker's job performance is acceptable to his or her colleagues. Herbert gives several examples of the extremes to which some minorities will go to be accepted by their peers. For instance, minority police officers may be more forceful in order to gain the attention of their peers and get promoted. Minority welfare workers will apply rules rigidly to clients in order to be perceived as omnipotent. Minority teachers will blame students rather than the quality of the academic experience in order to be accepted by colleagues. These examples demonstrate that minorities are subject to pressures to assume traditional roles that are compatible with dominant group organizational behavior. Resisting the pressures to conform means not responding to the dominant culture's values that are the basis of organizational practices and behaviors. Carried a step further, practices and behaviors become professional standards that all administrators are expected to incorporate into their professional value systems.

The price for resisting is to be labeled a non–team player. Accepting the bureaucratically motivated role determinants means duplicating the behavior of the administrators who may favor homogeneous organizations. The diversity literature ignores this demand that determines whether an administrator remains a member of the organization. This kind of idealism means that administrators who diversify organizations can also be put in a position where values that are presumed to be a positive contribution of the diverse workplace are negated by bureaucratic homogeneity. In sum, the ability to dictate behavior means that how we understand differences is being determined by bureaucratic expectations.

Social Equity: The Second Challenge

Creating diversity is an important first step, but its true rationale promotes a commitment to social equity. David K. Hart (1974, 3) defines social equity as the "habit of fairness, justness and right-dealing" that would regulate the intercourse of men with men. Stressing fairness and justness means that administrators are relying on behavioral standards that emphasize more than instrumental conduct. More important, fairness requires that new administrators cannot criticize exclusionary action and later duplicate the actions of administrators who limited their access. To duplicate such behavior creates a situation where a minority administrator defends an executive whose agencies refused to hire and award contracts to minorities. This is a position that diversity newcomers want to avoid. Social equity is motivated by ethics. Ethics that "provide behavioral guidelines and are applicable to a variety of occupations in the same pro-fession, are necessary if administrators, whose presence creates workplace diversity, are to discharge their responsibilities" (Pugh 1991, 26). In this regard, the American Society for Public Administra-tion's (ASPA) current revised Code of Ethics is partially useful.

ASPA's Code of Ethics: The Balancing Capacity

ASPA's code is designed to influence the conduct of public adminis-trators in their delays with the public. ASPA's code includes five principles, but only the first, third, and fourth principles are relevant for our discussion. The first principle in the code calls for serving the public interest. This principle encourages behavior that promotes public and not private interests. Further, it engenders a focus be-yond that of the single administrator. Efforts to get administrators to conform to role determinants generally focus on pursuing private interests, personal survival, and acceptance. Conformance to role determinants is a problem that the code tries to avoid by clearly stating that the public's interest is the primary concern of public administrators. The third ASPA principle calls for personal integrity to inspire confidence and trust in the public sector. If we consider that trust and confidence in public sector leadership is waning, mem-bers of diverse organizations have an opportunity to change this perception; inspiring confidence and trust is a possibility for diver-sity newcomers who demonstrate that they are good leaders and stewards of the public trust. Their presence gives them an opportu-nity to demonstrate their leadership among members of that part of the population with which they identify. It also gives them an op-portunity to hear citizens stress their preference for ethical adminis-tration, policy, and management. Personal integrity has a major role in demonstrating that administrators are to be trusted. This means that personal integrity is used to engender qualities that inspire con-fidence and trust in the public sector.

The fourth ASPA principle calls for promoting ethical organiza-tions by improving the ability of organizations to apply ethics, ef-fectiveness, and efficiency when providing public service. This principle discourages system demands that manipulate administra-tors with rewards and sanctions. It also discourages efforts to in-timidate administrators to conform to organizational standards of acceptable behavior. Conversely, ASPA's fourth principle also calls for administrators to insure that organizations are providing services. Hence, what is needed is managerial balance that emphasizes ethical action, effective performance, efficiency, and promotion of diverse ideas that enhance the development and delivery of services. The fourth principle discourages an organization's leaders from believing that homogeneous thinking, and therefore conformity, is the key to efficient and effective performance. Instead, it promotes diversity that values differences. The challenge for leaders is to make sure that their organizations comply with the ASPA Code of Ethics. In turn, they embrace the code's promotion of an enhanced organizational capacity for open communication, creativity, and dedication. To comply, leaders need to avoid and discourage undue criticism that dampens effective performance. Undue criticism undermines a leader's credibility. Criticism creates the perception that a diversity newcomer's judgment is challenged. The results may be a managerial imbalance based on the perception that a diversity newcomer's judgment is impaired, creating an ethical problem that could have been avoided. The effect is to create an environment where diversity is symbolic.

There is a clear concern in the literature about diversity newcomers being ignored and not being taken seriously. This concern implicitly attributes to opponents of diversity a level of control that implies diversity newcomers are passive victims of individual and organizational opposition to diversity. Contrary to this line of thought, diversity newcomers can positively affect how they are received in organizations having to react to excessive behavior that is intended to diminish their importance to organizations. Diversity newcomers must assume that their experiences are sometimes influenced by the need to protect historical advantages or the need to control individual and collective behavior or the need to protect one's position by controlling results. White colleagues are not the only ones guilty of this behavior. Our earlier discussion that some African-Americans can develop an unrealistic expectation for other African-Americans is an example of this kind of controlling behavior. For diversity newcomers who would conclude that my group is not included in these examples, there are no exceptions.

ASPA's code (1994) calls for "enhance[ed] organizational capacity for open communication, creativity, and dedication." Diversity newcomers are obligated to promote open communication. Yet they cannot do so if they become administrators whose conduct is motivated by a need to control individual and collective behavior. In other words, ASPA code establishes ethical standards that are higher than those of the individuals who would discourse diversity. The ASPA code promotes ensuring that others receive credit for their work and contributions. Leaders undermine diversity newcomers when their need for control diminishes the contributions that a diverse perspective adds to policy-making, decision-making, and implementing policy. To comply, leaders need to make sure that diversity newcomers take the lead in presenting their program issues in staff meetings and public settings. Conversely, leaders should avoid reporting developments in the diversity newcomer's area of responsibility while others report developments in their areas. This situation is exacerbated when a leader later asks the diversity newcomer if there is additional information to add to the report. Such action diminishes the diversity newcomer's contribution and creates the perception that the newcomer is not trusted, consequently creating an ethical problem that could have been avoided. This is another example where the effect is to create an environment where diversity is symbolic.

ASPA's code can be useful in promoting the professional development of diversity newcomers. By positively acknowledging each diversity newcomer's judgment and creating trust, an organization's leader is taking an important step toward developing future leaders. If the projection that a significant number of future employees will be women and people of color is correct, then developing future leaders for diverse organizations is a major responsibility. A diversity newcomer's success is dependent on support and encouragement toward the ethical action that ASPA's Code of Ethics promotes. The effect is to create an environment where diversity is substantive. This is a desirable outcome based on a managerial balance that is ethically motivated.

Conclusion

Achieving diversity involves some rewards and some barriers. Yet, creating a setting where diversity newcomers are welcomed is essential if we are to have well-integrated and productive organizations. We contend that ethical standards that provide behavioral guidelines for the public administration community are starting points. Ethical standards assure that administrators entering organizations today can satisfy demands from two sets of values, ethical and organizational. New public servants and administrators are in a position to respond to existing bureaucratic values, but also to establish higher standards than their predecessors. Advocates of diversity are ignoring this challenge. Advocates must recognize diversity newcomers may face demands that compromise the benefits that they claim that diversity offers. The excitement in this literature suggests that diversity newcomers can contribute to the public sector. Their contributions need not be compromised, and will not be, if we encourage diversity newcomers to conclude that their responsibility starts with being aware of their moral responsibility as public servants and administrators.

References

Allison, M.T. 1999. "Organizational Barriers To Diversity in the Workplace." *Journal of Leisure Research* 31: 78–101.

American Society for Public Administration. 1994. *Code of Ethics*. Washington, DC: ASPA.

Bendick, M. Jr. et al. 2001. "Workforce Diversity Training: From Anti-Discrimination Compliance To Organizational Development." *Human Resource Planning* 24: 10–25.

Carnevale, A., and S.C. Stone. 1995. *The American Mosaic: An In-depth Report on the Future of Diversity at Work.* New York: McGraw-Hill.

Carrell, M.R., and E.E. Mann. 1995. "Defining Workforce Diversity in Public Sector Organizations." *Public Personnel Management* 24 (1): 99–111.

Cox, Taylor, Jr. 1993. *Cultural Diversity in Organizations*. San Francisco: Jossey-Bass.

Dominguez, C.M. 1992. "The Challenge of Workforce 2000." *The Bureaucrat* 20 (4): 15–18.

Easley, C.A. 2001. "Developing, Valuing, and Managing Diversity in the New Millennium." *Organizational Development Journal* 19: 38–50.

Fine, Marlene G. 1995. *Building Successful Multicultural Organizations*. San Francisco: Quorum Books.

Friedman, R.A., and M.N. Davidson. 2001. "Managing Diversity and Second Order Conflict." *Internal Journal of Conflict Management* 2: 132–53.

Gibson, C.J., and E. Lennon. 2001. "Historical Census Statistics on the Foreign-Born Population of the United States: 1850–1990." *U.S. Bureau of the Census, Population Division, Working Paper No. 29.* www.census.gov/ population/www/documentation/twps0039.html

Griggs, Lewis Brown. 1995. "Valuing Diversity: Where From . . . Where To?" In Lewis Griggs, Louis Brown, and Lente-Louise Louw, eds. *Valuing Diversity: New Tools for a New Reality.* New York: McGraw-Hill, 1–14.

Hart, David K. 1974. "Social Equity, Justice, and the Equitable Administrator." *Public Administration Review* 34: 3–11.

Herbert, A.W. 1974. "The Minority Public Administrator: Problems, Prospects, and Challenges." *Public Administration Review* 34: 556–63.

Hughes, G.F. 1992. "A Categorized Workforce." *The Bureaucrat* 20 (4): 23–26.

Jamieson, David, and Julie O' Mara. 1991. *Managing Workforce 2000: Gaining the Diversity Advantage.* San Francisco: Jossey-Bass.

Johnston, William B., and Arnold H. Packer. 1987. *Workforce 2000: Work and Workers for the 21st Century.* Indianapolis: Hudson Institute.

Kendall, Francis E. 1995. "Diversity Issues in the Workplace." In Lewis Brown Griggs and Lente-Louise Louw, eds. *Valuing Diversity: New Tools for a New Reality.* New York: McGraw-Hill, 77–113.

Kirby, S.L., and O.C. Richard. 2000. "Impact of Marketing Work-Place Diversity on Employee Job Involvement and Organizational Commitment." *Journal of Social Psychology* 140 (3): 367–77.

Koehler, Berrett, and S. Blake. 1991. "Managing Cultural Diversity: Implications for Organizational Competitiveness." *Academy of Management Executives* 5 (3): 45–56.

Leach, Joy, B. George, T. Jackson, and A. Lebelle, eds. 1995. *A Practical Guide To Working with Diversity: The Process, the Tools, the Resources.* New York: Amacom.

Loden, Marilyn, and Judy B. Rosener. 1991. *Workforce America: Managing Employee Diversity as a Vital Resource.* Homewood, IL: Business One Irwin.

Minors, A. 1996. "From University to Poly-Versity: Organizations in Transition to Anti-Racism." In C. James, ed., *Perspectives on Racism and the Human Services Sector.* Buffalo: University of Toronto Press.

Mobley, Michael, and Tamara Payne. 1992. "Backlash! The Challenge To Diversity Training." *Training and Development* 46 (12): 46.

"One Florida." n.d. www.//oneflorida.org/myflorida/government/governor-initiatives/one florida/education.html

Peters, B.G. 1995. *The Politics of Bureaucracy,* 4th ed. White Plains, NY: Longman.

Prasad, P., and A.J. Mills. 1997. "From Showcase to Shadow: Understanding the Dilemmas of Managing Workplace Diversity." In P. Prasad et al., eds., *Managing the Organizational Melting Pot: Dilemmas of Workplace Diversity.* Thousand Oaks, CA: Sage, 3–27.

Pugh, Darrel L. 1991. "The Origins of Ethical Frameworks in Public Administration." In James S. Bowman, ed. *Ethical Frontiers in Public Management,* San Francisco: Jossey-Bass, 9–33.

Scruggs, Floydette, and Mylon Winn. 1996. "Diversity Newcomers and the Challenge of Balancing Organizational Expectations: A Perspective on Assuming an Ethical Responsibility." In Mitchell F. Rice, ed. *Diversity and Public Organizations: Theory, Issues, and Perspectives.* Dubuque, IA: Kendall Hunt.

Smith, Janet Farrell. 1994. "A Critique of Adversarial Discourse: Gender as an Aspect of Cultural Difference." In Lawrence Foster and Patricia Herzog, eds. *Defending Diversity.* Amherst, MA: University of Massachusetts Press.

Soni, Vidu. 2000. "A 21st Century Reception for Diversity in the Public Sector: A Case Study." *Public Administration Review* 60 (5): 395–408.

Swanger, Clare C. 1994. "Perspectives on the History of Ameliorating Oppression and Supporting Diversity in United States Organizations." In Elsie Y. Cross et al., eds. *The Promise of Diversity: Over 40 Voices Discussing Strategies for Eliminating Discrimination in Organizations*. Burr Ridge, IL: Irwin.

Thomas, Percy. 1995. "A Cultural Rapport Model: Fostering Harmony in the Workplace." In Lewis Brown Griggs and Lente-Louise Louw, eds. *Valuing Diversity: New Tools for a New Reality*. New York: McGraw-Hill, 136–57.

Thomas, R. Roosevelt, Jr. 1990. "From Affirmative Action To Affirming Diversity." *Harvard Business Review* 90 (2): 107–17.

———. 1991. *Beyond Race and Gender: Unleashing the Power of Your Total Workforce by Managing Diversity*. New York: Amacom.

———. 1992. "The Concept of Managing Diversity." *The Bureaucrat* 20 (4): 19–22.

Tsui, A.S. et al. 1992. "Being Different: Relational Demography and Organizational Attachment." *Administrative Science Quarterly* 37: 549–80.

U.S. Office of Personnel Management. n.d. *Monthly Report of Federal Civilian Employment* (SF 113–A): Office of Workforce Information. www.opm.gov/feddata/factbook/html/fb-p08.htm

Weech-Maldonado, R. et al. 2002. "Racial/Ethnic Diversity Management and Culture Competency: The Case of Pennsylvania Hospitals/Practitioner Application." *Journal of Healthcare Management* 47: 111–27.

8

Networking, Career Management, and Diversity in the Public Sector

Wilbur C. Rich

Over the last four decades diversity in the workplace has generally become an accepted American norm. This decisive change started in the late 1960s when the federal government began supporting the fight against job discrimination launched by African-Americans. By the 1970s the women's movement joined the fight against job discrimination. The 1980s saw these efforts mired in a debate over the efficacy and fairness of affirmative action. The 1990s turned into a period of fits and starts, bewildered by conflicting court decisions. Yet progress was made, presaging the end of the all-white-male workplace. An inevitable correlate of this change is more interaction among people of different skin colors, ethnic backgrounds, and genders. The future work environment will include even more of a blend of what Anthony Carnevale and Susan Stone (1995) call the *American Mosaic.*

As the United States enters the early twenty-first century, it faces new challenges. Consequently the nation must prepare its workforce for a globalized labor market. Politicians are no longer championing national guaranteed employment or the use of government resources to create such a worldwide market. Part of the retreat from the "jobs, jobs, jobs for all Americans rhetoric" is tied to anxieties produced by recurrent recessions and the changing international economy. All levels of government are cutting back on hiring and finding ways to use online and other technology methods to replace employees. This change comes at a time when a new generation of minority professionals faces more uncertainty in government service than ever before. During this era of uncertainty, government employees can ill afford to isolate themselves in their cubicles and offices. They must stay connected to their graduate schools, class-mates, and professional associates, and their counterparts in other parts of government. In other words, networking is an occupational imperative. This chapter examines how minority public servants can widen contacts in their occupations and improve their marketability. It attempts to meld the literature on professional networks with the growing diversity in the workplace. More specifically, the chapter provides minority public professionals with an overview of the research in network behavior.

Diversity and the Incomplete Transformation

In *Workforce America,* Marilyn Loden and Judy B. Rosener (1991) offer a broad definition of diversity in the workplace. Such a workforce includes individuals with all types of human characteristics. For Loden and Rosener diversity has both primary and secondary dimensions. The primary dimensions consist of "those immutable human differences that are inborn and/or that exert an important impact on our early socialization and ongoing impact on our lives" (1991, 18). These include age, ethnicity, gender, physical abilities, race, and sexual orientation. These characteristics are our given human attributes and we are stuck with them. There is more hope with our secondary dimensions as they are characteristics that we can change. These include educational background, geographical location, income, marital status, military experience, religious beliefs, and work experience.

These two sets of dimensions shape our basic self-image, or how we see ourselves. Self-image is also a critical part of how we present ourself to others. This is a part of a person's self-promotion. One's attitude toward self-promotion is related to one's personality. Not everyone is equally good at self-promotion—or equally motivated to put the effort into it. Introverts have figured out that if they leave socializing to the extroverts, they will end up at the bottom of the pile. So they learn how to practice the art of self-promotion, though it does not flow as naturally for them. Extroverts see that everyone is playing the same game—and assume the world is full of extroverts like themselves (Nicholson 2001).

The American workplace changes to adapt to the changing social environment. In the old industrial labor market the employer had a limited interest in the worker's profile or biography. In the contemporary workplace, employers are required to take into consideration workers' rights and be governed by them. The legal system has made it practically impossible to discriminate openly, with impunity, against a worker for his or her primary dimensions. Yet, as was suggested earlier, the goal of an open labor market has not been realized. People are still in some way discriminated against on the basis of their primary dimensions. Few women or minority workers can boast of never having experienced job discrimination. Many organizations still prefer white males to all other types of applicants. White males continue to enjoy more career success, more organizational status, and higher incomes than their minority cohorts. Part of their success is related to the traditional white male networks that exclude others. White male advantage is also helped by accepted discrimination on secondary characteristics (or dimensions) of individuals. With the exception of religious beliefs, employers are relatively free to discriminate on the grounds of education levels or even to the particular college applicants attended. Veterans are given preference in government jobs. The requirement of a certain kind of work experience is sometimes a matter of interpretation. Minority workers can overcome this type of discrimination by utilizing strategic career planning. Investing heavily in education and networking can be a way to overcome this type of discrimination. One must become a *careerist* in this new market.

Careerists and Postmodern Labor Market

The postmodern labor market is a by-product of the postindustrial economy. In the old labor market, professionals were considered a part of the primary labor market. The whole concept of professionals was defined in rigid and binary terms. Professionals were independent, nonprofessionals were not. They were highly educated and well paid; nonprofessionals were not. Professionals were innovative and creative and nonprofessionals were the opposite. These descriptions of professionals were used to denigrate nonprofessionals and add status to white-collar work. Managers in the old labor market came to the workplace with MBA and MPA degrees in hand. They did not start in the mailroom. Although they were expected to spend their careers in a single agency, upward mobility was determined by highly individualized performance ratings. If one worked hard and long, one would be promoted to the top. These professionals became William H. Whyte's *Organization Man* (1956).

The postmodern labor market accords fewer privileges to professionals who enter the company as midlevel managers. The MBA or MPA degree is just an insurance policy against downward mobility to blue-collardom. Job security belongs to those who are willing to move from job to job. Sociologist Ruth Pape calls moving from job to job *diversity skills "tourism"* (Pape 1954). Job tours allow these professionals to become flexible, multitalented, and well connected. They have little choice but to become enlightened careerists. C. Brooklyn Derr (1986) outlines five types of careerists. *Getting ahead* careerists are goal-oriented and aware of the appropriate strategy to get them to the top of their profession. The *getting secure* types are oriented toward achieving job security and lifetime employment. The third type is called a *getting free* careerist who strives toward personal autonomy and enjoys solving problems independently. The fourth type, the *getting high* careerist, is interested in the challenge of work and is happiest with the excitement of work. The fifth type, called a *getting balanced* careerist, pays equal attention to his career and personal life.

The coming of the postmodern labor market poses different challenges for each of these types. For the *getting ahead* type, the strategy of working hard and long may be less effective than it was in the old labor market. The *getting secure* type will find it more difficult to locate the organization that offers permanent or surprise-free jobs. Even in the highly classified public service, the promise of lifetime employment is less reliable. One can be laid off in a fiscal exigency or kept on but with more duties. The *getting free* careerist who covets loose supervision and more space may find teamwork is the norm. The latter two types, the *getting high* types and the *getting balanced* careerists, may be the best prepared to enter the postmodern labor market. These individuals are excited by their work. The *getting balanced* persons are not only excited by the work and are willing to work hard, but also know how to achieve balance in their lives. To Derr's five types of careerists can be added a sixth: *getting networked*. This type of individual combines work with that of creating opportunities for relationships within and outside the organization. Rather than seeking autonomy, this type of careerist seeks connections. The careerist who is well connected inside and outside of the organization will have an advantage over those isolated within organizations. This well-traveled, multiskilled, and glorious generalist will be the most effective careerist in the new labor market.

The Need for Networking in the Early Twenty-first Century

For public sector employees, networking represents one way to overcome social isolation and organizational provincialism. Yet Susan Hanson asserts that "effective networks are rarely grounded in blatant utilitarianism" (Hanson 2000, 752). There are both personal and professional rewards in networking. Professional networks consist of individuals organized around shared interests. They provide members with opportunities to shop for and exchange ideas. Services offered by networks also include career tips, useful gossip about rival organizations, and linkages with prestigious professionals. Hanson concludes, *"Networks affect career outcomes not only by helping one connect with job opportunities (the lubricating function) but also by providing support (the glue function)"* (Hanson 2000, 755, italics added).

Sociologists, psychologists, and anthropologists continue to be fascinated by the adaptations human beings make in response to changing social conditions. The need of human beings to belong continues despite changes in the workplace. It is impossible to further one's career and grow professionally without some contact outside the workplace.

At first glance networking seems to be an old idea repackaged. Support groups, cliques, and caucuses have been around for a long time (see Dalton 1959). How are networks different? A closer look reveals that modern professional networks are engaged more explicitly in career promotion than were earlier informal groupings. Networks promote careers by facilitating the use of human and social capital. *Human capital* refers to the amount and quality of formal education and training an individual possesses. The concept of human capital, developed by Gary Becker (1964), holds that an educated worker is more productive and is worth more to the organization. The more educational credentials one obtains, the greater the attention one receives from employing organizations. Educational credentials signal the employer that the applicant is a potential productive worker (Spence 1974). The returns on the educational investment are measured by income and status (see Schultz 1961). *Social capital* refers to the nurturing of personal characteristics that are organizationally valued. While one brings human capital to an organization, social capital is gained through interaction with one's peers. Organizations reward such personality traits as dependability, reliability, probity, and leadership. Eva Meyerson (1994), a sociologist, claimed that over time social capital is more important than human capital. She found that top managers were judged by subjective criteria such as "trustworthiness." In other words, educational credentials will get one a place in the organization, but positive peer evaluations are necessary for mobility. Prudent professionals develop social capital inside and outside the organization just in case they choose to leave or are pushed out the door.

Investing in oneself is not so easy or selfish as it sounds. Some people find it difficult to introduce themselves to others. Others believe that open careerism is crass. Still others never become good networkers. Few continue to question the need to network if they produce consistently high quality work. Many first generation white-collar minority professionals fall in the latter group. They equate networking with a glorified chattering. This is a false impression, as minority professionals need networking more than ever. First, there is a growing demand for mobile minority professionals who are willing to change jobs and locations to advance their careers. Second, modern communication has shrunk the spatial distance among organizations. Public and private organizations around the world can locate talent within seconds. Networks are excellent sources of talent identification and promotion because they are relatively risk-free and loosely organized.

Networking and Loose Coupling

Openness and freedom are the operating norms of professional networks. Openness facilitates relationships within and among networks. Freedom is derived from weak ties or *loose coupling* in organizations. Such organization creates multiple interactive opportunities because contacts are nonbinding and nonredundant. Network members have the freedom to move in and out of networks. One is not obligated to talk only with a particular network member. In fact, the more one moves around and interacts with people outside the group, the more contacts are created for one's home network group. Multinetworking provides the greater payoff in terms of information and opportunities.

Can grouping based on racial affinity be harmful to good networking? Tightly coupled groupings that stress group identification and cohesion can isolate their members because they do not encourage them to interact with other groups. For example, an African-American caucus, organized as a reaction to exclusionary practices of a larger white organization, could run the risk of becoming a tightly coupled group. Caucus leadership often insists on total loyalty of members as a way to keep the group viable. This is not to gain the psychological benefits from "hanging out with one's own kind," but conferences are designed to maximize networking in a short period of time. Minorities may find themselves commiserating among themselves and not networking. Herminia Ibarra (1995, 675) observes: "From a career development perspective, close relationships are more likely to fulfill psychosocial functions. Psychosocial functions are aspects of a relationship that enhance an individual's sense of competence, identity, and effectiveness in a professional role; they include serving as a role model, acceptance, and friendship. Psychosocial functions are distinguished from purely instrumental functions, such as providing exposure to senior management and advocacy for promotion, in that they involve benefits that stem from the nature of the relations rather than the positional power of the contact."

Most loosely structured networks do not require members of minorities to represent their ethnic or racial groups. Therefore, African-Americans can meet whites, women can meet men, and Latinos can meet Asians, and so on. Loose organizations are also self-measuring for members: a member evaluates the performance of the network, not vice versa. A member can leave a network and rejoin it without adverse career implications. An individual can remain an attending member or become a part of the network's leadership structure. Sociologist Mark S. Granovetter, the most notable advocate of loose relationships or what he calls "weak ties," believes that such ties are not "generative of alienation" but are "indispensable to individuals' opportunity and to their integration into communities; strong ties, breeding local cohesion, lead to overall fragmentation" (Granovetter 1973, 1378). Weak ties are the strength of the network. Strong ties compromise the purpose of networks: to provide opportunities to meet as many people as possible.

In some cultures, developing strong ties is the norm. Some people take umbrage at casual, favor-seeking friendships. They are more comfortable with personal relationships. For example, in some Latino cultures there is a very strong orientation toward close ties, particularly among first-generation professionals. Powell and Smith-Doerr (1994) believe such close ties can bind as well as blind. They can blind one to opportunities. Since Latinos are relative newcomers to professional life, they are less likely to attend professional conferences, where most of the outside networking takes place. The best way for professionals to stay connected is to attend professional membership organizations.

The Role of Professional Association Meetings

Most professional organizations (e.g., the American Society for Public Administration, the International Personnel Management Association, and the International City and County Management Association) can be described as loosely structured. At their national conferences there is a formal program, but people are expected to pursue their own private agendas. Nicholson regards professional conferences as "huge circuses devoted almost exclusively to official and unofficial gossip" (Nicholson 2001, 44). People move among networks to seek influence and alliances. Gossip performs several functions for attendees. It exposes who is doing what, who is unhappy, and who is vying for what job. Where else can one get professional gossip except at conferences? Conferences also allow one to be someone different than their day-to-day working self. In a fascinating study of behavior at bars, sociologist Sherri Cavan found that people take a "liquor license" when they present themselves at bars. Drinking gives them the right to exaggerate their accomplishments (Cavan 1966). This is also true of association conventions. Conferences are opportunities to "peacock," that is, look good and attract attention. One can inflate one's verbal resume, take credit for one's organization success, and shift blame for failures to others. These presentations are done in good spirits and no one is expected to believe everything they hear.

Since the formal parts of the meetings (e.g., paper presentations and workshops) rarely take all of the attendee's time, they become a linking mechanism for an array of networks. Granovetter (1973) calls these linkages "bridge ties," which connect individuals and networks that otherwise would not be linked. Because these networks are nonredundant (different people in different networks), an individual can spend the entire time at the organizational meeting making new connections without losing old ones.

Professional conferences are a combination of giant job fairs, training sessions, exhibits, and social events. During the conference a temporary community is formed, and it is left up to the individual to determine how to make the most of it. A first-time attendee is accorded nearly equal treatment as the veterans and is allowed to make alliances, obligations, and contacts at relatively low cost (i.e., in energy, time, and resources). First-time attendees will find the business card swapping, brief visiting, and clustering baffling, but this is the essence of networking. One is to meet as many people as possible in the short time of the conference. Veteran conventioneers often arise very early for a group breakfast, plan a separate group lunch, attend receptions, and organize an entirely new group for dinner. It is a long day, but it exposes one to the maximum amount of contacts.

Returning attendees play a variety of roles. Some attendees spend the entire meeting advertising their availability for other jobs. Others devote considerable time attending panels. Still others focus on socializing. A few vie for leadership positions within the organization. Yet the looseness of the group is its most important asset. Information is its most important currency. However, the individuals who profit most from making contacts are those with self-command capital.

Self-command Capital and Networking

Siegwart Lindenberg has introduced the notion of *self-command capital* as the capacity to take authoritative direction (cited in Baron and Hannatt 1994). Self-command individuals know what they want and how to get it. Such individuals are very attractive to networks. They are often aggressively recruited. It is not difficult to understand why the most successful networkers are those who are self-motivated. Although self-command capital is in part a product of personality, it can also be taught. The skills needed include verbal facility, self-confidence, an attractive appearance and self-presentation. Some introverts can use the professional conference to experiment with a different part of their personality. There is little or no risk. One can talk, act, and even dress differently at a professional conference.

Are minority professionals self-command capital deprived? Obviously, given the history of this country, it is unlikely that minorities will feel comfortable in every setting. Being a *token* is often very uncomfortable. Nevertheless, minorities who break network barriers may have to pay the price of being a token or "the first of his group" in order to educate network members to a larger pool of potential minority members. Networks will be receptive to them to the extent that minorities bring something to exchange. Bringing oneself is not enough. Some confident minority professionals are reluctant to approach an all-white network because they fear rejection. As networks become more multiracial, rejection will become less likely. Besides, to be an effective networker, one must take risks. There are so many networks that one can shop around. The point is to accomplish three important goals: improve job mobility, find new opportunities, and attract mentors.

Attracting National Mentors

In the postmodern era, minority professionals cannot afford to be "too local." They must seek a more national profile and perhaps an international one. To become a professional with national visibility, one may need a powerful patron. In our society patrons can facilitate a client's career by simply endorsing their bids for power and prestige. Sponsorship is made easier if the client has the talent to match the support. However, the lack of certifiable talent is not a complete barrier to a successful career. Persons with few discernible intellectual attributes have scaled the pyramid of success. They were able to do so with a strategic use of social capital or with the assistance of a powerful sponsor.

The mentor-client relationship is one of the oldest relationships in organizations. David Thomas's (1993) research found that racial compatibility is not a requirement for good mentoring. People, regardless of background, help each other either because they enjoy the psychological rewards of giving or they expect something in return. Alvin Gouldner (1960) calls the latter implicit obligation the "norm of reciprocity." For every gift or favor, there is an implied obligation. In effective networks, obligations are the currency to engage in continuous exchange. A good client understands the obligatory nature of work relationships and works hard to keep the confidence of the mentor. A client also knows that his access to opportunities is being charged to his sponsor's account (the social capital the sponsor has accumulated in networks). The client is often aware that his success reflects well on his sponsor. A good sponsor not only helps a client's career but also assists in finding job vacancies. Job vacancies are created by structural holes.

Finding the Structural Hole

Ronald Burt's notion of a structural hole is concerned with how the individual identifies and takes advantage of opportunities in organizations. One has to be in the right place at the right time. In addition, one must have enough contacts to be able to mobilize them at a critical moment. Vacancies, or structural holes, are only episodically available. Finding such holes increases the likelihood of upward mobility. Burt (1992) suggests that individuals can fill these holes by altering the structure of the organization. For example, minority employees can volunteer their services to improve communication in the organization. This can be done with a workshop. The information created by the workshop could alter the organizational dynamics. The volunteer could conceivably create a new job niche in the organization. Attending national conferences, finding mentors, and creating structural niches is not easy even for loose organizations and willing individuals. Networking consists of recognition of career goals, a plan of action, and solicitation of others. Ultimately, networking is about self-promotion and presentation. Yet there are still barriers that may inhibit minority professionals.

Barriers to Networking

Despite the fact that most professional networks are relatively open organizations, a lack of social skills can be a barrier to networking. People who are not naturally gregarious and who do not enjoy meeting other people will find networking difficult. A person who may have excellent human capital but who cannot handle a simple self-introduction will not go far up the career ladder. Since these skills can be taught, network members can teach others.

A second barrier to networking is a lack of financial resources. Without adequate resources, a professional cannot travel to national meetings. Many ambitious minority professionals do not have the disposable income necessary for distant travel. A trip to a conference can cost a thousand dollars for four days. Some agencies will not pay for such travel. If an ambitious employee wants to maximize her national marketability, then her first employment choice should be an agency that encourages its employees to keep current with their profession or that requires them to participate in associations. Local and regional meetings are not good substitutes.

An additional barrier is time. To be an effective meeting participant, one must be willing to give speeches, write papers, participate in panels, and accept committee assignments. Anyone expecting to gain a national reputation after one convention appearance is in for a big disappointment. The rewards of networking go to those willing to put in the time. Finally, women are not welcome in all networks. Some are prevented from becoming important players in networks. In some cases women have created their own networks. As early as 1980 books such as Mary Scott Welch's *Networking* appeared, advising women to network. In 1994, Carolyn Steele reported that professional black women were networking themselves into better job and business opportunities (Steele 1994). As long as women stay connected to other mixed-gender networks, they will not have problems. Although gender bias is changing, exclusive networks still exist. The new economy may make gender as well as racial quotas obsolete.

Conclusion

Diversifying the workforce may prove easier than convincing some minority professionals of the efficacy of networks. If the postmodern labor market promises a more open recruitment pool, then the once-closed professional networks will also be unlocked. White males still dominate the managerial job markets, but glass ceilings and color lines are being broken every day. Thanks to new discrimination laws and more progressive attitudes, we are diversifying our workforce. Patronage, favoritism, and bias are no longer openly promoted or condoned. If we are in the twilight of the exclusive array of all-white-male networks, then it is imperative that minorities prepare themselves for membership. The dawn of *mosaic networks* (i.e., multiracial, multicultural, and open to women) will create new opportunities for minority professionals. It is incumbent upon these newcomers to link up with other networks. Networks are proven career builders. Remember, professionals who refuse to participate in them can achieve only local visibility. In this changing job market it is very risky to remain local because agencies change/merge, political parties get defeated, management ideology shifts, and budgets cave in. One must maintain outside contacts if one is to manage a fulfilling and effective professional career. The openness and looseness of networks makes easy entrance possible and exit painless. However, the initiative must come from the individual. Also, remember that networks are self-regulating and voluntary.

We are surely moving toward a global workforce. Accordingly, minorities must prepare for an open job market that will be even larger and more diverse than now. Given my comments at the beginning of the chapter about the size of government, the future of public service is unpredictable. Diversification of one's career investment is the only way to avoid unwelcome surprises. The only thing certain in this new economy is uncertainty. Minorities cannot afford to feel secure in their jobs.

References

Baron, J.N. and M.T. Hannatt. 1994. "The Impact of Economics on Contemporary Sociology." *Journal of Economic Literature* 32 (3): 1111–46.

Becker, Gary. 1964. *Human Capital.* New York: National Bureau of Economic Research.

Burt, Ronald. 1992. *Structural Holes: The Social Structure of Competition.* Cambridge, MA: Harvard University Press.

Carnevale, Anthony, and Susan Stone. 1995. *The American Mosaic: An In-Depth Report on the Advantage of Diversity in the U.S. Workforce.* New York: McGraw-Hill.

Cavan, Sherri. 1966. *Liquor License: An Ethnographical Study of Bar Behavior.* Chicago: Aldine Publishing Company.

Dalton, Melville. 1959. *Men Who Manage.* New York: John Wiley, Inc.

Derr, Brooklyn C. 1986. *Managing the New Careerists.* New York: Jossey-Bass.

Gouldner, Alvin. 1960. "The Norm of Reciprocity: A Preliminary Statement." *American Sociological Review* 25 (2) (April): 161–78.

Granovetter, Mark. 1973. "The Strength of Weak Ties." *American Journal of Sociology* 78 (6) (May): 1360–80.

Hanson, Susan. 2000. "Networking" *Professional Geographer* 52: 751–58.

Ibarra, Herminia. 1995. "Race, Opportunity, and Diversity of Social Circles in Managerial Networks." *Academy of Management Journal* 38 (June): 673–703.

Lindenberg, Siegwart. 1992. Self-Command Capital and the Problem of Agency. Paper presented at the Annual Meeting of the American Sociological Association, Pittsburgh, PA.

Loden, Marilyn, and Judy B. Rosener. 1991. *Workforce America!: Managing Employee Diversity as a Vital Resource.* Homewood, IL: Business One Irwin.

Myerson, Eva. 1994. "Human Capital, Social Capital, and Compensation: The Relative Contribution of Social Contacts To Manager's Income." *Acta Sociologia* 37 (4): 383–99.

Nicholson, Nigel. 2001. "The New Word on Gossip." *Psychology Today* (May/June): 41–45.

Pape, Ruth. 1954. "Touristry: A Type of Occupational Mobility." *Social Problems* 11 (2): 336–44.

Powell, Walter, and Laurel Smith-Doerr. 1994. "Networks and Economic Life." In N. Smelser and R. Swedbert, eds. *The Handbook of Economic Sociology.* Princeton: Princeton University Press.

Schultz, Theodore. 1961. "Investment in Human Capital." *American Economic Review* 51 (March): 1–17.

Spence, Michael A. 1974. *Market Signaling: Informational Transfer in Hiring and Related Screening Processes.* Cambridge: Harvard University Press.

Steele, Carolyn Odom. 1994. "Setting a New Agenda for Women's Network." *Black Enterprise* 25 (3): 126–32.

Thomas, D.A. 1993. "The Dynamics of Managing Racial Diversity in Developmental Relationships." *Administrative Science Quarterly* 38 (2): 169–94.

Welch, Mary Scott. 1980. *Networking: The Great Way for Women to Get Ahead.* New York: Harcourt Brace Jovanovich.

Whyte, William H. 1956. *The Organization Man.* New York: Simon & Schuster.

9

Responding to the Health Needs of a Diverse Population

The Need for Diversity in the Health Professions

B. Lee Green, Rhonda K. Lewis,
and Daphne C. Watkins

The health care system over the past few decades has seen significant changes in the way business is conducted. The literature continues to highlight the challenges that are faced by the health care system and the changes that are being made (Monheit and Vistnes 2000). This enterprise has seen rising health care costs, shortages of critical health professionals, and rising concerns and criticisms by the public (LaVeist et al. 2000). It is apparent that the health care system must confront these challenges and make the necessary adjustments to gain back the trust of the public. It is hoped that changes are made that will allow the system to be as effective as possible in delivering the best possible health care to all individuals who utilize the services. To be the most effective health care system, health professionals must always consider how they deliver services and determine how services can be delivered more effectively. In order to meet the new challenges and demands of the health care environment it has been recommended that health professional groups do five things: (1) change professional training to meet the demands of the new health care system; (2) require interdisciplinary competence in all health professionals; (3) continue to move education into ambulatory practice; (4) encourage public service for all health profession students and graduates; and (5) ensure that the health profession workforce reflects the diversity of the nation's population (Gragnola and Stone 1997; PEW 1995).

The Right Thing to Do, The Smart Thing to Do. This is the title of the 2001 Institute of Medicine (IOM) report that discusses the need to enhance diversity in the health professions (Smedley et al. 2001). It is clear from the report that diversity is a necessary component of health professions of all kinds. The IOM report outlines in a very clear and succinct way the benefits of diversity and the strategies for achieving diversity (Smedley et al. 2001). The IOM report is responding to the fact that after more than twenty-five years of making significant efforts, minorities are still underrepresented in health-related fields. Many minority groups, including African-Americans, Hispanics, and Native Americans, are poorly represented in the health professions relative to their proportions in the overall U.S. population (Grumbach et al. 2001). Additionally, these groups tend to have more health problems, experience more barriers to health care, and when receiving care often experience a poorer quality of care (Kington 2001). Further, based on recent census reports, the proportion of these groups is rising significantly, thereby increasing the need to be prepared to respond to their health needs (Smedley et al. 2001). An examination of current trends indicates that this problem will not be easily solved. We continue to see the number of minorities enrolling and completing health-related professional schooling remaining constant or declining in some cases. The pipeline of students who are enrolled in health-related schools has declined over the years as well. Many agencies, institutions, and foundations have been interested in this issue and are working to address the problem.

Efforts to increase the number of minority scientists, researchers, and health professionals are ongoing in colleges and universities all across the United States. The scarcity of minority scientists, researchers, and health professionals is not a new issue and continues to be a major problem in most academic disciplines including the biomedical and health fields. The present pool of minority U.S. doctoral degree holders is woefully underrepresented in the biomedical fields, and efforts are under way to ameliorate this problem (Trickett et al. 1994). The need to increase diversity in the health professions has been a major concern of the federal government and many private groups and organizations. However, efforts to increase diversity have been met with challenges. For example, lawsuits were brought forward that challenged affirmative action policies, and public referenda were initiated to counter affirmative action. These include the *Hopwood v. Texas* case, California Proposition 209, and Initiative 200 in Washington State (Murdock et al. 1998). The lawsuits and public referenda have forced educational institutions to reexamine how they use race and ethnicity as factors in decisions regarding admissions. Despite these challenges, many believe that there is a need for greater diversity in the health professions and that more resources are needed to eliminate this problem.

Rationale for Diversity

Dr. Jordan J. Cohen, president of the Association of American Medical Colleges (AAMC), in 2003 noted four important reasons why preserving diversity in medical colleges is important: (1) adequate representation among students and faculty of the diversity in U.S. society is indispensable for quality medical education; (2) increasing diversity in the physician workforce will improve access to health care for underserved populations; (3) increasing the diversity of the research workforce can accelerate advances in medical and public health research; and (4) diversity among managers of health care organizations makes good business sense (Cohen 2003).

1. *Adequate Representation Among Students and Faculty of the Diversity in U.S. Society Is Indispensable for Quality Medical Education*

With the U.S. population increasing, the numbers of multiracial and multicultural people in need of quality healthcare are also increasing. Future physicians will be expected to have knowledge about all types of people, American-born or not, and will need to know how to deal with patients from all racial and ethnic backgrounds. With this in mind, the quality of health care that is expected from physicians will depend on their competence of medicine as well as their cultural competence. Obtaining the skills necessary to care for multicultural populations requires knowledge about one's own culture in addition to information about the cultures of others. These factors and many others contribute to the way patients respond to their illnesses, how they interact with their physicians, and their path to a better quality of health. The skills that medical students need in order to assist patients in their quest for better health cannot be confined to the information found in their textbooks. But rather, medical students will need to immerse themselves into diverse populations so that they experience working alongside diverse populations.

2. Increasing the Diversity in the Physician Workforce Will Improve Access to Health Care for Underserved Populations

Evidence has documented that physicians who are members of underrepresented minority populations usually dedicate their work to serving underrepresented populations. This is supportive of the view that increasing the number of minority physicians will lead to more detailed explorations of health issues in underrepresented minority populations. Personal relationships with health issues that plague one's community will most likely make that individual passionate about those issues and will encourage efforts to seek answers.

3. Increasing the Diversity of the Research Workforce Can Accelerate Advances in Medical and Public Health Research

Any health research conducted by a physician will eventually affect the health concerns of all Americans. But the challenge is allowing individuals who are passionate about a specific area to explore that particular area. "Since what people see as problems depends greatly on their particular cultural and ethnic filters, it follows that finding solutions to some of our country's most recalcitrant health problems, even being able to conceptualize what the real problems actually are, will require a research workforce that is much more diverse racially and ethnically than we now have" (Cohen 2003). Since it is believed that people conduct research on the problems they see, diverse research will be achieved if more diverse students are admitted into medical schools.

4. Diversity Among Managers of Health Care Organizations Makes Good Business Sense

The various workers a business employs should reflect that of the business clientele. More and more professionals in health care as well as other business endeavors are realizing this as the United States becomes more widely and diversely populated. What corporations are discovering is that their quality of service and success is magnified when they decide to make their atmosphere multicultural. This can also be applied to professionals in health care, as they too can benefit from interactions with diverse health professionals. In regard to the health care professional-patient relationship, as the patients diversify, so too should the physicians.

A symposium on diversity in the health professions was conducted by the IOM in 2001. The purposes and goals were to: (1) reexamine and revitalize the rationale for diversity in health professions, particularly in light of the rapid growth of racial and ethnic minority populations in the United States; (2) identify problems in underrepresentation of U.S. racial and ethnic minorities in health professions, and discuss the strategies that are being developed to respond to underrepresentation; (3) assess the impact of anti–affirmative action legislative and judicial actions on diversity in health professions and health care service delivery to ethnic minority and medically underserved populations; (4) identify effective short-term strategies for enhancing racial and ethnic diversity in health professions training programs; and (5) identify practices of health professions schools that may assist in improving the preparation of racial and ethnic minority students currently underrepresented in health professions, thereby enhancing the long-term likelihood of greater diversity in the health professions. The major outcome of the symposium was that diversity in the health professions is critically important and that there is a need to adequately address this issue (Smedley et al. 2001).

Louis Sullivan, former secretary of Health and Human Services, says, "If we are to improve the delivery of health care for all Americans, including the poor and our minority citizens, we need to open the doors of our classrooms, our laboratories, and our clinics. Members of our minority communities understand and have experienced directly the problems confronting poor and underserved areas. Many of these students will eventually practice in such underserved areas" (Sullivan 1995). Clearly, a diverse pool of health professions scientists and researchers will bring a unique perspective that includes personal and professional insight into a minority culture (Hunttlinger and Drevdahl 1994). According to Ready and Nickens (1994), there are four major reasons why diversity in health professions is important.

1. *Diversity and equity:* Minorities make up a larger proportion of the total U.S. population. According to the U.S. Census, by the year 2020 minority youth will make up 40 percent
   of the school-age population.
2. *Access to care:* Some evidence suggests that minority physicians have higher proportions of minority patients in their
   practice. Lack of minority physicians limits the choices that
   minority patients have in selecting physicians.
3. *Leadership in the medical enterprise:* The health care system or medical enterprise is one of the largest industries in
   the world. The United States alone spends over $900 billion
   a year on health care. Many important decisions are being
   made about the way the health care system will work. It is
   important for the individuals who are making those decisions to reflect the population in which they serve.
4. *Desegregation of elites:* Many look to physicians and other
   health care professionals as leaders in the community as well
   as individuals who can make significant change in the community. It is important that these individuals have a composition that is comparable to the American population (Ready
   and Nickens 1994). Additionally, we live in a world in which
   public health threats are numerous and there is a need for
   our public health system to be as effective as it has ever
   been. In order to have the best public health system and
   health care system, we must make significant improvements.
   One major improvement will be a more diverse workforce
   in medicine and public health. Our system cannot be as effective as possible without a diverse team of individuals
   working together to solve the health threats of the world.
   This diversity must begin in the classroom.

Research shows that the MCAT scores and GPAs of underrepresented minority medical school applicants are typically lower
than those of white and Asian students. Yet, one must still acknowledge the fact that all medical school applicants, minority or nonminority, are examined under a microscope. Factors such as an
applicant's leadership abilities, ability to handle a heavy workload,
overcoming adversity, participation in community service, compas-
sion, willingness to help others, empathy, and communication skills

all play a part in their attractiveness to medical school admission committees. As much as admission committees like to emphasize MCAT scores and GPAs, they are not the only determining factors in selection processes. It is no mystery that students entering medical school with a lower MCAT score and GPA are expected to encounter academic difficulty in pursuit of their degree. However, there is no concrete evidence that suggests that high MCAT scores and GPAs guarantee outstanding academic achievement, nor does it suggest that the physician's quality of care will ascend above that of another. Despite their lower MCAT scores and GPAs, over the past few years an elite class of underrepresented minorities has been identified by medical school admission committees to the degree where these individuals have successfully completed medical school and proceeded to enriching medical careers.

Medical educators are convinced that patients do not want their physician's education to be confined to what they receive from textbooks, but rather their entire contribution to the profession as it reflects their own attributes. The biggest fear of medical admissions committees is that as they attempt to eliminate the racial and ethnic disparities in matriculation, they are faced with the number of underrepresented minorities who *do* have low qualifications and who *do* take longer to graduate. The question is, what should be done about these medical students? Should we just accept the fact that these happenings occur, or lower the standards of medical school qualifications so that minorities have an easier transition into the physician workforce? Whatever the medical admissions committees decide to do, the outcome must be an improvement in all aspects of the health care system. This is especially important because an increasingly multicultural society and future is ahead of us.

A number of studies indicate that diversity in higher education settings seems to be associated with positive social and academic outcomes. For example, a landmark study in 1998 investigated career outcomes for two cohorts of white and minority students who attended twenty-eight selective colleges and universities in the 1970s and 1980s. The results were that minority graduates at these institutions attained levels of achievement that were equal to their nonminority students. Additionally, minority graduates obtained professional degrees in law, business, and medicine at rates much higher than the national average for all students (Bowen and Bok 1998). This study suggests that the learning environment that includes diverse students adds more richness to the experience, thereby developing health professionals who have a greater appreciation for other ideas and experiences. This is further highlighted in a quote by Lisa Tedesco, vice president and secretary of the university and professor of dentistry at the University of Michigan. She says, "Students who experience the most racial and ethnic diversity in classroom settings and in informal interactions with peers show the greatest engagement in active thinking processes, growth in intellectual engagement and motivation and growth in intellectual and academic skills" (Tedesco 2001).

A Focus on the Numbers: The Current Trends

The support for affirmative action was revived in the early 1990s when the AAMC launched its *Project 3000 by 2000*. This program simply stated that access to quality health care for more people would be achieved if the physician workforce were more diverse. Not only did the AAMC encourage all medical schools to increase their efforts in identifying more qualified minority applicants, it also pushed other educational institutions to better prepare students for the medical school process.

Recent legislative and judicial decisions such as Proposition 209 in California and *Hopwood v. Texas* have restricted the use of special consideration taken toward race and ethnicity in the medical school student selection process. Although these two activities had some impact around the country, the evaluation process was felt more heavily in Texas and California allopathic medical schools in the late 1990s. For example, in Texas, underrepresented minorities, or URMs (a term used by the AAMC as early as the 1970s that refers to African-Americans, Mexican-Americans, Native Americans, and mainland Puerto Ricans), dropped from 21.0 percent matriculants in 1996 to 15.6 percent by the year 2000. In California the percentage of matriculants who were URMs decreased from a high of 21.9 percent in 1992 to 15.6 percent in the year 2000. Since California and Texas are where large numbers of U.S. minorities reside, these numbers are especially disturbing. To reach numbers of population proportion, California would need 40 percent of its matriculants to be URMs and Texas would need 43 percent. All in all, the number of URMs in the health professions is not reciprocal to the number of URMs in the United

States. Trends in matriculants and enrollees differ across the health professions. Nursing, public health, and pharmacy have experienced a steady increase in the proportion of matriculants who are URMs. Dentistry, on the contrary, has experienced a steady decrease in its proportion of diverse matriculants over the past decade.

Of all the health professions analyzed, dentistry is the only one that has experienced a decrease in its proportion of matriculants throughout the 1990s. As a result of the surge in total number of applicants from 1989 to 1999, matriculation rates of both URMs and non-URMs steadily decreased. For URMs the matriculation rate went from 69.3 percent to 42.4 percent while the non-URM rate fell from 75.3 percent to 46.7 percent. Similar to the rest of the United States, California and Texas also experienced a decrease in matriculants throughout the 1990s. In Texas the proportion of URM matriculants fell from 16.5 percent to 12.9 percent between 1989 and 1999. Already exceptionally low, California's proportion of URM matriculants in dental school decreased from 6.7 percent to 3.6 percent (Grumbach et al. 2001).

Nursing is the only field (of the ones analyzed) that does not require a graduate degree for and initial license to practice. In fact, nursing is unique in that it allow its students to enter from a wide range of educational points. This reflects the outstanding increase in the proportion of URM students and, as a result, nursing has the highest number of URM enrollees among the health professions, with the exception of public health. In baccalaureate nursing programs between 1991 and 1999, there was a steady URM increase. The increase in URM enrollment and minimal increase in non-URM enrollment resulted in a growing percent of URMs in baccalaureate nursing programs, rising from 12.2 percent in 1991 to 16 percent in 1999.

Public health programs have the highest proportion of URM applicants and enrollees of the health professions (Grumbach et al. 2001). Throughout the 1990s, URMs accounted for 19 percent to 21 percent of admitted applicants to public health programs. In the past decade the proportion of URMs in public health programs has been consistently higher than in any other health profession in the United States, and there is no evidence of this percentage decreasing. In 1990, URMs represented 15.3 percent of public health students, and in 1999 that percentage was 19.5.

The class entering medical school in 2001 was among the most diverse classes ever, with nearly 34 percent of all matriculants being racial and ethnic minorities. URMs, however, accounted for less than 11 percent of new entrants. Throughout the 1980s the total number of matriculants into medical school remained relatively flat and only began a steady increase in 1992. In contrast, the number of Asian and Pacific Islander matriculants has increased nearly fivefold since 1980. Between 1996 and 2001 the ability of schools in several states to use race/ethnicity as one element in the admissions process was limited by public referenda or court challenges. This had a negative effect on URM's matriculation rates.

Examining the Pipeline

Problems of isolation, alienation, and lack of support make it very difficult for minority students to succeed on predominantly white campuses. The educational system is partly responsible for the problem in that it fails to retain minority students at all points in the pipeline. This seems to be especially true at the undergraduate level (Massey 1992). Career choices of minorities are often cited as a reason for the low numbers of scientists and researchers. Frequently minorities will choose careers and professions that offer a clear employment opportunity and that do not require additional schooling and a doctorate degree as the minimum criteria to enter the profession. Minority students may come from environments of lower economic gains, which may significantly decrease the likelihood of a career choice that may require additional years to complete. Students in general are drawn to professions where the potential for immediate and continued financial success is clear. Minority students are no exception (Johnson-Thompson et al. 1996).

Part of the reason for the low numbers of minorities as scientists, researchers, and health professionals is the poor academic preparation by the current K–12 educational system. This is indicated by high drop out rates from high school, social factors such as drugs and crime, teachers who are ill-prepared to teach necessary subjects such as math and science, and learning environments that are not conducive to a quality education (Johnson-Thompson et al. 1996). Therefore, minority high school students, when compared to white students, tend not to take and have a diminished opportunity to enroll in advanced math and science classes and are less likely to select courses and careers in biological/

life sciences, computer information sciences, and engineering (Malcolm 1996). The poor preparation at this level tends to have an effect at all levels of academia and is very evident when examining the numbers of Ph.D. and M.D. degrees awarded to minorities.

Studies have documented the disparities in educational outcomes between minority students and white students. In order for more students to be in the pipeline to careers in the health professions, our educational system must improve the quality of the students who are present. Some of the discrepancies show that white students are twice as likely as African-Americans to earn a college degree, and Asian students are more than five times as likely as Hispanics to earn a college degree (U.S. Department of Education 1997). This will only escalate with the growing numbers of minorities in the United States. It has been noted that African-American and Hispanic children are more likely than white children to have multiple risk factors for school failure. African-American, Hispanic, and Native American children are more than twice as likely as Asian and white children to be in the lowest quartile in reading and math skills during their kindergarten year. By elementary school, 39 percent of white students score at or above proficiency in reading while only 10 percent of African-American and 13 percent of Hispanic children do so (National Center for Educational Statistics 1994). African-American, Native American, and Hispanic children are underrepresented in programs for "gifted and talented" students (Gandara 2001). Additionally, white and Asian-American students are much more likely to be assigned to algebra in grade 8 compared to African-American and Hispanic students. By the time these students reach high school it is very difficult to catch up and they are often lost somewhere in the pipeline. Minority students are not well represented in four-year colleges (Gandara 2001) despite making up nearly one-quarter of the U.S. population. It will be necessary to increase the number and quality of students in the pipeline to ensure that the pool of minority students to draw from for health professions is adequate.

Diversity in Health Professions: Promoting Health Parity

It is clear that minorities experience a greater burden of disease and death when compared to the rates of white Americans. The causes of the excess burden of morbidity and mortality can be attributed to socioeconomic status, greater health risk factors, discrimination, environmental and occupational exposures, and access to care issues (Kington et al. 2001). Drastic improvements have been made to public health and medical practice such that the results have increased the longevity of the U.S. population. Between the years 1900 and 1996 alone, the number of years an American was estimated to live leaped from fifty to seventy-six years (Council of Economic Advisors 1998). Although longevity has increased in the United States, the quality of life among ethnic and racial groups is not as profound. Blacks, American Indians, and Hispanics all fare worse in health status when compared to their white counterparts, while Asians fare as well as and sometimes better than non-Hispanic whites on most measures of health.

Research into why these and other health disparities exist has depended largely on the work conducted in socioeconomic status among ethnic and racial groups. White Americans have proved to have more access to the social and economic resources needed for health care and medical services. Education leading to better jobs and increased income also play a part in the health care access of white Americans. Other research has noted that discriminatory behavior and racism toward patients has contributed to poorer health among members of underrepresented minority groups. For example, personal discriminatory experiences have been linked to the prevalence of hypertension among African-Americans more than whites. Along with the idea that lack of access to health care will contribute to ill health, the lack of proficient health insurance has also proved to be correlated with ill health. According to the Department of Health and Human Services Office of Minority Health, Hispanic and African-American men are less likely to have health insurance than non-Hispanic whites (Council of Economic Advisors 1998). Insurance coverage correlates with income, and the disparity in insurance status between African-American and white men is largely due to differences in income.

It has been proposed that increasing the numbers of minorities who become physicians and who work in health care settings can provide some remedies to the health disparities issues that we face (Kington et al. 2001). Over the past decade we have seen a decrease in the number of minority physicians and physicians who work in minority communities (Carlisle et al. 1998). There is evidence that physician biases and stereotypes may influence the relationship between the health care professional and the patient. Finucane and Carrese (1990) found that physicians were more likely to make negative comments when discussing minority patients' cases than when discussing the cases of "other" patients. J.M. Abreu (1999) concludes that mental health professionals and trainees were more likely to evaluate a hypothetical patient more negatively after being "primed" with words associated with African-American stereotypes. Van Ryn and Burke's (2000) study in clinical settings found that doctors are more likely to assign negative racial stereotypes to their minority patients. These stereotypes are ascribed to patients even when differences in minority and nonminority patients' education, income, and personality characteristics are considered. These studies illustrate that the sources of racial and ethnic disparities in America are rooted more deeply than what is assumed. Disparities are historic and contemporary, and include not only health systems but also administrative and bureaucratic processes, utilization managers, health care professionals, and patients.

The 2003 publication of the IOM, *Unequal Treatment: Confronting Racial and Ethnic Disparities in Healthcare*, concludes that more research is needed on ethical issues and other barriers to eliminate disparities and to further identify sources of racial and ethnic disparities and assess promising intervention strategies. When health care professional-patient relationships are analyzed, evidence of stereotyping, biases, and uncertainty on the part of the health care professional all contribute to unequal treatment in health care. Minorities, even when insured at the same level as whites, are found to experience a range of other barriers to accessing care, such as barriers of language, geography, and cultural familiarity. In addition to these, financial and institutional arrangements of health systems and the policy environment in which they operate may have negative effects on minorities' access to quality care.

The issue of health professions diversity and its relationship to health disparities has been characterized in three ways: (1) the effect of practice choices of minority providers; (2) the quality of training in health professional training; and (3) the quality of communication between minority patients and providers (Kington et al. 2001). Regarding practice choices, minority physicians are more likely to work in communities that have high numbers of minorities. This phenomenon appears to be by choice of the minority physicians. Minority physicians on average treat four to five times the number of minority patients than white physicians do (Kington et al. 2001). The quality of the training experience may also prove to be beneficial to potential physicians because of the exposure to different cultures and experiences. This in turn may improve communication between physicians and patients who are of different ethnic and racial groups. However, it must be noted that no rigorous studies have been conducted to support this notion. Finally, the issue of better physician-patient communication seems to be the result of minority physicians serving minority patients. Several studies have supported the idea that patients communicate better with physicians who are of the same racial and ethnic group. It was found that patients experience greater patient satisfaction, greater use of preventive services, and better communication (Kington et al. 2001).

Successful Programs to Increase Diversity in Medicine and Health Related Fields

It is critical that the pipeline of underrepresented minorities be addressed. A number of national initiatives, institutional programs, and local efforts have been implemented to increase the number of underrepresented minorities in the pipeline of health-related fields. MGT of America (1999) conducted a study of programs to recruit minorities in science and medicine and submitted the report to Florida State University. In the report a number of national programs are outlined. They include:

- The College Reach-Out Program (CROP) operated by the Florida Department of Education
- Project 3000 by 2000 sponsored by the Association of American Medical Colleges (AAMC)
- Health Professions Partnership Initiative funded by the Robert Wood Johnson Foundation
- Upward Bound funded by the U.S. Department of Education
- Health Careers Opportunity Program (HCOP) funded by the U.S. Department of Health and Human Services
- Minority Medical Education Program (MMEP) funded by the Robert Wood Johnson Foundation.

Each program offers an innovative approach to recruit minorities into health-related fields. The programs are highlighted below.

College Reach-Out Program (CROP)

This statewide program targets educationally disadvantaged students in middle and high school in Florida who would not ordinarily attend college. The primary focus is to strengthen these students' educational motivation and preparation to be successful in college. Program components include summer programs and field trips, after-school activities (i.e., homework and tutoring), summer career exploration, time management, financial aid awareness, college visitation, self-esteem-building classes, ACT/SAT workshops, goal-setting, test-taking, and recognition of learning styles. Results of this program show that program participants are "more likely to perform at levels comparable to or better than non-program participants and are also more likely to enroll in postsecondary education than non-program participants" (MGT 1999).

Project 3000 by 2000

This program, sponsored by the AAMC, was started in 1991 with the goal of having 3,000 underrepresented minorities enroll in medical schools by the year 2000. In the 1990s it appeared that the target would be met by 2000, but in the late 1990s minority enrollments started declining. In order to address the declining enrollment, the AAMC adjusted its goals and is focusing on increasing minority applicant pools and preparing minorities for the rigors of medical school (MGT 1999).

Health Professions Partnership Initiative (HPPI)

This program is sponsored by the Robert Wood Johnson Foundation. Established in 1996, this program in collaboration with AAMC is designed to increase the preparedness of underrepresented minority students for careers in medicine. The aim of this program is to ensure that more minority students graduate from high school and are prepared academically for the rigors of studying medicine, the rationale being that the applicant pool must be increased in order to reach the diversity goals of the medical profession (MGT 1999). The HPPI program was able to establish partnership programs across the country including the Medical College of Georgia School of Medicine, the University of Connecticut Health Center, the University of Louisville Health Science Center, the University of Massachusetts Medical Center, the Medical College of Pennsylvania and Hahnermann University, the University of Nebraska Medical Center, the University of North Carolina at Chapel Hill, the Oregon Health Sciences University, the Medical University of South Carolina, and the University of Wisconsin-Madison Medical School. This program has not been evaluated to determine its success in increasing the minority applicant pool.

Upward Bound

This program is funded by the U.S. Department of Education and its goal is to prepare disadvantaged (i.e., low-income and first-generation) high school students to enroll in and graduate from college. A total of 681 programs are funded throughout the United States. Program components include weekly tutoring sessions after school throughout the academic year; social, academic, and cultural activities; career development and assistance with college preparation; and financial aid and scholarships. Students also participate in field trips and summer programs where they actually stay in college dorms and take classes at the college level. High school seniors can earn six college credits at no cost. Overall results show that participants in Upward Bound have a 91 percent national success rate of graduating from high school and entering college. Upward Bound students are four times more likely to earn an undergraduate degree than students from similar backgrounds who did not participate in the program (MGT 1999).

Health Careers Opportunity Program (HCOP)

This program is funded by the U.S. Department of Health and Human Services. The goal of this program is to increase the number of disadvantaged students who enter and graduate from health professional programs. The program basically has two components: one is a career development component that includes exploring health careers firsthand, opportunities to improve academic skills, realistic experience of college living, study skills development, health professions mentoring, job-shadowing activities, and financial aid sources for college. The second component involves a summer enrichment component. Participants are involved in programs over the summer that include gaining experience from health professionals and attending classes on campus. Overall the results are positive in regard to students enrolling in medical school (MGT 1999).

Minority Medical Education Program (MMEP)

The Minority Medical Education Program is another program funded by the Robert Wood Johnson Foundation. The aim of this program offers summer programming for promising and highly motivated minority students interested in medical school to help them gain a competitive edge to gain admission to medical schools. The summer program lasts for six weeks and includes academic enrichment in the biological sciences, mathematics curriculum, problem-solving, preparation and review for the MCAT, and practical counseling on the medical school application process. In addition the program provides access to people in the medical field as well as practical experience in the lab (clinical and research). Approximately 60 percent of participants in the program have been accepted into medical schools (MGT 1999).

Other programs at the national level include the National Institutes of Health programs to increase minorities in the mental health fields. Many of the institutes at NIH have supplemental funding for underrepresented minorities, including programs for high school students, undergraduates, graduate students, and faculty development opportunities for minorities.

Taken together, these programs were all designed to either increase the pool of minority applicants, increase preparedness of minority applicants, or increase enrollment and graduation rates of both middle and high school students. The results of these programs have been fairly positive with the exception of the AAMC 3000 by 2000 program. These programs have a number of common components: summer enrichment programs, tutoring, exposure to health professionals, and campus or residential stays on college campuses. More programs as well as more coordination between these programs are needed to address the issue of diversity in the health professions.

A publication by Gandara and Maxwell-Jolly called *Priming the Pump: Strategies for Increasing the Achievement of Underrepresented Minority Undergraduates* identified five major components of successful programs: mentoring, financial support, academic support, psychosocial support, and professional opportunities (Gandara and Maxwell-Jolly 1999). It notes that programs that are successful are concerned with both the academic and social development of students. In summary, programs that have demonstrated success in improving academic performance of underrepresented minority students are found to:

- stress scholastic excellence;
- encourage each student to do his or her best;
- emphasize helping students succeed in their freshman year;
- focus on mastery in foundation courses;
- help students build strong academically oriented peer groups;
- build strong student/faculty relationships;
- focus on providing good ongoing academic advising services;
- encourage participation in research;
- provide strong support beyond the freshman year; and
- provide students with sufficient financial aid so they can concentrate fully on their studies (Ready and Nickens 1994).

Solutions/Recommendations

There are a number of solutions to help increase minority preparedness for the rigorous curriculum in medical schools and other allied health professions. One place to start is by establishing programs in elementary, middle, and high schools. What follows is a number of recommendations that address the lack of diversity in the health professions:

1. Programs should continue to offer tutoring and campus visits and stays.
2. Programs should be marketed appropriately so that low-income and underrepresented minorities know about these programs. Program planners may have to use nontraditional

approaches such as advertising to students to get them to participate.

3. Programs should provide small incentives or college credits as described in the Upward Bound programs. Often these students come from low-income families and need money or incentives to make ends meet. It is important that one of the reasons minority students may not be succeeding is that they do not have the networks and access to people outside of their environments to consider pursuing a health-related career let alone succeed in school. These programs allow youth to be exposed to people and resources to which they would not otherwise have access.

4. There should be more programs as well as a clearinghouse of all of the programs available, the number of slots available for student participation, and additional funding provided to rural and urban centers that would allow minority students to participate.

5. Policy changes are needed at the national, state, and local levels that would allow institutions of higher learning to leverage public funds to increase underrepresented minorities' preparedness for the rigors of health-related fields.

6. There needs to be a national committee that coordinates and evaluates the effectiveness of these programs in meeting program objectives and an effective dissemination strategy for all educators concerning the success of these programs and curricula designed to increase minority enrollment and graduation rates.

7. At the national level the government should expand current programs and increase the number of colleges and universities involved.

8. Establish minority health-related training centers in rural and urban settings that would be responsible for building community support and capacity and connections with tribal universities, reservations, churches, and community-based youth-serving organizations (i.e., Boys and Girls Clubs, Big Brothers, Big Sisters) that have large populations of underrepresented youth, Hispanic-serving institutions, and historically black colleges and universities.

9. Appoint statewide commissions in each state to address the

lack of diversity in the public health progressions and provide incentives for those commissions to increase enrollment and graduation rates.

10. Work with existing programs such as the Ronald E. McNair Programs and bring them to more students. Involve past graduates to serve as mentors to the upcoming classes at the elementary, middle, and high school levels.

It appears that a number of programs are designed to increase minority enrollment and graduation, but these are fragmented, available only at select universities, not widely disseminated, publicized, or evaluated, and no one is being held accountable for the programs' progress. Thus if progress is not being made after three or four years, the programs should be revamped and more intense efforts should be made to make a difference.

Many of the solutions to increasing diversity in the health professions will come from institutional initiatives. Institutions generally have the resources or access to resources to support initiatives to increase the diversity in the health professions. Institutions must have clearly defined policies regarding recruitment and retention of minority students and must visibly demonstrate this institutional commitment. Leadership of minority recruitment programs must come from individuals who are well respected in the university community, and minority faculty and staff must be involved in the process. Institutions must provide adequate financial support for innovative programs and services that might enhance the numbers of minorities who apply for matriculation into health professional schools.

When institutions are educating minority students, the approach must include confidence-building, incentives, role-modeling, mentoring, and adequate financial support. A national three-year study conducted by the National Center for Postsecondary Governance and Finance, funded by the Office of Educational Research and Improvement, found several effective strategies for helping minority students graduate from college and become successful. These strategies include institutional commitment; backing the priorities with adequate funding; employing minorities in senior leadership positions; providing an environment with minimal threats of racism, discrimination, and harassment; providing bridge programs to minimize educational gaps; reaching out to the community to make it a community-wide effort; emphasizing quality in all aspects of the curriculum and program; supporting services that are comprehensive; and tracking progress to keep detailed information for review (Smedley et al. 2001).

The importance of role models and mentors in successful recruitment and retention of minority students cannot be underestimated. Mentoring has been identified as an important aspect of increasing diversity in health professions. Mentoring is an informal system that provides students with support and guidance during their training and serves as additional support once they graduate. Mentoring has been described as a dynamic, reciprocal relationship in a work environment between an advanced career incumbent (mentor) and a beginner (protégé) aimed at promoting the career development of both. Mentoring at the graduate level has been described as a process by which novice individuals are provided support and protection during training and additional support once moved to the professional world. Some educators believe that mentoring is very important to the overall educational experience and may be a major factor for success. Yet, only one in eight black doctoral degree recipients have the benefit of a true mentoring situation while in graduate school (Blackwell 1983). Students who have matched up mentors have been found to be more productive; additionally, the lack of this type of relationship can hamper or negatively affect professional development. Other solutions call for changes in how students are admitted into the program, changing the delivery and content of the curriculum, and having services that are supportive to increasing diversity. Below are more suggested changes.

- Health professions schools should incorporate diversity as a part of their overall objective and mission statement. It must be clear that the institution embraces the need for diversity, and this must come through when communicating to students and their families.
- Institutions must be a part of developing a pipeline of minority students. This may include developing enrichment programs for students in middle to high school to get them prepared and interested in health professions.
- Scholarships and loans must be made available for students who lack the financial support necessary to gain entry into graduate

school. Institutions must be willing to commit adequate resources for a significant amount of time. These scholarships may be used as a recruitment tool to attract students into these programs.

- Programs should be established for students who may be identified as at risk early in the educational process. The earlier these students are identified, the more likely they can be assisted and retained in the program.
- Institutions must be committed to bringing in more diverse faculty members who can serve as role models for minority students.
- Various departments on campus, such as deans, department chairs, minority affairs, and so on, should work together to attempt to control attrition during the first few years of study.

Records should be kept to document different aspects of the minority students' experiences at the institution. This data might prove very useful in making major decisions regarding recruitment and retention issues.

Conclusion

Increasing diversity in the health professions will continue to be a major issue until there are significant numbers of minorities in these areas. Having a diverse healthcare workforce is necessary at every level of the delivery of health-related services. Institutions, health agencies, and organizations must demonstrate their commitment to achieving diversity within their individual groups. They must also be committed to an educational system that will adequately prepare students to deal with complex health issues such as health disparities in an environment that is becoming more and more diverse. Many universities, colleges, organizations, and individuals are seeking to address the underrepresentation of minorities in the health professions and are working to increase those numbers. The current unfavorable climate for affirmative action and special programs for minority students may hamper efforts to increase minority representation. Because of the current climate it is important that efforts to encourage minority student recruitment and retention in the health professions be strengthened. Some progress is evident, but much work is still needed. The lack of significant progress may lead some to believe that the problems are too difficult to solve. However, this line of thinking is nothing less than destructive to the process. Instead, building on the success of other programs and efforts is essential, and (as stated at the beginning) it is "the right thing to do, the smart thing to do."

References

Abreu, J.M. 1999. "Conscious and Nonconscious African-American Stereotypes: Impact on First Impression and Diagnostic Ratings by Therapists." *Journal of Consulting Clinical Psychology* 67 (3): 387–97.

Blackwell, J.E. 1983. *Networking and Mentoring: A Study of Cross-Generational Experiences of Blacks in Graduate and Professional Schools*. Atlanta: Southern Education Foundation.

Bowen, W.G. and B.D. Bok. 1998. *The Shape of the River: Long-Term Consequences of Considering Race in College and University Admissions*. Princeton: Princeton University Press.

Carlisle, D.M. et al. 1998. "The Entry of Underrepresented Minority Students into U.S. Medical Schools: An Evaluation of Recent Trends." *American Journal of Public Health* 88 (9): 1314–18.

Council of Economic Advisors. 1998. "Changing America: Indicators of Social and Economic Well-Being by Race and Hispanic Origin." *Council of Economic Advisors for the President's Initiative on Race*. Washington, DC.

Cohen, J.J. 2003. "The Consequences of Premature Abandonment of Affirmative Action in Medical School Admissions." *Journal of the American Medical Association* 289 (9): 1143–49.

Finucane, T.E. and J.A. Carrese. 1990. "Racial Bias in Presentation of Cases." *Journal of General Internal Medicine* 5: 120–23.

Gandara, P. 2001. "Lost Opportunities: The Difficult Journey To Higher Education for Underrepresented Minority Students." In B.D. Smedley, A.Y. Stith, L. Colburn, and C.H. Evans, eds. *The Right Thing to Do, the Smart Thing to Do: Enhancing Diversity in the Health Professions*. Washington, DC: National Academy Press.

Gandara, P., and J. Maxwell-Jolly. 1999. *Priming the Pump: Strategies for Increasing the Achievement of Underrepresented Minority Undergraduates*. New York: College Entrance Examination Board.

Gragnola, C.M. and E. Stone. 1997. "Considering the Future of Health Care Workforce Regulation." University of California at San Francisco Center for Health Professions, December.

Grumbach, K. et al. 2001. "Trends in Underrepresented Minority Participation in Health Professions Schools." In B.D. Smedley, A.Y. Stith, L. Colburn, and C.H. Evans, eds. *The Right Thing to Do, the Smart Thing to Do: Enhancing Diversity in the Health Professions*. Washington, DC: National Academy Press.

Hunttlinger, K., and D. Drevdahl. 1994. "Increasing Minority Participation in Biomedical and Nursing Research." *Journal of Professional Nursing* 10 (1): 13–21.

Johnson-Thompson et al. 1996. "NIEHS/AACR Task Force on the Advancement of Minorities in Science: Vision for a Model Program." *Cancer Research* 56: 3380–86.

Kington, R.D. et al. 2001. "Increasing Racial and Ethnic Diversity Among Physicians: An Intervention to Address Health Disparities?" In B.D. Smedley, A.Y. Stith, L. Colburn, and C.H. Evans, eds. *The Right Thing to Do, the Smart Thing to Do: Enhancing Diversity in the Health Professions.* Washington, DC: National Academy Press.

LaVeist, T.A. et al. 2000. "Attitudes About Racism, Medical Mistrust, and Satisfaction with Care Among African-American and White Cardiac Patients." *Medical Care Research and Review* 57 (Supp. 1): 146–61.

Malcolm, S. 1996. "Science and Diversity: A Compelling National Interest." *Science* 271 (5257) (March 29): 1817–20.

Massey, W.E. 1992. "A Success Story amid Decades of Disappointment." *Science* 258 (Special Section: Minorities in Science) (5085): 1177.

MGT of America. 1999. "A Study of Programs to Recruit Minorities in Science and Medicine." Tallahassee, FL: MGT of America.

Monheit, A.C., and J.P. Vistnes. 2000. "Race/Ethnicity and Health Insurance Status 1987 and 1996." *Medical Care Research and Review* 57 (Supp. 1): 11–35.

Murdock, S.H. et al. 1998. "An Assessment of the Potential Needs Unmet and Opportunities Lost as a Result of Hopwood: Problems, Prospects, and the Impact on Minorities in Higher Education." Texas A&M University, College Station, Texas. Unpublished manuscript.

National Center for Educational Statistics. 1994. *Digest of Education Statistics.* Washington, DC: U.S. Department of Education, National Center for Education Statistics.

Pew Health Professions Commission. 1995. *Critical Challenges: Revitalizing the Health Professions for the Twenty First Century.* San Francisco, CA.

Ready, T., and H.W. Nickens. 1994. "Programs that Make a Difference." In B.H. Kehrer and H.C. Burroughs, eds. *More Minorities in Health.* Menlo Park, CA: Henry J. Kaiser Family Foundation.

Smedley, B.D. et al. 2001. *The Right Thing to Do, the Smart Thing to Do: Enhancing Diversity in the Health Professions.* Washington, DC: National Academy Press.

Sullivan, L.W. 1995. "Minority Student Recruitment: The Challenge and the Obligation." *Journal of Dental Education* 59 (6): 641–44.

Tedesco, L.A. 2001. "The Role of Diversity in the Training of Health Professionals." In. B.D. Smedley, A.Y. Stith, L. Colburn, and C.H. Evans, eds. *The Right Thing to Do, the Smart Thing to Do: Enhancing Diversity in the Health Professions.* Washington, DC: National Academy Press.

Trickett, E.J. et al. 1994. "Toward an Overarching Framework for Diversity." In E.J. Trickett, R. Watts, and D. Birman, eds. *Human Diversity: Perspectives on People in Context.* San Francisco: Jossey-Bass.

U.S. Department of Education. 1997. *Integrated Postsecondary Education Data System.* Washington, DC: U.S. Government Printing Office.

Van Ryn, M. and J. Burke. 2000. "The Effect of Patient Race and Socio-Economic Status on Physicians Perceptions of Patients." *Social Science and Medicine* 50: 813–28.

10

Cultural Competency and the Practice of Public Administration

Margo L. Bailey

The growing demographic changes and ethnic and cultural diversity within the United States is increasing the demand for culturally competent public servants. At its most basic level, *culturally competent public administration* is a "respect for, and understanding of, diverse ethnic and cultural groups, their histories, traditions, beliefs, and value systems" in the provision and delivery of services (Bush 2000). In practice, culturally competent public administration emphasizes the capacity of public organizations and their employees to effectively provide services that reflect the different cultural influences of their constituents or clients. Culturally competent practices have been used to: (1) develop recommendations for national standards on culturally and linguistically appropriate services in health care (U.S. Department of Health and Human Services 2001); (2) develop traditionally based conflict resolution processes for Native Hawaiian families (Hurdle 2002); (3) identify culturally competent social work practices for Native Americans (Weaver 1994); (4) provide training for home-based psychiatric services to Latino families (Zayas et al. 1997); (5) identify marriage and family therapy guidelines for non–African-American therapists working with African-American families (Bean, Perry, and Bedell 2002); and (6) integrate hip-hop culture into English curricula to help African-American youth improve their critical writing skills (National Education Association 2003).

Cultural competency is the final goal along the continuum of creating government organizations that fully represent all segments of the population. However, the path to culturally competent public sector organizations is filled with many challenges. This chapter considers some of these challenges. The chapter introduces the concept of the representative bureaucracy continuum by examining the relationship among equal employment opportunity (EEO), affirmative action, managing diversity, and cultural competency. The challenges of balancing the goals of cultural competency and public administration values are highlighted. The potential for organizations' human resource leaders to support the development of culturally competent organizations is discussed. The chapter concludes with some reflections about developing cultural competency skills within the field of public administration.

Cultural Competency: The Missing Link Between Passive and Active Representation

Representative bureaucracy is "the body of thought and research examining the potential for government agencies to act as representative political institutions if their personnel are drawn from all sectors of society" (see Dolan and Rosenbloom 2003). Mosher (2003) identifies two elements of representative bureaucracy—passive and active representation. *Passive representation* refers to the demographic composition of government workforces and the extent to which these workforces reflect the demographic characteristics of the clients they serve or the population from which the workforce is drawn. *Active representation* is the expectation that an individual will "press for the interests and desires of those whom he is presumed to represent" (Mosher 2003). Historically, the goal of passive representation in government workforces has been pursued through affirmative action and equal employment opportunities to increase the number and percentage of employees from the legally protected classes of gender, race, ethnicity, and disability. More recently, managing diversity initiatives have been used to mitigate the more controversial aspects of affirmative action and equal employment opportunity practices by expanding the scope of who is viewed as "different" among employees. Managing diversity programs acknowledge that employees' cultural differences are based upon work experiences and training, education, age, parental status, geographic location, religion, military experience, marital status, income (Riccucci 2002), and parental status as well as other factors. The cultural differences perspective allows organizations to increase the number of employees with an interest in changing policies and practices that affect how they carry out their work.

Equal employment opportunity, affirmative action, and managing diversity are viewed as critical elements for achieving passive representation. Without the legal force of equal employment laws and the threat of litigation, many organizations would not have implemented voluntary affirmative action efforts. Managing diversity programs can make it easier for organizations to strategically change human resource practices that benefit all employees. However, the empirical evidence linking passive and active representation is mixed (Dolan and Rosenbloom 2003). One possible explanation for why it is difficult to show a strong relationship between passive and active representation may be that the employment numbers of minorities cannot support it. Almost 90 percent of all teachers in the United States are white and only 7 percent identify themselves as African-Americans (National Education Association 2003). In 2001, 6.9 percent and 6 percent of medical school graduates were African-Americans and Hispanic Americans, respectively (Adams 2003). In the same year, members of minority groups constituted only 14 percent of the Federal Senior Executive Service workforce (U.S. Office of Personnel Management 2002). To achieve active representation, more government employees will need to become culturally competent when carrying out their responsibilities.

The Legal Foundation for Cultural Competency in Public Administration

Over the past sixty years, Congress has passed key legislation to require or promote cultural competence among federal employees or recipients of federal funds (see Table 10.1). The activist agendas of the New Deal and the civil rights movement brought about the passage of the Hill-Burton Act in 1946, Title VI of the Civil Rights Act in 1964, and the Social Security Act in 1965. The Hill-Burton and Social Security acts emphasize providing federal health services to individuals who have limited English proficiency. The goal of ensuring access for individuals who have limited English proficiency is integral to cultural competency within public administration. By requiring agencies and other federally funded service providers to reach out to these individuals, they are forced to confront and address the cultural barriers that exist in communication and in establishing effective service delivery.

Subsequent legislation in the late 1980s through the year 2000 provided more specific actions to expand the scope of cultural competency. The Disadvantaged Minority Health Improvement Act of 1990 led to the establishment of the Center for Linguistic and Cultural Competency in Health Care within the Department of Health and Human Services. Under the Emergency Medical Treatment and Active Labor Act of 1996, hospitals can be held liable for civil penalties if they do not provide language assistance to patients who have limited English speaking skills. President Clinton issued Executive Order 13166 in August 2000 to continue activities to improve access to federal programs and services for immigrant populations. Health care and education are fields most directly affected by federal cultural competency legislation. Several major health care professional associations have set standards for cultural competency or issued position statements within their fields. The National Association of Social Workers, the Council on Social Work Education, the American Psychological Association, the American Nursing Association, and the National Mental Health Association are examples.

Defining Cultural Competency

The Developmental Disabilities Assistance and Bill of Rights Act Amendments of 1987 set forth a definition for cultural competence: "Services, supports or other assistance that are conducted or provided in a manner that is responsive to the beliefs, interpersonal styles, attitudes, language and behaviors of individuals who are receiving services, and in a manner that has the greatest likelihood of ensuring their maximum participation in the program" (see Goode 2000). However, as agencies and organizations have worked to meet the guidance for Executive Order 13166 and the mandates of federal legislation, a variety of definitions have emerged. For example, in psychiatry, cultural competency is defined as "having the knowledge and interpersonal skills to understand, appreciate, and work with individuals and families from cultures other than one's own and using the knowledge and skills effectively to employ therapeutic techniques in achieving behavioral and social change" (Zayas et al. 1997). Other definitions are similar, with a focus on the extent

Table 10.1

Laws and Policies Relevant to Cultural Competence in Federal Agencies

Year	Name	Cultural competency relevance
1946	Hospital Survey and Construction Act (Hill-Burton Act)	Encouraged the construction and modernization of public and nonprofit community hospitals and health centers. In return for receiving these funds, recipients agreed to comply with a "community service obligation," one of which is a general principle of nondiscrimination in the delivery of services. This has consistently been interpreted as an obligation to provide language assistance to those in need of such services.
1964	Title VI of the Civil Rights Act	"No person in the United States shall, on ground of race, color or national origin, be excluded from participation in, be denied the benefits of, or be subjected to discrimination under any program or activity receiving Federal financial assistance."
1965	Social Security Act	Established Medicare and Medicaid. • Medicaid providers and participating facilities must provide "culturally and linguistically appropriate services." States must communicate "in a language understood by the beneficiary" and provide interpretation services at Medicare hearings. • Medicare "providers are encouraged to make bilingual services available to patients wherever the services are necessary to adequately serve a multilingual population." Medicare reimburses hospitals for the cost of the provision of bilingual services to patients.
1988	Hawaiian Health Care Improvement Act	Requires "culturally based health care, health education, and promotion" for Native Hawaiian Americans.
1990	Disadvantaged Minority Health Improvement Act	The Center for Linguistic and Cultural Competency in Health Care is a response to P.L. 101–527. It requires the Department of Health and Human Services, Office of Minority Health (OMH) to develop the capacity of health care professionals to address the cultural and linguistic barriers to health care delivery and increase limited English-speaking individuals' access to health care. The law directs OMH to support research, demonstrations, and evaluations to test innovative models aimed at increasing knowledge and providing a clearer understanding of health risk factors and successful prevention intervention strategies for minority populations.

Table 10.1 *(continued)*

Year	Name	Cultural competency relevance
1991–1992	Carl D. Perkins Vocational and Applied Technology Education Act	Congress amends and renames P.L. 98–524 (Perkins Act). Make the United States more competitive in the world economy by more fully developing academic and occupational skills of all population segments. The term "special populations" is expanded by this law to include disabled individuals, economically and educationally disadvantaged individuals (including foster children), those with limited English proficiency, individuals participating in sex-bias elimination programs, and persons in correctional institutions.
1994	Developmental Disabilities Assistance and Bill of Rights Act	Amended P.L. 100–146, the Developmental Disabilities and Bill of Rights Act Amendments of 1987, Defines "cultural competence" as "services, supports or other assistance that are conducted or provided in a manner that is responsive to the beliefs, interpersonal styles, attitudes, language and behaviors of individuals who are receiving services, and in a manner that has the greatest likelihood of ensuring their maximum participation in the program."
1996	Emergency Medical Treatment and Active Labor Act (Patient Antidumping Act)	Requires hospitals that participate in the Medicare program that have emergency departments to treat all patients (including women in labor) in an emergency without regard to their ability to pay. Hospitals that fail to provide language assistance to persons of limited English proficiency are potentially liable to federal authorities for civil penalties as well as relief to the extent deemed appropriate by a court.
2000	E.O. 13166: Improving Access to Services for Persons with Limited English Proficiency	The federal government is committed to improving the accessibility of federally assisted and federally conducted programs and activities for eligible persons with limited-English proficiency. Directs federal agencies to implement consistent standards of language assistance across agencies and for recipients of federal assistance. The Department of Justice (DOJ) will work with federal agencies to develop their guidance.

March 2002	OMB Report to Congress, "Assessment of the Total Benefits and Costs of Implementing Executive Order No. 13166"	Office of Management and Budget recommends that the federal government create clear and uniform standards defining how federal agencies and recipients of federal funds should implement E.O. 13166.
June 2002	DOJ Final Guidance to Federal Financial Assistance Recipients Regarding Title VI Prohibition Against National Origin Discrimination Affecting Limited English Proficient (LEP) Persons	Replaces guidance issued January 2001. Clarifies existing statutory and regulatory requirements for LEP persons by providing a description of the factors recipients should consider in fulfilling their responsibilities to LEP persons. It recommends but does not require written language assistance plans.

Sources: Center for Linguistic and Cultural Competence in Health Care, www.omhrc.gov/cultural/; Goode 2000; U.S. Department of Health and Human Services, Office of Minority Health; U.S. Department of Justice, Civil Rights Division, Coordination and Review Section, www.usdoj.gov/crt/cor/13166.htm

to which a provider possesses cultural knowledge about a client: "development of adequate professional skills to provide services to ethnic, racial, and cultural groups" (Hurdle 2002); "effectively operating in different cultural contexts" (Center for Effective Collaboration and Practice 2003); and "the capacity to relate to and to intervene effectively with individuals and families of different cultures" (Zayas et al. 1997).

The Cross et al. (1989) definition of cultural competence is notable because it states the need for culturally competent organizations. They define cultural competence as "a set of congruent behaviors, attitudes, and policies that come together in a system, agency or among professionals and enable that system, agency or those professions to work effectively in cross-cultural situations." Culturally competent organizations have five essential elements (Cross et al. 1989): they (1) value diversity; (2) have a capacity for cultural self-assessment; (3) are conscious of the dynamics inherent when cultures interact; (4) institutionalize culture knowledge throughout their activities; and (5) adapt service delivery to reflect an understanding of cultural diversity. An organizational focus for cultural competency considers the following questions: "What are the patterns of behavior that result in different or unfair treatment of different groups of people? What are examples of the written or unwritten policies, procedures, or customs that result in inequities that favor one group over another?" (Yee and Tursi 2002). Can we identify effective, culturally competent practices? How do we communicate success across the organization? The answers should lead to an organizational setting that uses formal structures and policies to create an environment where employees examine and develop their cultural knowledge or expertise by sharing information with their colleagues as well as access organization support systems.

The Representative Bureaucracy Continuum: EEO, Affirmative Action, Managing Diversity, Cultural Competence

Progress toward a representative bureaucracy should be viewed along a continuum because the implementation of EEO, affirmative action, and managing diversity programs create the capacity for agencies to become culturally competent. The continuum considers the differences between EEO, affirmative action, managing diversity (Riccucci 2002), and cultural competency across five elements: (1) expected outcomes; (2) the extent to which they promote access for employees and clients; (3) drivers for change; (4) the framework for change; and (5) strategies to bring about change (see Table 10.2). As agencies move from EEO to cultural competence, they increase opportunities for employees to perform their jobs better.

EEO and cultural competency share similar expected outcomes for ending discrimination in organizational practices. Managing diversity outcomes can provide a stable environment as employees develop procedures for meeting their cultural competence mandates. Cultural competency draws upon the increased access provided by affirmative action and managing diversity to allow more employees to participate in decisions to change organizational practices. The force of EEO legislation and strategic diversity initiatives combine to ensure culturally competent approaches that balance legal constraints and the desire for innovative service provisions. The capacity-building model for assessing cultural competence builds upon the lessons learned about identifying employee needs from the successes and failures of using the access, assimilation, and synergy models. Similarly, the organizational and behavioral strategies for achieving employee cultural competence must consider their experiences with structural changes that resulted from implementing EEO, affirmative action, and managing diversity policies.

The representative bureaucracy continuum is useful within public administration because it highlights how the five elements essential for becoming a culturally competent organization can be achieved in agencies. Valuing diversity is attained if agencies use their legal, managerial, and strategy drivers to develop a commitment to diversity initiatives across the agencies. A capacity model sustains this effort because the agency constantly assesses and responds to the diversity concerns of its employees. Agency assessment should lead to service adaptations that reflect new organizational demands for cultural competency skills. These skills are identified as agencies seek to institutionalize "best practices" for cultural competencies. Ultimately, culturally competent agencies are possible only when leaders and managers acknowledge the inherent tensions that occur when employees bring different cultural backgrounds to their workplaces and their client interactions.

Table 10.2

Representative Bureaucracy Continuum: Comparing EEO, Affirmative Action, Managing Diversity, and Cultural Competency

	EEO	Affirmative action	Managing diversity	Cultural competency
Expected outcome	*Fairness.* Seeks to end discrimination and create equal opportunities.	*Remedial and compensatory.* Specific voluntarily developed goals as well as court-ordered programs.	*Pragmatic.* The organization benefits in terms of morale and increases in productivity.	*Fairness and results oriented.* Seeks to end discrimination in service provision. Held accountable for meeting policy guidance.
Ensure access	*Level playing field.* Seeks to ensure equal opportunity and access.	*Opens doors.* Seeks to affect hiring and promotion decisions in organizations.	*Opens the system.* Seeks to affect managerial practices and policies.	*Opens and expands the system.* Seeks changes in organizational practices and policies to help more clients.
Driver	*Legally driven.* Mandated by federal law.	*Managerially and legally driven.* Involves voluntarily developed goals as well as court-ordered programs. Common law has defined its legality and constitutionality.	*Strategically driven.* Behaviors and policies are *seen as* contributing to organizational goals and objectives such as productivity.	*Legally and strategically driven.* Mandated by federal laws. Effective service provision achieve program goals.

187

Framework for change	*Access model.* Model assumes that protected-class persons will be able to access organizations.	*Assimilation model.* Model assumes that persons and groups brought into the system will adapt to existing organizational norms. Can result in "sink or swim" atmosphere/environment.	*Synergy model.* Model seeks to change organizational culture to accommodate diverse groups. Assumes people will develop new ways of working together in a pluralistic environment.	*Capacity-building model.* Model assesses organizations' strengths and weaknesses to address employee/client culture mismatches and employee needs.
Strategy	*Qualitative/Quantitative.* Emphasis is on *pre*-venting or ending discrimination.	*Qualitative/Quantitative.* Emphasis is on redressing past discrimination and achieving diverse, representative workforces.	*Behavioral.* Emphasis is on building specific skills and creating a productive work environment with the organization's human resources.	*Organizational and behavioral.* Focus on organizational structures and policies that help employees develop skills to work with clients.

Source: Derived from Riccucci (2002).

Competing Public Administration Values and Challenges for Culturally Competent Agencies

The practice of public administration is guided by core values that compete for primacy in agency decision-making (Rosenbloom 1983). *Efficiency*, "the relationship between inputs and outputs," emphasizes minimizing taxpayer cost (Denhardt 1995). *Effectiveness* is the extent to which an agency and its programs are achieving their mission and goals. *Equity* values the equal distribution and access to services across region, income, gender, and race/ethnic groups as well as other demographic variables (Starling 2002). Agency leaders, managers, and employees constantly balance the demands for responsiveness from citizens, elected officials, media, and other constituents. The quest for efficiency typically comes at the expense of effectiveness. As agencies look to cut costs, they sacrifice the additional resources to make its programs more effective. Increased effectiveness often warrants more resources and therefore more funding. Responsiveness can enhance effectiveness because the agency commits more time to addressing unique needs and concerns. However, increased responsiveness challenges the goal of equity. In contrast, responsiveness and effectiveness are complementary values that seek to provide services that best meet the different needs of clients. Efficiency and equity reduce responsiveness by limiting the discretion that allows for more effective responses.

Cultural competency promotes the values of effectiveness and responsiveness, but raises important issues about equity. Kaiser Permanente, a major health maintenance organization, recognized that Chinese immigrants are one of the fastest growing populations in San Francisco. Yet Kaiser saw that it was not successful at recruiting them as members. Over a five-year period, Kaiser nearly doubled its share of the Chinese market in San Francisco by acknowledging language barriers as a major obstacle to attracting Asian members. Kaiser's strategy included the use of multilingual signs at one of its major San Francisco centers and the hiring of physicians, technicians, and staff fluent in different Chinese dialects. "We were prompted into action by our members' expressed needs, then we recognized the importance of the changing demographics and saw an opportunity to execute an improved business plan" (Suro 2000). In government agencies, while the success of this approach would have been applauded for its effectiveness at meeting the needs of Chinese immigrants, the approach would immediately be questioned concerning equitable treatment for other immigrant groups and its cost to taxpayers. The expectation would be to provide the same type of response for other client groups regardless of the cost.

Equity is also a concern for agency employees. Culturally competent employee and client interactions require employee discretion in order to develop unique interventions. Clinicians and other health care providers have much more discretion to develop unique responses for their clients. Within agencies, employees follow rules and regulations; who has the "opportunity or flexibility to do anything other than strictly follow dictates from above"? (Dolan and Rosenbloom 2003). Employees' commitment to using cultural competency skills to best meet client needs can be outweighed by the agency's overall commitment to equitable treatment for all client groups.

The Role of Human Resource Management

Federal and state laws, and demands for increased efficiency and effectiveness make it difficult to answer the question of "How can public organizations become culturally competent?" The human resource function is an essential part of the answer. Kim (1999) contends that "human resource management can and should make a contribution to the competitive strategy of a global village." His argument focuses on the likelihood of American public managers working with individuals from other countries and the increased need to train them to be successful in these interactions. This argument can be extended to the development of culturally competent public managers and employees working within the United States.

The human resource function has four critical roles: (1) strategic partner; (2) change agent; (3) employee champion; and (4) administrative expert (Ulrich 1997). As a strategic partner, human resource leaders "sit at the table" and develop strategic goals with other organizational leaders. Knowledge and expertise about the organization's human resource strengths and challenges are integrated into organization-wide strategies. The change agent role asks human resource professionals to work with management to put into place activities to help the organization successfully implement major change initiatives. Human resource professionals are employee champions when they consistently seek input and feedback from employees and use this information when serving as strategic partners and change agents. Administrative expertise fulfills human resources' traditional role of developing and monitoring the organization's formal human resource policies and rules. The effective use of these human resource roles can help organizations develop the *five elements they need to become culturally competent: (1) valuing diversity; (2) self-assessment; (3) acknowledging the impact of cultural interaction; (4) institutionalized culture knowledge; and (5) adapting services and activities.* Table 10.3 summarizes where the human resource roles might best assist the goal of organizational cultural competency.

The employee champion role is the crux of human resources' ability to support culturally competent organizations. Through this role, human resources are able to acquire from employees the information about the skills, policies, support, and guidance they need to become culturally competent. This knowledge can then be used to help human resources carry out its other roles and develop strategies for organizational cultural competence. For example, employees frequently complain to human resources when their managers do not demonstrate a commitment to valuing diversity. Through their change agent responsibilities, human resources works with managers to help them understand how their actions affect employees' perception of the organization's commitment to diversity. Therefore, human resources brings a valuable perspective to developing a strategic approach to valuing diversity because it aggregates the experiences of its managers and employees.

The strategic partner and administrative expert roles can work together to institutionalize culture knowledge and adapt activities. Institutionalizing knowledge and changing activities are organization-wide processes that require strategic development and coordination. If an organization wants to establish a formal process for sharing and applying "best practices" for providing culturally competent services to African-American teenagers, it must work with human resources to assess training programs that help employees working with this client group. At the same time, human resources must be part of strategic discussions that consider how changing services to one client group affects how employees work with other client groups to avoid allegations of inequitable treatment.

Table 10.3

Developing Culturally Competent Organizations and the Role of Human Resources Management

	Strategic partner	Change agent	Employee champion	Administrative expert	Culturally competent:
Value diversity	—				Attitudes
Self-assessment		—	—	—	Structures
Cultural interaction		—	—		Policies
Institutionalized culture knowledge	—		—		Services
Adapt activities	—			—	

An assessment of an organization's cultural competency status highlights the extent to which it understands the impacts of cultural interaction upon its employees and their clients. As employee champions, human resources gains considerable insight into the common challenges managers and employees face as they confront cultural tensions. Self-assessment identifies organizational practices and skills that are most effective at addressing cultural tensions. This information is used to develop appropriate training, and revise job descriptions as well as the knowledge, skills, and abilities to perform these jobs. At the same time, human resources personnel must work as change agents with managers to help employees understand the need for increased expertise in resolving cultural tensions with their clients. This has benefits for improving client and organization relationships as well as manager and employee relationships. Employees will enhance their cultural competence skills and provide better services to clients. Just as important, managers are expected to support the organization's commitment to diversity by using the same skills with their employees.

Human resources professionals are key to developing culturally competent public organizations. In their roles as employee champions, administrative experts, change agents, and strategic partners, they interact with employees and managers in a variety of ways that provide opportunities to know what the organization needs to support cultural competency. But they cannot do it alone. Managers have the daily contact with employees to reinforce the value of cultural competency. They see the impact of service adaptations designed to promote cultural competence and quickly learn about ineffective culturally competent practices. Ultimately, the senior management team has the primary responsibility for establishing the commitment and support for a culturally competent organization. Alexander (2002, 31) offers a good indicator to determine if this is occurring: "If you ask employees to name their facility's chief diversity officer and they say the chief executive officer, you've found an organization that's truly striving for cultural competence."

Culturally Competent Public Administration

Representative bureaucracy is the primary lens through which the field of public administration has examined the impact of diversity upon public sector organizations. Passive representation will remain an important goal as long as minority groups are underrepresented in public sector workforces. However, the presumed direct link between passive and active representation that is based upon shared demographic characteristics may become less important as more agency employees are required to increase their cultural competency. This responsibility confronts *cultural chauvinism*, the belief that "only members of the same ethnic, racial, or cultural group are qualified to serve individuals from the particular group" (Taylor-Brown, Garcia, and Kingston 2001, 185).

Dean (2001) argues that cross-cultural competence may be a myth, a flawed concept founded upon the "metaphor of American 'know-how'" and the assumption that "knowledge brings control and effectiveness." Dean proposes a framework that supports "lack of competence," not cultural competence, as a goal. The result is "the act of respectful, nonjudgmental, and deeply interested questioning and the exchange of beliefs" to strengthen trust and understanding that can lead to improved client interventions. Dean (2001, 624) says, "Our goal is not so much to achieve competence but to participate in the ongoing processes of seeking understanding and building relationships. This understanding needs to be directed toward ourselves and not just our clients. As we question ourselves, we gradually wear away our own resistance and bias. It is not that we need to agree with our clients' practices and beliefs; we need to understand them and understand the contexts and history in which they develop." She acknowledges that information about history and culture can be a starting point. However, it is difficult to become culturally competent because culture is constantly changing.

Culturally competent public administration faces many obstacles. In addition to the competing demands of equity, effectiveness, efficiency, and responsiveness, it will be challenged by constantly changing cultures because bureaucracies are slow to respond to change. This leads us to the problem of measurement. Geron (2002) identifies several measurement issues. Different definitions of cultural competency and organizational cultural competency make it difficult to measure cultural competency practices across government agencies. A related concern is developing valid and reliable measures to operationalize cultural competency concepts. A better understanding of how clients define cultural competency is essential for developing valid measurement tools. However, getting honest feedback may be difficult because clients may not want to jeopardize continued service delivery.

Despite these challenges, public administration will need to move forward and establish culturally competent agencies and employees. In the short term most agencies will be reactive, creating culturally competent strategies, policies, and practices in response to client and employee needs. In the long term, public administration should consider how its current training methods meet the future demand for culturally competent organizations, managers, and professionals. Teacher education curricula are using training in a second language to help preservice teachers prepare for working with culturally diverse and multilingual school populations (Ward and Ward 2003). Undergraduate and graduate programs that prepare students for careers in the public sector should consider how they will change their curricula to provide graduates with the skills needed to develop and work within culturally competent agencies.

References

Adams, D. 2003. "Minority Mistrust Still Haunts Medical Care." Amednews. com, January 13. www.ama-assn.org/sci-pubs/amnews/pick_03/pr120113.htm

Alexander, G.R. 2002. "A Mind for Multicultural Management." *Nursing Management* 33 (10): 30–34.

Applied Technology Education Act of 1992. P.L. 102–3.

Bean, R.A. et al. 2002. "Developing Culturally Competent Marriage and Family Therapists: Treatment Guidelines for Non-African American Therapists Working with African American Families." *Journal of Marital and Family Therapy* 28 (2): 153–64.

Bush, C.T. 2000. "Cultural Competence: Implications of the Surgeon General's Report on Mental Health." *Journal of Child and Adolescent Psychiatric Nursing* 13 (4): 177–78.

Center for Effective Collaboration and Practice. 2003. "How Does Cultural Competency Differ from Cultural Sensitivity/Awareness?" cecp.air.org/cultural/Q_howdifferent.htm

Cross, T. et al. 1989. *Towards a Culturally Competent System of Care.* Vol. 1. Washington, DC: Georgetown University Child Development Center, CASSP Technical Assistance Center.

Dean, R.G. 2001. "The Myth of Cross-Cultural Competence." *Families in Society* 82 (6): 623–30.

Denhardt, R.B. 1995. *Public Administration: An Action Orientation.* 2d ed. Belmont, CA: Wadsworth.

Developmental Disabilities Assistance and Bill of Rights Act of 1994. P.L. 103–230.

Disadvantaged Minority Health Improvement Act of 1990. P.L. 101–527.

Dolan, J., and D.H. Rosenbloom. 2003. *Representative Bureaucracy: Classic Readings and Continuing Controversies.* Armonk, NY: M.E. Sharpe.

Emergency Medical Treatment and Active Labor Act of 1996. 42 USC 1395dd.

Executive Office of the President, Office of Management and Budget. 2002. *Assessment of the Total Benefits and Costs of Implementing.* OMB Report to Congress.

Executive Order No. 13166. 2000. *Improving Access To Services for Persons with Limited English Proficiency.* March 14. www.usdoj.gov/crt/cor/lep/omb-lepreport.htm

Geron, S.M. 2002. "Cultural Competency: How Is It Measured? Does It Make a Difference?" *Generations* 26 (3): 39–45.

Goode, T.D. 2000. *Definitions of Cultural Competence.* Washington, DC: National Center for Cultural Competence, Georgetown University Child Development Center, Center for Child Health and Mental Health Policy, University Affiliated Program (UAP).

Hospital Survey and Construction Act (Hill-Burton Act) of 1946. P.L. No. 79–725. www.hrsa.gov/osp/dfcr/about/aboutdiv.htm

Hurdle, D.E. 2002. "Native Hawaiian Traditional Healing: Culturally Based Interventions for Social Work Practice." *Social Work* 47 (2): 183–92.

Kim, P.S. 1999. "Globalization of Human Resource Management: A Cross-Cultural Perspective for the Public Sector." *Public Personnel Management* 28 (2): 227–42.

Mahiri, J. 1998. "Streets to Schools: African-American Youth Culture and the Classroom." *Clearing House* 71 (6): 335–38.

Mosher, F.C. 2003. "Democracy and the Public Service" In J. Dolan and D.H. Rosenbloom, eds. *Representative Bureaucracy: Classic Readings and Continuing Controversies.* Armonk, NY: M.E. Sharpe, 19–22.

National Education Association. 2003. *Status of the American Public School Teacher, 2000–2001.* Washington, DC: National Education Association.

Native Hawaiian Health Care Improvement Act of 1988. P.L. 100–579.

Riccucci, N. 2002. *Managing Diversity in Public Sector Workforces.* Boulder, CO: Westview Press.

Rosenbloom, D.H. 1983. "Public Administrative Theory and the Separation of Powers." *Public Administration Review* 43 (3): 219–27.

Starling, G. 2002. *Managing the Public Sector.* 6th ed. Orlando, FL: Harcourt College Publishers.

Suro, R. 2000. "Beyond Economics." *American Demographics* 22 (1): 48–54.

Taylor-Brown, S., A. Garcia and E. Kingston. 2001. "Cultural Competence Versus Cultural Chauvinism: Implications for Social Work." *Health and Social Work* 26 (3): 185–87.

Title VI of the Civil Rights Act of 1964. 42 USC §§ 2000d. www.justice.gov/crt/cor/coord/titlevistat.htm

Title XIX of the Social Security Act of 1965. §§1396–1396v, subchapter XIX, chapter 7, Title 42. www.ssa.gov/OP_Home/ssact/title19/1900.htm#fn001

Ulrich, D. 1997. *Human Resource Champions: The Next Agenda for Adding Value and Delivering Results.* Boston: Harvard Business School Press.

U.S. Department of Health and Human Services. 2001. *National Standards for Culturally and Linguistically Appropriate Services in Health Care: Final Report.* Washington, DC: Office of Minority Health.

U.S. Department of Justice. 2001. "Memorandum from Assistant Attorney General Ralph F. Boyd, Executive Order 13166, Improving Access To Services for Persons with Limited English Proficiency." Washington, DC.

———. 2001. "Background and Questions and Answers." DOJ Clarifying Memorandum Regarding Limited English Proficiency and Executive Order 13166. October 26. www.usdoj.gov/crt/cor/13166.htm

———. 2002. "Memorandum from Assistant Attorney General Ralph F. Boyd, Executive Order 13166, Improving Access to Services for Persons with Limited English Proficiency." July 18. www.usdoj.gov/crt/cor/lep/Boyd Jul82002.htm

U.S. Federal Register. 2000. "Department of Justice, Enforcement of Title VI of the Civil Rights Act of 1964–National Origin Discrimination Against Persons with Limited English Proficiency; Policy Guidance" 65 (159): 50123–25. August 16.

———. 2002. "Department of Justice, Guidance To Federal Financial Assistance Recipients Regarding Title VI Prohibition Against National Origin Discrimination Affecting Limited English Proficient Persons" 67 (117): 41455–72. June 18.

U.S. Office of Personnel Management. 2002. "Senior Executive Service Member Profile, 1991–2002." *Federal Civilian Workforce Statistics Fact Book.* Washington, DC: U.S. Printing Office.

Ward, M.J., and C.J. Ward. 2003. "Promoting Cross-Cultural Competence in Preservice Teachers through Second Language Use." *Education* 123 (3): 532–36.

Weaver, H.N. 1994. "Indigenous People and the Social Work Profession: Defining Culturally Competent Service." *Social Work* 44 (3): 217–25.

Yee, D., and C. Tursi. 2002. "Recognizing Diversity and Moving Towards Cultural Competence: One Organization's Effort." *Generations* 26 (3): 54–58.

Zayas, L. et al. 1997. "Cultural Competency Training for Staff Serving Hispanic Families with a Child in Psychiatric Crisis." *Families in Society* 78 (4): 405–12.

11

Cultural Diversity and Productivity

Audrey Mathews

Whether an organization, public or private, shows a profit or an increase in outcomes and productivity at year end is directly connected to how well human resources, cultural diversity, and their corollaries, strategic workforce planning and succession, are managed. The most important issue facing governments and businesses is how well human resources will be managed. Critical areas of human resources include personnel practices; cost; capacity to operate effectively and undertake change; productivity; and customer services (Ospina 1992, 53). Governments and corporate executives who do not understand the significance of well-managed human resources and cultural diversity programs are experiencing costly outlays for employee replacement, workforce stability, and lost productivity (Ospina 1992, 53). Because of this, key actors in organizations need to rethink critically and debate the reasons for increases in U.S. productivity ratios. Business and governments are producing more with fewer people. Today's better productivity is catalyzed by layoffs, and therefore the positive effects of corporate and government management of cultural diversity is overshadowed by these layoffs. In the seven quarters since the recovery supposedly started, through September 2003, the real gross domestic product was up 6.2 percent and payroll employment was down 0.8 percent (Shilling 2003, 224).

Government and corporate human resources managers, middle management, supervisors, and other key actors who still expressed views that activities devoted to strategic workforce planning and cultural diversity are unimportant need to be trained and educated about the significant impact these issues can have on their organization's operations (Elmuti 1993, 19; Bendick, Egan, and Lofhjelm 2001, 11–12). Before governments and corporations can cheer about the increase in productivity, everyone involved must

197

first understand that there are problems inherent with the current method of counting productivity increases. Counting the benefits of technology innovations as the major source of the increase is failing to value the benefits of a workforce trained to appreciate cultural diversity. Cultural diversity management and strategic workforce planning processes directly impact productivity in governments and corporations. Therefore, human resources and cultural diversity training and education and strategic human resources are essential to any organization actively competing in the global marketplace. The United States experienced a productivity boom in the 1990s. Economists attribute the increase to being powered chiefly by technology. But better labor training, more efficient staffing structures (fewer managers), smarter government and corporate cultural diversity management, and other strategies are major contributors to this increase. With the downturn in the economy, corporations and governments used the power of doing more with less as a method of increasing their bottom lines without increasing their workforces (Shilling 2003).

This chapter is presented as a guide to human resources and middle management supervisors, professionals, and students of human resources management who have or want responsibility for hiring and increasing productivity and outcome levels in their organizations. Using cultural diversity management policies and practices, the ultimate goal is to foster a thoughtful dialogue among human resources managers and other stakeholders who have the power to influence organizations' culture (Weimer and Vining 1992, 13). The long-term goals of organizations, of ultimately increasing profits and outcome levels while sustaining the increase in productivity ratios without counting the benefits of technology innovations, is achievable using the methods and tools presented herein. Changing demographics affects workforce quality, hence productivity. This chapter presents evidence from existing research that indicates the importance of examining capital investment levels (defined to include human capital) (Lansing 1995, 2). By examining past and present conditions, an understanding is gained about the driving forces and barriers to productivity and diversity management along with causal circumstances and events (Allison 1971, v). Therefore, on one hand, current human resources and cultural diversity practices that prevent or hamper organizations from accomplishing established productivity goals and objectives resulting in reduced bottom lines are discussed. On the other hand, case studies, solutions, and action plans that can be used to reduce barriers and increase the driving forces to increased productivity are presented (Weimer and Vining 1992, 285; Napier and Gershenfeld 1973, 227). Finally, effective human resources practices are recommended that feature organizations' key actors' roles and responsibilities in managing and understanding these issues (Weimer and Vining 1992, 314).

Background

Although in 1993, Vice President Al Gore's national performance review report and all subsequent reports called for strategic planning, performance measurements, and accountability, it should be noted that a few corporations and governments have not incorporated or engaged in human resources or cultural diversity management as a core ingredient of strategic planning. Since these core ingredients are directly linked and negatively impact national productivity rates and global competitiveness, this should be enough justification to call for a national debate about the value of diversity management to the country's productivity ratio and standing in the global marketplace (Morrison 1992; Ospina 1992; Klingner and Nalbandian 1993; Bendick, Egan and Lofhjelm 2001, 11–13). Yet, this debate has not occurred.

The reluctance of executives to engage in a discourse about this subject is understandable since most governments and corporate environments are political in nature (Ospina 1992). No definitive estimate is available concerning the prevalence of diversity training and management in the American workplace today; however, it appears to be undertaken by the majority of large employers in both the public and private sectors. A substantial proportion of medium-size and smaller entities have also joined the larger group. The ideas associated with strategic workforce planning are no longer considered luxuries, especially when other work tasks are executed in a crisis-oriented environment. The impact of human resources decisions upon organizational effectiveness needs to be strongly emphasized. Strategic workforce planning has become relevant because governments and corporations realize the direct connection between the workforce, cultural diversity management, and productivity.

Context of Reality

A 1995 survey of the fifty largest U.S. industrial firms indicates that 70 percent had a formal diversity management program, typically including training. An additional 8 percent were developing a formal diversity management program (Bendick, Egan, and Lofhjelm 2001, 12–13). Another 1995 survey reports that 50 percent of the members of the American Management Association (AMA) have formal programs for managing diversity, with training a usual component. This figure is an increase from 46 percent in 1992 (AMA 1995). The federal government has also provided training in diversity management to its supervisors, mid-management, and senior executive service (Bendick, Egan, and Lofhjelm 2001). In a 1994 survey of members of the Society for Human Resource Management, 33 percent reported that their employers provided training on workforce diversity, making it about as common as training in sales techniques (35 percent) or clerical skills (31 percent). Unfortunately, despite diversity training's popularity as indicated by these surveys, little systematic research is available to resolve often vocal debates about its effects and affects. One side of these debates argues the continuing need for and effectiveness of diversity training. Some authors emphasize the benefits for employees in terms of reduction of discrimination while others emphasize the benefits for employers in terms of productivity (see Bendick, Egan, and Lofhjelm 2001).

Accomplishing strategic missions through the effective use of employees happens when key organization executives, elected officials, and others respond to external pressures. Specifically, the external global marketplace clamors for improved productivity, bottom line profits, work measurements and outcomes, and political accountability (Klingner and Nalbandian 1993; Fryklund 1994, 4–8). However, before executives, human resources, middle managers, and supervisors can influence their organizations into adopting and successfully carrying out human resources and productivity policies, these organizational actors' reality must be brought into context. Perhaps visiting the past will help in understanding present and future conditions and circumstances.

Shifting Environments

In the 1920s, legislation caused personnel departments to move past political responsiveness and curtail the use of "spoils systems" as a way to hire employees, especially technical and professional. Personnel departments were directed to start testing and selecting the best candidate for the job using the hiring criteria established by management (Klingner and Nalbandian 1993). Governments and corporations operated their personnel departments that way until the 1970s. In the late 1970s, traditional personnel departments found that performing record-keeping function was not enough. Organizations shifted into environments of change and uncertainty in the 1980s. As their responsibilities broadened in the late 1980s and early 1990s, personnel departments became human resources management departments and made quantum transitions in the way personnel functions were performed. Organizational goals changed from knowing laws (regulations) and managing positions within a particular personnel system to accomplishing missions that reconciled workplace value conflicts by developing and managing human resources systems (Klingner and Nalbandian 1993, 32–38). But no matter the type of personnel system used, positions, employee, or work management, organizations found that the right numbers of people still needed to be hired, with the right qualifications, for the right jobs, in the right locations (Klingner and Nalbandian 1993, 71; Schuler 1984, 79). The impetus for government changes to human resources management was Public Law 101–576, *Chief Financial Officers Act of 1990*, and the Office of Personnel Management, *Manage to Budget Programs (1989)*. The changing workforce demographics caused the private sector to make the same transition in their human resources management activities.

During this period the definition of workforce diversity changed. The new definition recognized the need to factor organizations' skills, knowledge, and ability requirements (SKAs) into personnel decisions. In organizations that understood the positive impact SKAs had on productivity, hiring based on the jobs needed to carry out and accomplish the organizations' goals became the norm for personnel departments, middle management, and supervisors. SKAs defined occupations and acceptable education and training. Managers defined the important tasks and specified the combination of SKAs needed to accomplish these tasks. Good middle managers and supervisors' special talents were hiring and assigning the right employee with the right SKAs to the right job (Klingner and Nalbandian 1993, 71; Schuler 1984, 79).

Workforce Planning and Cultural Diversity

Accomplishing outcome and productivity goals requires managers and supervisors to understand the problems of workforce planning and cultural diversity management policies (Weimer and Vining 1992, 13). At stake are customer services and organizational effectiveness. According to Dennis L. Dresang (1991), the "completion" of workforce planning is an ongoing function and part of the first step of employee selection function. Furthermore, workforce planning identifies and devises strategies for meeting organizational goals, human resources managements' role, and assessing whether the desired goals have been met (Dresang 1991, 85; see also Wholey et al. 1994, 15–40). When used correctly, workforce strategic planning analyzes the workforce skills, retirements, turnover, and retention of employees while considering the balance of social representation and affirmative action (Dresang 1991, 85). However, many program, line, and middle managers view workforce planning as irrelevant chores imposed for the purpose of generating "paper" rather than real work. According to human resources literature, organizations can use the "top-down" or "bottom-up" approach to workforce planning. The top-down approach defines organizational goals and then translates them into human resource requirements (objectives) according to work needs. The bottom-up approach emphasizes information on employees and social representation within the organization. Successful organizations are using both approaches to ensure that cultural diversity policies are incorporated into the planning process (Dresang 1991, 89).

Organizations are learning how to turn a culturally diverse workforce into a competitive advantage. An effective diversity program begins with training at all levels of the organization. The best training programs focus on inclusion and are professionally developed. Providing eye-opening experiences such as temporary assignments in cultures foreign to specific groups of employees is recommended as a means of helping them better understand the challenges faced by others. Competitive advantage rests on innovation, and to succeed the public and private sectors must bring together talented and committed people from diverse perspectives. Productivity increases and innovations are accessed from a workforce that is diverse in all dimensions (Salomon and Schork 2003). From this examination of past and present conditions, circumstances, and methodologies that impact workforce management and planning, it would appear that nothing prevents increased productivity ratios except the organizations themselves.

Productivity Ratios

A look at capital investment trends would suggest a corollary between the lack of U.S. capital investment and the slowdown in productivity ratios. Arguments that address the slowdown in U.S. productivity rates include the decrease in the growth rates of public capital investment (definition includes human capital). It should be noted, there is no proven causal link between human capital (workforce) and productivity because some researchers say that the United States's productivity slowdown is responsible for the lack of workforce capital growth (Lansing 1995, 2). To the contrary, between 1947 and 1969, workforce productivity (defined as real gross national product [GNP] divided by total labor hours) increased and grew at an average rate of about 2.7 percent per year (Lansing 1995, 2). The growth rate dropped to less than 1 percent per year from 1970 to 1992. But the nation saw a productivity boom in the 1990s chiefly powered by diversity management and training, technology, and fewer managers (Shilling 2003).

Do not count on government or business to step up capital spending (including human capital) in the near future. Inventories are low in relation to sales, and there is too much excess and vacant industrial and commercial capacity in cities' economic development tool chests. Of course, these are not the only explanations for productivity slowdown in the United States. Although considered theoretically flawed by some researchers, other appealing arguments include return to normal growth from the high growth during the Depression and World War II years, fallout from the rate of research and development spending (defined as training and education), compliance with laws and regulations, and changing demographics reducing the quality of the workforce (Lansing 1995, 2). The United States's productivity problems as defined match the behavior of people or groups (humans) in organizations. Organizations are often seen as both dependent and independent variables that influence human behavior just as human behavior shapes the organization (Ott 1989,

---

Table 11.1

Barriers: Costs/Capacity to Operate Effectively and Undertake Change

Lost productivity
• Poorly defined SKAs
• Incomplete planning function
• Lack of employee involvement and satisfaction with work
• Negative implementation of EEO and AAP

Workplace fear
• Failure to treat employees as assets
• Uncertain work environment
• Poor employee job performance
• Forced assimilation

Source: Derived from Lewin (1951) and Napier and Gershenfeld (1973).

4–7). Consequently, organization and human behavior platforms form the base for examining driving forces and barriers to increasing organizations' productivity ratios. These barriers are shown in Table 11.1 and are discussed in more detail below.

Organization and Human Behavior Barriers

It is recognized that for corporations to be competitive in contemporary global markets, they must take advantage of the benefits a diverse workforce brings. Government and corporate managers are quoted repeatedly as saying that diversity is critical to business, outcomes success, and the bottom line. Further, with increased innovation being broadly accepted as one of the chief benefits of diversity, organizations must learn to embrace diversity and turn it into a competitive advantage. The chairman and CEO of Merck, Raymond Gilmartin, has said, "Competitive advantage in business as well as government rests in innovation. To succeed, we must bring together talented and committed people with diverse perspectives" (Salomon and Schork 2003; Mathews 1999).

Lost Productivity

A study by the General Accounting Office (GAO), *Federal Budget Choosing Public Investment Programs* (1993), suggests that workforce productivity contributes more to the economy than any other source. Therefore, it is logical to assume that if governments and corporations are going to increase productivity ratios, they must look internally for improvement. Barriers that challenge increased productivity and affect the bottom line are also concentrated in organizations' culture and behavior. Behind-the-scenes behavior problems (barriers) associated with human resources and cultural diversity management are conditions that can be altered to increase productivity ratios (Weimer and Vining 1992, 205; Napier and Gershenfeld 1973, 227). Poorly defined SKAs are derived from traditional job analyses that are faulty and contain minimum information about tasks employees will perform. Traditional job descriptions are developed from this information, which includes: responsibilities, duties, minimum qualifications, SKAs, job title, occupational classification, salary, and location in the hierarchy.

There are no standards for minimally acceptable employee performance, and that causes problems for supervisors who are trying to improve productivity goals (Klingner and Nalbandian 1993, 73–80; Weimer and Vining 1992, 206–12; Abbasi and Hollman 2000, 333–42). Incomplete planning functions often cause breakdowns in the employee selection process simply because this function is the first step. Activities like job standards, seeking productivity improvements, and motivating employees are often not considered as part of the planning process. Failure to consider these activities when planning often leads to functional breakdowns in budgeting, cost-benefit analysis, and forecasting for personnel programs such as affirmative action, labor-management, and performance rewards (Klingner and Nalbandian 1993, 49–55; Weimer and Vining 1992, 218; Abbasi and Hollman 2000, 333–42). Lack of employee involvement and dissatisfaction with work can create pockets of malcontents, rumor mills, and fear due to noninvolvement in work process decisions that affect employees' quality of life. This type of work environment and culture results from organizations' failure to gather employee input on ways to solve practical work problems and lack of respect for cultural differences (Weimer and Vining 1992, 98–99).

Embedded within the individual members of the workforce are levels of expectancy. Organizations' failure to fulfill employees' needs and expectations for inclusion often produce unexpected outcomes and lost productivity (Ott 1989, 183; Abbasi and Hollman 2000, 333–42). Negative implementation of equal employment opportunity (EEO) and affirmative action programs (AAP) results from inappropriate hiring practices along with improper interpretation of EEO laws, rules, and regulations by human resources staff, middle managers, and supervisors. The real intent of the law as written by executive, legislative, and judicial systems is "Equal Employment Opportunity." According to the Bureau of National Affairs, Inc. (1973), "AAPs are seen as enforcement tools used to meet the requirements that bring minorities, women, and others into the workforce." Actions (initiatives, referenda, court decisions) occurring periodically in the Congress and in states like California, Texas, Florida, and Washington forgo the increased productivity that properly managed cultural diversity brings to organizations.

Workplace Fear

Workplace technology, organizational structures, and the international climate have created an unpredictable workplace climate of anxiety and fear. Employees' concerns about organization downsizing and personal emotional uncertainty permeates workplace environments and cultures. The responsibility for developing policies that allay workplace fear rests with the leaders of governments and corporations (Weimer and Vining 1992, 102). Human resources managers provide the employment forecast and describe it in a way that should dispel fears. Human resources planners stress that their role is to eliminate anxieties and fears of displacement. Middle managers and supervisors who are responsible for policy application and implementation, however, are seen as the bearers of bad news and become the brunt of workplace fear (Klingner and Nalbandian 1993, 74; Schuler 1984, 80; Schein 1978, 191). Further, governments and corporations often fail to treat employees as assets that impact their productivity. The basic issue facing organizations' managers during this period of downsizing is "whether to respond to the productivity problems by treating employees as valuable assets or continue to regard them as expendable (Elmuti 1993, 19). Uncertain work environments have been created by organizations that believe demographics changes, globalization, and current economic policies (reductions in health benefits) negatively impact government's and corporations' productivity and bottom. There are also some who support the theory that, concurrent with these anticipated changes, the size of the workforce pool is decreasing (Jorgensen 1993, 72; Shilling 2003).

High employee absenteeism and turnover can often be attributed to workplace rumors, fears, and anxieties. Employee expectations have risen to include job security, a decent wage, and health benefits, among others. Organizations' demands for increased productivity and profits have created environments where the norm is layoff, declining benefits, reduced rights, and inadequate communication. This type of environment breeds absenteeism and turnover (Robinson, McClure, and Terpstra 1994, 9; Abbasi and Hollman 2000, 333–42).

Poor employee job performance often occurs when the impact of managing cultural diversity issues is not considered in the strategic planning process. Frustration and tension invade the planning process, causing vulnerability, instability, and high uncertainty about the work environment. Generally organizations have costly, negative, and unanticipated consequences from using quick solutions to mend lost motivation. This tension leads to a loss of employee motivation and ends with low productivity (Ospina 1992, 57). Forced assimilation is used by some organizations to create an adaptive work environment. Managers of this type of work environment wonder why all the commotion. There have always been workers of different races, religions, and genders in organizations. R. Roosevelt Thomas (1991, 8) points out the frailties of organization assimilation: "Newcomers are expected to adapt so they fit; the burden of making the change falls to them." Managers have insisted that people who are different bear the brunt of adjusting. "We have determined in this company that there is a specific culture and that people who fit a given mold do better than those who do not. . . . If you fit, fine. If you don't, we invite you to allow us to shape you to the appropriate mold."

Times and Attitudes Are Changing; Forced Assimilation Is Unattainable Now and Considered Bad for Business

Where there is action there is also reaction. Building defenses against coercive or threatening barriers is normal behavior for or-

Table 11.2

Productivity Driving Forces

Production costs
• Diversity is a business issue
• Budgetary limitations

Capacity to operate effectively
• Public good
• Customer service

Undertake change
• Diversity training and education
• Reward structure

Source: Derived from Lewin (1951) and Napier and Gershenfeld (1973).

ganizations and the workforce. However, negative reactions do not occur when concerted efforts are made to reduce perceived organizational barriers. Successful organizations force, push, or drive down production costs, increasing their capacity to operate and undertake change (Napier and Gershenfeld 1973, 227). Nearly every U.S. government and corporation has a policy on diversity. Most define diversity in broad terms: "All the unique talents and capabilities possessed by individuals in the workforce" (Dow Corning, Inc.), or "All of the differences that we bring" (Agilent, Inc). As indicated in the book *Sum of the Difference*, diversity is more than the clearly visible parameters of race, age, and gender. It includes religion, education, sexual orientation, personality type, and a variety of other factors that may or may not be obvious at first (Mathews 1999); for example, the management of Indian rights, endangered species, agriculture, and immigrant rights (Mathews 2003). Ultimately it is the diversity of perspective and thought that will benefit government and corporations. This productivity and diversity is accessed from a workforce that is diverse in all dimensions. Most creative new ideas tend to be generated from these driving forces. Driving forces as depicted in Table 11.2 can be an important factor in any movement toward change. Problems can be created when new driving forces are introduced (Napier and Gershenfeld 1973).

Production Cost

Most organizations' cultures contain disturbing levels of intolerance and exclusionism (*Personnel Management* 1993, 15). Line managers often do not recognize the importance of diversity programs despite managing rapidly changing workforces. On the one hand, some managers believed these programs are motivated by a desire to avoid litigation. On the other hand, white males in the workplace see cultural diversity programs as tantamount to preferential treatment (*Personnel Management* 1993). Lost productivity costs are offset by organizations that emphasize appreciating, respecting, and enjoying each person's uniqueness. Consequently, the presence of differences in these governments and corporations is the norm, and managing diversity means respecting culture, age, gender, the physically and mentally challenged, and lifestyle differences. By valuing diversity, management seizes the productivity benefits differences bring.

Diversity Is a Business Issue

The demographic changes and trends predicted in *Workforce 2000* affect the public sector and the private sector, causing competition for and greater emphasis upon attracting and retaining qualified employees. Many corporate managers believe that it is absolutely clear that diversity must be managed not only now but much more so in the future. However, managing diversity must extend beyond mere tolerance (ProQuest ABI 1994). For competitive organizations, diversity management is not just the latest catchword in the series of organizational jargon. David Kearns, president and CEO of the Xerox Corporation, says, "The company that gets out in front of managing diversity will have a competitive edge not because they have become kinder and gentler toward minority groups, but because they want to survive and remain competitive" (cited in Elmuti 1993). Budgetary limitations must be considered when managers evaluate proposed program costs. Factors considered are numbers and types of employees, pay, benefits, and training needed. Also considered are comparisons of performance and productivity data against organization goals and budgetary limitations. Some corporate and government leaders have laid aside their biases and recognized the need to grant human resources, middle management, and supervisors budget and resource flexibility. One final step is holding these managers accountable for results (Schein 1978, 90; Klingner and Nalbandian 1993, 331).

Capacity to Operate Effectively

One key point of conflict within human resources management is the extent personnel systems should be driven by market models, or concerns of social equity and individual rights (EEO, AAP, and diversity) (Weimer and Vining 1992, 104). Compliance with the law was the impetus to implement affirmative action; on the other hand, diversity is seen as valuing each person as an individual and has no specific law driving it. It is said that workplace diversity is a direct result of EEO and affirmative action programs. In keeping with the economic concept of market and government failure and the fact that the market does not allocate this particular good efficiently, managing human resources and cultural diversity can be viewed as a public good (see Aronson and Schwartz 1987, 401–6; Weimer and Vining 1992, 41). Public-good benefits are not always measurable because benefits can be intangible in nature. This is one reason that enforcement of equal employment opportunity programs is left to the government. Human resources and cultural diversity usefulness is still considered quasisocial and not easily determined in monetary terms, although cost remains a theoretically correct criterion for investment in the public sector (Weimer and Vining 1992, 46). Human resources and cultural diversity are both nonrivalrous in consumption and nonexcludable in use. It is highly unlikely that their nonrivalrous good can or will be observed. Managing human resources and cultural diversity is something that can be produced by one manager but consumed by all members (Weimer and Vining 1992, 43). For example, one person can supervise a diverse work group that produces more work by using their diversity to be innovative and creative. Maintaining a culturally diverse organization may be costly to individual members because it requires them to expend extra effort to understand a complex workforce, increase productivity, and meet clientele demands quickly, effectively, and cheerfully (Weimer and Vining 1992, 44–45; Stockley and Zeckhauser 1978, 305–8).

Customer service is a major thrust in organizational goal development. Many managers believe human resources and cultural diversity programs are important to customer service, contributing to corporate innovation and providing an enhanced company image. To these managers, diversity has a definite place in the wider context of human resources management and workforce planning (Muir 1993, 26). Employees are considered customers and assets of the organization. In progressive organizations, "supervisors are learning not just to cope with diversity, but also to use it as a stimulus, increasing organizations' customer base, service levels, and productivity, consequently calming workplace anxieties" (Van Auken 1993, 11).

Undertake Change

Often training and education is used to initiate and induce culture change, resulting in solutions to performance and productivity problems in organizations. Training is a critical part of the preparation stage and must be kept in tune with the needs of employees and the organization as a whole. Diversity training and education should be supported by training needs assessment. To help employees understand their own feelings as well as the feelings of others about human resources and cultural diversity issues, a systematic follow-up is required. It is an investment in increased productivity and should be based on comparisons of computerized skills inventories against the jobs' required SKAs. The result is increased productivity. Management and human resources managers feel that middle managers and supervisors need skills and knowledge obtained from diversity training about managing human resources. This type of training should portray management's full support and the objectives of the programs, thus allowing managers and supervisors to learn and fully understand that diversity is a business issue for their organizations (Klingner and Nalbandian 1993, 196).

Reward structures in most organizations do not hold managers and supervisors accountable for results. The performance appraisal system can be used for tying rewards to performance and productivity. Private organization's managers can use a variety of rewards and punishments to try to induce "hiring" cultural diversity. In the public sector, managing diversity is more difficult for the public manager because of civil service rules. An avoidance of "acculturating" a department or unit can be seen as resulting from the public manager's inability to match individual rewards to organizational contributions (see White et al. 1985, 206; Klingner and Nalbandian 1993, 132).

Problem-Solving Sequence

The problems that contribute to organizations' low growth productivity are conditions that exist with forces impinging upon them. Solutions to low growth productivity in these economic domains are highly sensitive to critical output elasticity estimates used to decide optimal level of public investment (Lansing 1995, 2; Weimer and Vining 1992: 40–58). Capital investment solutions will require national policy and law changes. Costs, and the capacity to operate effectively and undertake change are also conditions created by organization and human behavior barriers and driving forces. Reality clearly suggests that most organizations do not have the power to influence normal capital investment solutions without legislative assistance. This long-term process involves many actors and success is highly unlikely. Therefore energies should be spent on problems that organizations have the power to change, such as human resources and cultural diversity management practices and policies (Weimer and Vining 1992, 225).

Objectives, Assumptions, Criteria

Traditional approaches to job analyses, descriptions, and classifications frequently conflict with organizational goals of surviving and remaining competitive, whereas the results-oriented approach supports goal accomplishment (Klingner and Nalbandian 1993, 77). Organizations have the capacity to initiate change in workforce planning during the strategic planning processes. Employers must do more to analyze the data provided by others and better define the demand side of the workforce equation. Two strategic factors—lack of investment in human capital and inappropriate corporate culture—can be directly related to a lack of understanding about diversity (Kemmerer and Arnold 1993, 39). The question is how we translate organizations' concerns about productivity goals, customer services, workforce skills, competencies, and abilities into the capacity to operate effectively and undertake changes required by the marketplace.

Workforce Planning

Organizations need to assess the differences in the two approaches to job analysis, descriptions, and classifications. The traditional approach to these activities requires human resources and personnel managers in collaboration with supervisors to observe or interview the worker and record information about work performed (Klingner and Nalbandian 1993, 225). From these observations, job descriptions are formulated that describe duties and qualification standards (minimum education and/or experience) needed to carry out the duties satisfactorily. The operative word in this activity description is observed. Progressive organizations are transitioning from traditional job descriptions to the newer results-oriented descriptions and a formal competency-analysis program based on forty-five different behaviors deemed essential to the organization's success, including clear business thinking, the ability to manage change, and good interpersonal relationships. Organizations then offer adult learning curriculum and training based on the needs of both employees and the organization (Greengard 2001).

Results-oriented job descriptions are considered more useful because they contain information on tasks, conditions, standards, knowledge, skills and abilities, and qualifications. The organizations' linkages and expectations of the employees are clarified. Executives are no longer handicapped, because results-oriented job descriptions describe personnel inputs and resultant outputs in terms of productivity, which is the intended outcome (Klingner and Nalbandian 1993, 74). Another key to planning and managing the workforce of the future is "flexibility. Flexibility includes work hours, rewards, accommodating family responsibilities, dealing with individual differences, and matching competencies with job requirements." Developing career paths for minorities and women, job-sharing, and subsidizing day and elder care is also considered key when managing diversity (Jorgensen 1993, 72). All are positive ingredients that allow culturally diverse employees to shape collectively the culture of the organization and the way work is done to meet the organizations' goals and objectives. The only limitation to securing appropriate talent would be a shortage in the workforce supply, based upon skills and competencies. If this occurs, personnel management must search for alternatives such as rechecking

---

Table 11.3

Four Phases of Resource Planning

1. Determining of objectives (productivity)
2. Analyzing of critical variables (effort and motivation of employees)
3. Selecting strategies
4. Evaluating results

Source: Derived from Dresang (1991).

---

required skills and competencies against the job, seeking a trainable population, marketing jobs sufficiently ahead of needs, and extending the workforce boundaries to include other nationals' countries. The organization will prosper because of the linkages that treat employees as valuable assets and provide job satisfaction, resulting in increased productivity and "bottom line" profits.

Sonia Ospina (1992, 63) uses the consequences of nonstrategic public personnel management to explain why the general purposes of workforce planning are so vital to governments and organizations. McGregor (1991, 52) calls it the "workforce management" to highlight its strategic importance as a managerial function . . . "to ensure that the right people needed to accomplish the organizational mission are in place." This logic would seem applicable to businesses as well. Workforce planning increases productivity and motivation levels by emphasizing that employees are treated as human beings. A resulting effect is increased service delivery and customer satisfaction (Dresang 1991, 86). Human resources managers generally consider the four- and five-step models shown in Tables 11.3 and 11.4.

What it comes down to is: How good are human resources professionals at strategically determining what needs to be done to staff effectively, manage diversity, and operate companies and firms next year and for the next decade or two to come? Ann Morrison (1992) describes the diversity practices of sixteen successful corporations and public sector organizations that can be related to workforce planning. When the top ten diversity practices used in these organizations are ranked by importance, as seen in Table 11.5, evidence is provided that the four- or five-step models for workforce planning (see Tables 11.3 and 11.4), the functions and steps in personnel management, can be linked with managing cultural diversity. For

Table 11.4

Five-Step Model: Workforce Planning

1. Linking strategic organizational plans to human resource plans
2. Assessing the current human resource demand
3. Assessing the current human resource supply
4. Comparing demand and supply
5. Developing the right human resource programs necessary to close the gap

Source: Derived from Dresang (1991).

Table 11.5

The Top Ten Diversity Practices

1. Top management's personal intervention
2. Targeted recruitment of nonmanagers
3. Internal advocacy groups
4. Emphasis on Equal Employment Opportunity (EEO) statistics and profiles
5. Inclusion of diversity in performance evaluation goals and ratings
6. Inclusion of diversity in promotion decisions and criteria
7. Inclusion of diversity in management succession planning
8. Diversity training programs
9. Networks and support groups
10. Work and family policies

Source: Derived from Morrison (1993).

organizations that plan their anticipated workforces as a progressive technique, the payback is tremendous. Employee retention, increased productivity, less absenteeism, better morale, expanded marketplace, and improved services rendered to consumers/customers are all benefits according to those who advocate workforce planning (Jorgensen 1993, 70). Hence, to ensure that this payback is achieved, organizations must look at innovative workforce planning to improve productivity and enhance quality.

Alternatives

Competitive and productivity problems faced by industry and governments are related to strategic factors. One strategic factor approach used to achieve societal needs and value is "benchmarking" (Kemmerer and Arnold 1993, 39).

Table 11.6

Benchmarking as a Strategic Process Involves Ten Steps

1. Identify the practice to benchmark
2. Identify companies that perform this practice the best
3. Identify variables to measure data collection method and collect data
4. Compare actual performance with the best practice company
5. Based upon these results, forecast future performance
6. Establish goals for the practice
7. Communicate benchmark findings to employees
8. Develop action plans
9. Implement action plans and monitor performance
10. Revise benchmarks, if necessary

Source: Derived from Kemmerer and Arnold (1993).

Benchmarking

Benchmarking is used to identify successful processes and practices, including inventory control, product development, quality practices, robotics, warehousing, and distribution. Managing diverse workforces is improving because appropriate changes have been made to integrate employees from different backgrounds into the organization (Kemmerer and Arnold 1993, 38). Personnel managers who successfully identify and benchmark successful practices are contributing greatly to their organizations' ability to balance productivity, operate effectively, and undertake change. This does not preclude the fact that policies and procedures that are benchmarked may need to be adapted to fit the specific organization. Benchmarking is not necessarily the cure-all; organizations and governmental agencies that adopt benchmarking should be aware that certain problems exist in doing so. Benchmarking must have a strategic perspective. Unless an organizational culture of valuing diversity is continuously communicated, rewarded, and encouraged, turnover and intergroup conflict can result. The ten steps in successful benchmarking are shown in Table 11.6.

Flex-management

Flex-management is a philosophy of core values that treat people as assets to be valued, developed, and maintained. Executives who

Table 11.7

Flex-management Actions and Methodology Plan

Actions methodology

- Define the organization's employee composition including age, gender, ethnicity, diversity, education, and disability.

- Understand the organization's value. Hold discussions, set up task forces, and interview and survey employees.

- Describe the desired future state. What programs will be offered, and what policies, systems, and services can deliver them?

- Plan and manage transactions. Design specific plans that consider methods, people, and timeliness. Consider how to overcome any resistance to change.

- Evaluate results. Monitor and measure elements to evaluate the program.

Source: Derived from Jamieson and O'Mara (1991).

have integrated flex-management into their corporate culture are tuned into employees' needs. Options are created that give choices. Diverse individual desires are balanced with the organization's. Management, for example, is free to customize compensation and benefits programs. There is also freedom to build flexibility into performance planning, evaluation, recruiting, job design, and training (Jamieson and O'Mara 1991, 69).

When moving to flex-management, an important decision to be made is deciding who will guide and manage this change project. The open options range from an individual to various groups coordinated by a steering committee. Many organizations entering the flex-management change option use task forces, change teams, or internal and external consultants. However, commitment is more important than the decision of who will manage the change project. Deciding to use flex-management requires a major commitment from the manager or supervisor. Under flex-management, reformative corporations such as Apple Computer and 3M and some governmental agencies create ways to help their workforces. This includes "test-driving jobs," working on projects of choice, and helping people who have changing needs or goals provide valuable services. The process of change begins with the steps shown in Table 11.7 once the structure of the project is in place.

Positioning Diversity

There are several viewpoints centered on positioning diversity. The first viewpoint is maintaining the status quo. Equal employment opportunity and affirmative action programs operate when a gross disparity exists between the numbers of minority or female employees in an agency and their numbers in a relevant community labor pool. It also operates when the organization has resisted the voluntary adoption of techniques that reduce that disparity. Although considered to have reduced discrimination and opened doors for minorities and women, statistically it is hard to marshal evidence to that effect. The driving force to implement EEO and AAP is compliance with the law to solve workplace conflicts (Klingner and Nalbandian 1993, 132–6). A second view coming to the managing diversity forefront is that human resources managers should function as a strong right arm of the executive. How and where organizations position diversity and EEO initiatives are human resources management concerns. There are varied techniques for positioning diversity based upon organizational structure and needs. Mary L. Winterle (1993, 48) outlines techniques used by some top firms in the United States.

Mobil Oil Corporation uses a hierarchical organizational structure separating EEO and diversity functions, which are managed by two separate sections of the human resources department. Mobil did this when "EEO initiatives became more compliance-driven and externally focused, while workforce diversity became more focused on recruiting, career development and outreach." IBM Corporation created a functional link between diversity and EEO by moving the separate departments that are responsible for EEO/affirmative action and work-life issues to one department. One IBM executive points out that "moving the functions into one organization, reporting to the same director, enhances the synergy. The broader the umbrella, the more effective it is." A different organizational strategy was used by Hershey Foods Corporation. Diversity was mainstreamed, integrating responsibilities for diversity initiatives into other management functions within the organization. The Chevron Corporation, a matrix organization, Winterle (1993, 48) continues, "is moving from a highly centralized organization to a decentralized organization and, simultaneously, embracing the concept of

---

Table 11.8

Functions of Line Supervisors/Managers

- Planning, such as the responsibility for managing within the budget.

- Acquisition involved in the hiring and firing of employees, and performance appraisal, which should also evaluate the employee as a "human being" as well as job performance. While this humanistic evaluation may not be considered job-related in decisions regarding promotions or rewards systems, it is overall job-related in terms of understanding employee productivity.

- Development contributing to organizational goals being met by ensuring that necessary job skills needed by the employee are present and evaluated, and provides feedback to both the employee and management.

- Sanctions, counsels, and disciplines employees.

Source: Derived from Klingner and Nalbandian (1993).

Total Quality Management (TQM)." To do so, they have made management of diversity one of several "key strategies each business unit must address in the TQM process."

Training and Educating Managers

Personnel management has the function of training and educating managers and supervisors to understand their importance in human resource management and the application of organization policy. That training must be grounded in adult learning theory (Mathews 2002). Learning theorists describe context as a focus on reality which is the physical, emotional, and intellectual environment that surrounds an experience and gives it meaning. Workplace training must address the contextual issues of class, gender, culture, ethnicity, sexual orientation, and the physically and mentally challenged (Mathews 2002). Managers and supervisors are responsible for the day-to-day activities that determine the relationship between employees and organizations, an important factor of personnel management (Klingner and Nalbandian 1993, 26). The most transformational learning experiences occur through personal experience, group support, or mentoring. They are also the bottom line of accountability, the implementer and enforcer of workplace culture, setting values, and where diversity management begins (Mathews 1999). Table 11.8 reflects the functions of managers and supervisors.

The three areas of expertise that managers and supervisors are required to have and what makes them invaluable to the workforce planning and management functions are: (1) *yechnical expertise*— which ensures that the supervisor knows what the worker is doing and what is expected of the employee; (2) *conceptual expertise*— the ability to grasp the big picture and think both proactively and strategically. This expertise includes the ability to diagnose and analyze, and also identify cause and effect; and (3) *human expertise* is the ability to communicate about the quality and quantity of work and the values and culture of the organization to others. Supervisors use these same skills to motivate employees and build cooperative relationships among individuals and groups (Klingner and Nalbandian 1993, 169–75).

Changing Organization Culture

The direct connection between human resources practices and productivity can be linked by diversity using the theories of leadership described by Ann Morrison (1992, 159–266) and the competing values framework of organization effectiveness (OE) by James L. Perry (1989). The literature of OE and organizational design provides the conceptual framework for designing systems and actions that increase the ability to adapt to changing conditions (Morrison 1992, 160; Perry 1989, 152; Weimer and Vining 1992, 341). Workforce planning and managing diversity functions of personnel management fall neatly into the confines of organization effectiveness.

Competing Values Model

Often, organizations and their managers fail to place sufficient importance on the competing values that combine the models, "Human Relations (cohesion, morale, human resource development), Open Systems (flexibility, growth, resource acquisition, external/ environmental support), Rational Goals (planning, goal accomplishment, productivity, competitiveness), and Internal Process (monitoring, stability, controls)" (Perry 1989, 149). Table 11.9 explains effective diversity processes, and Perry (1989, 149) suggests that at the core of personal identity is a set of assumptions about how the world around them operates. Using these assumptions, individuals

Table 11.9

Effective Diversity Processes

Process steps

- Shared mind-set: Assesses the current mind-set and identifies the one required. Uses institutional practices to instill a "diversity" mind-set.

- Controlling behavior: Encourages and reinforces spending time behaving in ways consistent with organizational "diversity" goals.

- Market controls performance and incentives linked to "diversity" outcomes.

- Bureaucratic controls: Link "diversity" policy and rules to performance standards and behavior.

- Clan controls: Organizational "diversity" values derived through selection, training, communication, and reinforcement. Behavior shaped common organizational values.

- Accountability: Allocate "diversity" accountability and responsibility.

- Specify key "diversity" tasks that need to be accomplished. Define options about where "diversity" tasks can be done. Assign "diversity" tasks to specific levels.

Source: Derived from Perry (1989).

filter and process information, make decisions and allocate time for activities. Likewise, organizations have identities or mind-sets. Organizational mind-sets focus employees' attention, generate employees' commitment to key activities, and generate an organization's capability of responding to change. When a mind-set focused on change exists in each member of the organization, the organization is more likely to adapt to changing conditions. The competing values model is an organizational process for instilling mind-sets, establishing control systems, and instituting processes for allocating the accountability and responsibility for managing diversity (Perry 1989, 153–59). There are three models of corporate response to workforce diversity and productivity in the private sector that can be applied by other organizations and personnel managements (Laudicina 1993, 458).

Education/Training Model

The education/training model within the corporation is the range and scope of education expanded well beyond traditional skills training. Basic literacy, math, and English as a second-language course are now offered by many corporations. Public and private partnerships have been formed to strengthen educational systems. The business sector may advocate a reform of the educational system as well as "enhanced tax incentives for training-related expenses and federal- and state-sponsored job training programs.

Benefit/Reward Model

The benefit/reward model requires adaptations in the traditional structure of rewards and inducements. "Cafeteria" benefits packages, changes in retirement policies, allowances, on-site facilities for child and elder care, and work-at-home provisions are all characteristic of increasing flexibility in policies and procedures (Laudicina 1993, 458).

Organizational Culture Model

The organizational culture model entails fundamental changes in the systems, policies, and practices of the workplace. This model emphasizes managerial training to understand the needs, values, and concerns of a diverse workforce.

Education/Training and the Rewards/Benefits Models

This model represents expansion rather than redirection of corporate policies and procedures. Both represent efforts to assure a continuing supply of workers to meet corporate needs (Laudicina 1993, 458). Thomas (1991, 53–57) notes that organizational culture approaches look at the organization of work, job design, mobility patterns, and the broad network of relationships within the workplace to enhance the intrinsic rewards of the job besides expanding external motivators. Nine elements characterize most organization culture initiatives:

1. Redefinition of diversity
2. Fundamental reassessment of organizational culture
3. Diversity management being recognized as a "business issue"

4. Creation of a separate organizational entity for diversity management
5. Separation from the human resource function
6. Top-level initiation and support
7. Integration within the managerial reward structure
8. Program/results monitoring
9. Integration with total quality management (TQM) initiatives.

Conclusion

Of the three models adopted by the private sector, the organizational culture model combined with the competing values model has the potential to change fundamentally both business and government organizational culture (Weimer and Vining 1992, 228). However, for governments, there are some serious structural impediments to implementation of key elements of this approach, including: top-level indifference to management issues, change-resistant organizational cultures, and budgetary limitations that must be conquered. Below are two cases from the business sector.

Owens Corning

In 1992, Glen Hiner, an executive from General Electric, was hired as the first "outsider" chief executive officer in Owens Corning (OC) Inc. history. Owens Corning is a manufacturer of fiberglass insulation and other building materials with 24,000 employees and $4.3 billion in annual revenues. For fifty years the company experienced slow but steady growth based on innovative products and promote-from-within management. In the 1980s the company's conservative style made it a target for a hostile takeover. Hiner transformed the company, radically raising expectations for individual performance and making profound changes in the firm's culture. New, modern buildings featured open offices, six senior executives were replaced, and a new sense of possibility pervaded the firm.

For Hiner, diversity was above all else a way to support his ambitious goals by promoting broader vision, flexibility, openness to new ideas, and continuous learning. He argued that a more diverse workforce would promote internationalization, assist in penetrating demographically diverse domestic markets, and bring in talented employees. In his first meeting with senior executives, he bluntly stated, "We are too white and too male, and that will change." He appointed two women to the all-male board of directors, and five women, including one of color, to the all-white corps of fifty vice presidents. He ordered business cards that stated the company's core values and set diversity values equal to customer satisfaction and shareholder values. He held conferences, devoting several days to diversity in the first one and making it a recurring theme in others. In reviewing hiring practices he constantly questioned whether minorities, women, or citizens of other countries were being considered as candidates. In senior managers' annual performance reviews he paid prominent attention not only to financial goals but also to nonfinancial aims, including diversity. He hired a consulting firm to deliver diversity management training, but the consulting firm considered itself not just a trainer, but an organization-development change agent, devising and implementing strategies for cultural change. OC today is an organization in transition. Management remains predominantly white and male, however, women and minority employees now occupy several positions unprecedented for them half a dozen years ago. While women and minorities still tend to sit apart from their white male coworkers in the cafeteria, crude gender humor and racial epithets on the shop floor have been substantially curtailed. Within a broad process of organization development, diversity training contributed significantly to these results (Bendick, Egan, and Lofhjelm 2001). Human resources managers and general management should seek to identify new policies and strategies, using competing values techniques to balance productivity and diversity (Otto 1992, 53–54). Otto, too, describes how a major corporation, Tenneco, Inc. of Houston, Texas, utilized the competing values model to progress to integrated leadership.

Tenneco, Inc.

Tenneco, Inc., a major manufacturer in Houston, Texas, provides an example of how an organization can put into action a combination of personnel management functions to fit their specific organizational needs in workforce planning and managing diversity. Tenneco uses normal affirmative action planning to determine the availability of women and minorities in both the internal and external labor market. At year end, the actual percentage of women and minorities hired or promoted into each of the categories [of positions] is compared to the goal percentages. In addition, divisions are evaluated on the basis of programs and long-term efforts using five categories: *Tracking and reporting* using quantitative tools to manage the programs, that is, turnover analysis, jobs-filled records, and progress reports; *accountability* considering the extent to which the division pushes down the levels of accountability; *development* that evaluates division human resource development systems such as succession planning; *communication and training*; and *community involvement*, which includes the involvement of the division in internal and external educational and community organizations. In addition, Tenneco outlined five specific strategies for bringing women and minorities at Tenneco into the management and executive mainstream: *appointment* for both corporate and divisional CEO levels; *empowerment* by broadening participation of women and minorities in the policy- and program-making process of decisions affecting their lives; *strong system of measurements* and checks and balances; *design programs and policies* to meet broader employee needs, such as family-friendly benefits; *expand organizational capacities and opportunities* through employee training and development. The functions of personnel management and applications of personnel and organizational theories, the management of cultural diversity, human resource planning, and the willingness of management to listen to a strong right hand of personnel management can be seen in the initiatives enacted by Tenneco.

Even when initiatives such as those used by Owens Corning and Tenneco are established, there still remains a fact of life that must be considered by organizations. Any initiative prescribed that makes diversity management training an essential tool will fail without the direct help and support of managers and supervisors (Weimer and Vining 1992, 236–37). Van Auken (1993, 11) notes that the training for supervisors should be centered on what may be called the "secret to understanding culturally diverse workers." He says: "Concentrate on basic human needs, both personal and professional. Cultures may vary, but people's basic needs and motives are remarkably universal." Van Auken (11–12) identifies four universal principles: (1) The Job Mastery Principle (a desire to be successful in performing duties); (2) the Feedback Principle (employees need to know where they stand on the job in terms of performance); (3) the Role Principle (the importance of group membership and teamwork to the employee); and (4) the Appreciation Principle (wherein positive reinforcement yields desired behavior).

Supervisors who are trained to understand these principles as they apply to their employees will be better enabled to transform diversity into productivity. One strategy for achieving diversity training is through peer training. As an example, the National Coalition Building Institute (NCBI) uses a program titled Peer Training Strategies for Welcoming Diversity. This program is "designed to assist participants in understanding the dynamics of institutionalized racism by working through a series of personal and small group explorations" (Brown and Mazza 1994, 1–4). These peer training programs are based on NCBI's operational assumptions: (1) training teams of peer leaders will empower people to take a leadership role in reducing racism; (2) programs to welcome diversity require an ongoing institutional effort; (3) establishing proactive training programs that build strong intergroup relations are more effective than programs that respond to specific racial incidents or crises; (4) programs that welcome diversity need to include all of the visible and invisible differences found in the workplace; and (5) prejudice reduction programs that are based on guilt, moralizing, or condemnation result in prejudicial attitudes (Brown and Mazza 1994, 14).

In a world of changing programs and culture, the only source of experience for managers has been implementation. The actors involved in implementation are boards, top management, human resources personnel, middle managers, and supervisors. A most important factor in the implementation phase is educating participants from the top down and from the bottom up. Educating must be claimed by organizations and then delegated to peers, universities, and colleges. For human resources and diversity management, the emphasis is on educating, says Roosevelt Thomas (1991, 38): "It has to do with what we think." Managing human resources and diversity's goal is to change mind-sets. It requires that organizations and employees shift their mind-sets, and that takes ongoing and repetitive education (Thomas 1991, 39). Adapting the results-oriented strategies to organizations' cultures presented in this chapter reinforces implementing training and education to obtain full utilization of middle managers and supervisors.

Key steps in understanding and evaluating the worth of any process, according to Joseph Wholey (1994, 18), are "involving the users, clarifying the intent, program reality, change agreements, alternative evaluation designs and agreement of priorities and intended uses of information on program performance." To achieve this goal, organizations' management needs to bring managers and supervisors fully into the strategic workforce planning and education processes. The objective here is to ensure that middle managers and supervisors are committed to the organizations' goals and plans. Increased productivity comes from the successful management of diverse workforces managed by fully involved middle managers and supervisors. Part of the management team, these managers are responsible for explaining change and its implication on work processes. It should be noted that many organizations do not bring the middle managers and supervisors fully into the picture. These organizations are seriously undermining the ability of their organization to meet the goals set for productivity. After appropriate education and training in competing values techniques, human resources, and diversity management, and after the implementing of these techniques has been completed by organizations, an evaluation process should be developed and initiated. Organizations will need to evaluate these programs for their long-term outcomes. The evaluation categories are outlined in the Tenneco, Inc. case study and are adaptable to any organization's needs.

References

Abbasi, Sam M., and Hollman, Kenneth W. 2000. "Turnover: The Bottom Line" *Public Personnel Management* 29 (3): 333–42.

Allison, Graham T. 1971. *Essence of Decision: Explaining the Cuban Missile Crisis.* Boston: HarperCollins.

American Management Association. 1995. *AMA Survey on Managing Cultural Diversity.* New York: American Management Association.

Aronson, J. Richard, and Eli Schwartz. 1987. *Management Policies in Local Government Finance.* Washington: Published for the ICMA Institute by the International City Management Association.

Bendick, Marc Jr., Mary Lou Egan, and Suzanne M. Lofhjelm. 2001. "Workforce Diversity Training: From Anti-Discrimination Compliance To Organizational Development." *Human Resources Planning* 24 (2): 10–25.

Brown, Cherie R., and George J. Mazza. 1994. "Peer Training Strategies for Welcoming Diversity." *Leadership for Diversity Initiative, Training Institutes, National Coalition Building Institute*, Washington, DC.

Dresang, Dennis L. 1991. *Public Personnel Management and Public Policy*, 2d ed. New York: Longman.

Editorial Staff of the Bureau of National Affairs, Inc. 1973. *The Equal Employment Opportunity Act of 1972*. Washington: Bureau of National Affairs, Inc.

Elmuti, Dean. 1993. "Managing Diversity in the Workplace: An Immense Challenge for Both Managers and Workers." *Industrial Management* 35 (4) (July–August): 19.

Fryklund, Inge. 1994. "Privatization American Style." *Business Forum* (winter/spring): 4–8.

Gore, Al. 1993. *Creating a Government that Works Better & Costs Less: Report of the National Performance Review*. Washington, DC: U.S. Government Printing Office (September).

Greengard, Samuel. 2001. "Make Smarter Business Decisions: Know What Employees Can Do." *Workforce* 80 (11): 42–46.

Jamieson, David and Julie O'Mara. 1991. *Managing Workforce 2000: Gaining the Diversity Advantage*. San Francisco: Jossey Bass.

Jorgensen, Barbara. 1993 "Diversity: Managing a Multicultural Workforce." *Electronic Business Buyer* 19 (9) (September): 72.

Kemmerer, Barbara E., and V. Aline Arnold. 1993. "The Growing Use of Benchmarking in Managing Cultural Diversity." *Business Forum* 18 (1) & (2) (winter/spring): 39.

Klingner, Donald, and John Nalbandian. 1993. *Public Personnel Management*. Englewood Cliffs, NJ: Prentice Hall.

Lansing, Kevin. 1995. "Is Public Capital Productive? A Review of the Evidence." *Economic Commentary*. Federal Reserve Bank of Cleveland (March 1): 2.

Laudicina, Eleanor V. 1993. "Diversity and Productivity: Lessons from the Corporate Sector." *Public Productivity and Management Review* 4 (summer): 457–63.

Lewin, Kurt. 1951. *Field Theory in Social Science: Selected Theoretical Papers*. Westport, CT: Greenwood Press.

"Line Managers Out of Step on Dealing with Diversity at Work." 1993. *Personnel Management* 25 (7) (July): 15.

Mathews, Audrey L. 1999. *The Sum of the Differences*. New York: McGraw-Hill.

———. 2002. "Mentoring's Mosaic: Traits and Characteristics." Dissertation, University of Southern California.

———. 2003. Diversity Management PowerPoint notes. |FCO|Hyperlinkwww.csusb.edu/blackboard/PA619|FCC|

McGregor, Eugene B. 1991. *Strategic Management of Human Knowledge, Skills and Abilities: Workforce Decision-Making in the Post-Industrial Era*. San Francisco: Jossey-Bass.

Morrison, Ann. 1992. *The New Leaders: Guidelines on Leadership Diversity in America*. San Francisco: Jossey-Bass.

Morrison, Ann, interview by Patricia Galagan. 1993. "Leading Diversity: A Special Report on Diversity." *Training and Development* 47 (4) (April): 40.

Muir, John. 1993. "Employee Relations and the Line Manager." *Management Context and Strategies*. Englewood Cliffs, NJ: Prentice Hall.

Napier, Rodney W., and Matti K. Gershenfeld. 1973. *Groups: Theory and Experience*. Boston: Houghton Mifflin.

Office of Personnel Management. 1989. *Manage to Budget Programs*. Washington, DC: Office of Systems Innovation and Simplification, Personnel Systems and Oversight Group (PSOG-203) (August).

Ospina, Sonia. 1992. "When Managers Don't Plan: Consequences of No Strategic Public Personnel Management." *Review of Personnel Administration* 12 (2) (January–April): 51–63.

Ott, Steven. 1989. *Classic Readings in Organizational Behavior*. Pacific Grove, CA: Brooks/Cove Publishing.

Otto, Kenneth L. 1992. "Integrated Leadership: Tenneco Breaks the Barriers." *Resources Professional* 4 (2) (winter): 53–54.

Perry, James L. 1989. *Handbook of Public Administration*. San Francisco: Jossey-Bass.

ProQuest ABI/Inform. 1994. *Chief Financial Officers Act of 1990*. University Microfilms, Inc., Access No. 00746238. Washington, DC: Library of Congress, Public Law 101–576 (1990), November 15.

Report by an Academy Panel. 1993. *Leading People in Change: Empowerment, Commitment, Accountability*. Washington, DC: National Academy of Public Administration (NAPA): 34–35.

Robinson, Robert K., Geralyn McClure, and David E. Terpstra. 1994. "Diversity in the '90s: Avoid Conflict with EEO Laws." *Human Resource Focus* 71 (1) (January): 9.

Salomon, Mary F., and Joan M. Schork. 2003. "Turn Diversity To Your Advantage." *Research Technology Management* 46 (4): 37–44.

Schein, Edgar H. 1978. *Career Dynamics: Matching Individual and Organizational Needs*. Reading, PA: Addison-Wesley Publishing.

Schuler, Randall. 1984. *Personnel and Human Resources Management*. 2d ed. St. Paul: West Publishing.

Shilling, Gary A. 2003. *Forbes* 172 (13): 224.

Stockley, Edith, and Richard Zeckhauser. 1978. *A Primer for Public Analysis*. New York: W.W. Norton.

Thomas, R. Roosevelt, Jr. 1991. *Beyond Race and Gender: Unleashing the Power of Your Total Workforce by Managing Diversity*. New York: Amacom.

United States General Accounting Office (GAO). 1993. *Federal Budget Choosing Public Investment Programs*. Report to Congressional Requesters (July 23).

Van Auken, Phillip M. 1993. "Supervising Culturally Diverse Employees." *Supervision* 54 (8) (August): 11.

Weimer, David L., and Aidan R. Vining. 1992. *Policy Analysis: Concepts and Practice*. 2d ed. Englewood Cliffs, NJ: Prentice Hall.

White, Michael J. et al. 1985. *Managing Public Systems: Analytic Techniques for Public Administration*. Lanham, MD: University Press of America.

Wholey, Joseph S. et al., eds. 1994. *Handbook of Practical Program Evaluation*. San Francisco: Jossey-Bass.

Winterle, Mary L. 1993. "Positioning Diversity." *Across the Board* 30 (8) (October): 48.

12

Embracing Workplace Diversity in Public Organizations

Some Further Considerations

Mitchell F. Rice and Harvey L. White

The chapters in this book suggest that achieving and managing diversity in public organizations (and all organizations) requires a comprehensive strategy. It is our view that this strategy must emphasize a shift from looking at hiring numbers (affirmative action) and assimilation to focusing on valuing difference (multiculturalism) and managing diversity in public organizations. This strategy would allow public organizations to transform themselves into employers of choice for the best and brightest of individuals from all racial, ethnic, and gender backgrounds (Barak 2000). Traditional affirmative action programs, while needed and necessary, do not guarantee workplace diversity. Nor do affirmative action programs promote cultural change and effective integration (Thomas 1991–92; Shin and Mesch 1996; Rice 2001). This chapter argues that implementing and managing diversity involves a transformation process that takes into account four major elements. They are: (1) conversion from a monocultural to a multicultural organization; (2) adoption of a participatory shared approach to leadership; (3) urgent pursuit of organizational diversity objectives; and (4) a marketing approach for proper design and execution. These four elements are briefly discussed below.

Conversion from a Monocultural to a Multicultural Organization

A future condition for public organizations is to have a multicultural (as opposed to monocultural) and diverse cadre of employees who work in a nurturing and caring environment. Jun (1996, 354) argues that "Multiculturalism in organizations refers to the organizational phenomenon that occurs when people of different cultural backgrounds, with many different values, life experiences, and ways of expressing themselves, work together." Multiculturalism is not assimilation. Rather it is a "transmutational process in which different ideas, values, and experiences of organizational members are integrated and transformed into a constructive [and productive] force" (Jun 1996, 355). Underlying this process is a proactive approach to multicultural problem-solving that emphasizes organizational change, sharing, and learning. The objective is to remove elements of a monocultural organization-domination of one group over another and exclusionary hiring and membership practices (Miller and Katz, 1995).

Adoption of a Participatory Shared Approach to Leadership

In a multicultural organization, participatory shared leadership and supervision is a necessary element. Shared leadership in public organizations would assist in creating and fostering a milieu where all employees are respected, appreciated, and accepted for their contributions and perspectives. In this kind of environment, employees' efforts are likely to be more productive, effective, and rewarding. Further, all employees would have an equal chance at participation, career enhancement, and career advancement. This type of leadership and supervision would also allow the organization to take advantage of the diverse backgrounds and abilities of its employees. Therefore, organizational leadership must not only value diversity but must also lead and manage in a way to seize the benefits that differences bring. Jun (1996, 357–58) identifies five factors that are crucial for organizational leadership to understand and intervene with when dealing with culturally diverse employees: (1) reframing cultural perspectives; (2) facilitating social learning; (3) learning interpersonal skills; (4) empowering employees; and (5) promoting participation and representation. Through these five factors, "effective [leadership] support for diversity" can be evident in both the processes and outcomes of organizational work if diversity changes include a representation component, an interactional component, and an organizational culture component (Bond and Pyle 1998).

Urgent Pursuit of Organizational Diversity Objectives

A comprehensive diversity strategy in public organizations, while a long-term process, must be implemented quickly and thoroughly to gain a hiring advantage over other organizations and to provide better and more efficient services that the public customer demands. Choudhury (1996, 406) argues that "the purpose of MD [managing diversity] is to transform the organizational culture, ridding it of all unproductive biases, and creating an enabling environment for all employees to operate at full potential and contribute to organizational effectiveness." A major result of this diversity strategy is that individuals are fully integrated into all structures and activities of the organization.

Developing a Marketing Approach for Diversity Program Design and Execution

Diversity changes in public organizations must not only be far-reaching, they also involve dramatic changes in the interactions between public servants, how they see themselves, and how they accomplish their jobs. Therefore it is necessary that a marketing approach be implemented that considers both the employee and public service consumer as a vital tool in promoting these new changes.

Diversity Objectives in Public Organizations

This chapter recommends the adoption of eleven specific objectives for embracing diversity in public organizations. These objectives are:

1. Evaluate the status of leadership devoted to human resources and the establishment of a multicultural organization.
2. Effectively recruit and retain a multicultural workforce.
3. Develop an innovative, creative, and people-oriented work environment for employees.
4. Work to achieve community acceptance of a multicultural workforce.
5. Highly value, understand, and effectively manage diversity in the organization.
6. Provide outstanding support and first-line supervision to a multicultural workforce.

7. Establish a policy that enables employees to balance their career and personal needs in an increasingly complex society.
8. Develop an organizational vision and focus for training and development of the workforce.
9. Have effective accountability for managing a multicultural organization and for diversifying the workforce.
10. Clearly define goals and timetables for the organization to achieve within certain time frames and have a vision for future accomplishments—year 2000 and beyond.
11. Fully and appropriately recognize individuals and organizational units for their full range of multicultural accomplishments.

Components for Success

It should be recognized that, in addition to having a workable strategy and achievable goals, there are other necessary components for achieving and maintaining diversity in public organizations. These are: (1) communication, (2) leadership, (3) mission, and (4) marketing.

Communication

The success or failure of any endeavor, particularly one as sensitive as diversity, will depend heavily on clear and concise communications for all groups of individuals involved, especially those who are somewhat "traditionalists." Joel Barker (1992) mentions three keys to the twenty-first century—anticipation, innovation, and excellence. In public organizations these three keys require communications "par excellence" because by their very nature they induce a certain amount of anxiety. Such stimuli producing anxiety coupled with apprehension requires extra effort in assuring that full and complete communications are understood by all. Further, the Hudson Institute's report *Workforce 2000* (Johnston and Packer 1987) and the subsequent U.S. Department of Labor's report *Opportunity 2000* (1988) were unanimous in certain findings. These findings are: (1) the population and workforce will grow more slowly than at any time since the 1930s; (2) the average age of the population and workforce will increase while at the same time there will be a decrease in the pool of young workers entering the labor force; and (3) women, minorities, and immigrants will be a larger share of the workforce. Organizational communication will be an important component in dealing with these new workers. Communications in public organizations should focus on four areas for organizational diversity success: strategy, structure, operations, and culture.

Leadership

Tied directly to communications is leadership. Leadership is important from two perspectives. First, organizational leaders should know how employees feel. Leaders should look beyond their personal feelings and frames of reference. It is the responsibility of leaders to understand the unique experiences, knowledge, and cultures of employees to make sure that their needs are met. Second, organizational leaders must be strong proponents of employee training and development. This involves continuous education for both management and employees. The emphasis should be on diversity training, job enrichment, networking, and mentoring. Employee training and development must create an organizational culture and value for supporting diverse personnel.

Mission

A public organization's mission defines why it exists and what results it expects to achieve. A mission statement should describe what the public organization will contribute to society if it is to be successful in its goal. The mission statement should be up-to-date and developed through concerted discussion and decision-making by both management and employees. A multicultural organization's mission should address what the organization seeks to achieve in terms of workforce diversity and clarify its purpose and strategic objectives that make diversity important and necessary (Mello 1996).

Marketing the Changes

The changes needed to bring about diversity in public organizations will not be an easy task for many public organizations. Organizational leaders and employees can be assisted by marketing methods. We see marketing methods for designing changes and getting them accepted. Marketing arranges for mutually beneficial exchanges between the organization and society. Marketing in the private sector includes product development, pricing, promotion, and distribution based on customer needs and expectations. Marketing in the public sector should take into account service development and service delivery activities. If a marketing approach is used in a public organization, a strategic marketing plan will have to be prepared.

Conclusion

Achieving changes in communication, leadership, power arrangements, structure, values, and related behaviors for accomplishing a multicultural, diverse organization will require comprehensive and multiyear processes of organizational changes. Each of these areas of change necessitates careful analysis, clear decision-making, and major commitments followed by sustained and effective actions over a period of time throughout the organization. Some immediate actions are necessary for movement toward a multicultural, diverse organization. These are: training and development, outreach and recruitment, changes in the work environment, work standards for accountability, and recognition.

A public organization that is effective in reducing discrimination, achieving a diverse workforce, and becoming multicultural in its operations is one that will experience less friction and turbulence in a changing society. Further, a public organization that achieves and manages diversity is one that recognizes (1) demographic changes in which women and people of color are and will increasingly be a larger proportion of the workforce and the need of organizations to employ these people as a business necessity and (2) a growing realization of how diversity can result in more effective means of working and interacting in the interest of both organizational productivity and individual well-being and satisfaction.

References

Barak, Michael E. Mor. 2000. "The Inclusive Workplace: An Ecosystems Approach To Diversity Management." *Social Work* 45 (4): 339–52.

Barker, Joel A. 1992. *Future Edge of Discovering the New Paradigms of Success.* New York: Morrow Business Forecasting.

Bond, Meg A., and Jean L. Pyle. 1998. "The Ecology of Diversity in Organizational Settings: Lessons from a Case Study." *Human Relations* 51 (5): 589–623.

Choudhury, Enamul H. 1996. "The Native Significance of Workforce Diversity: Orientations of State and Urban Administrators." *International Journal of Public Administration* 91 (3): 399–423.

Johnston, William B., and Arnold H. Packer. 1987. *Workforce 2000.* Indianapolis, IN: Hudson Institute.

Jun, Jong S. 1996. "Changing Perspectives on Organizational Culture: Embracing Multiculturalism." *International Journal of Public Administration* 19 (3): 345–75.

Mello, Jeffrey A. 1996. "The Strategic Management of Workplace Diversity Initiatives: Public Sector Implications." *International Journal of Public Administration* 19 (3): 425–47.

Miller, Frederick A., and Judith H. Katz. 1995. "Cultural Diversity as a Development Process: The Path from a Monocultural Club to an Inconclusive Organization." *The 1995 Annual: Volume 2, Consulting*. San Diego: Pfeiffer, 267–81.

Rice, Mitchell F. 2001. "The Need for Teaching Diversity and Representativeness in University Public Administration Education and Professional Public Service Training Programmes in Sub–Saharan Africa." In *Managing Diversity in the Civil Service*. Amsterdam, Netherlands: IOS Press, 99–110.

Schubert, Jan. 1993. *Communications in Organizations*. Boston: JFK School of Government.

Shin, Roy W., and Debra J. Mesch. 1996. "The Changing Workforce: Issues and Challenges." *International Journal of Public Administration* 19 (3): 291–98.

Thomas, R. Roosevelt, Jr. 1991–92. "The Concept of Managing Diversity." *The Bureaucrat* (winter): 19–22.

U.S. Department of Labor. 1988. *Opportunity 2000: Creative Affirmative Action Strategies for a Changing Workforce*. Washington, DC: U.S. Department of Labor.

About the Editor and Contributors

Editor

Mitchell F. Rice is professor of political science in the Bush School of Government and Public Service and director of the Race and Ethnic Studies Institute of Texas A&M University. He is an elected Fellow of the National Academy of Public Administration in Washington, D.C. He is the author/coauthor of some one hundred scholarly and professional articles and five books. His research areas include: organizational diversity/diversity management; public administration/management; and social, health, and urban policy. Dr. Rice has served as president of the National Conference of Minority Public Administrators and the Southeastern Conference on Public Administration, and national chair of the Committee on the Status of Blacks in the Profession of the American Political Science Association. He is also a former member of the National Councils of the American Society of Public Administration and the American Political Science Association. He holds a Ph.D. in government from Claremont Graduate University.

Contributors

Dhananjaya M. Arekere is associate research scientist in the Race and Ethnic Studies Institute at Texas A&M University.

Margo L. Bailey is assistant professor of public administration at American University in Washington, D.C. Her research interests include cultural competency in public administration, diversity, and human resources management issues. Her writing has appeared in *Public Administration Review* and the *Journal of Public Management and Social Policy*.

Otha Burton, Jr. is chief administrative officer for the mayor's office in Jackson, Mississippi.

Kyle Farmbry is assistant professor in the School of Public Administration and Urban Studies at San Diego State University.

B. Lee Green is associate professor of health and director of the Center for the Study of Health Disparities at Texas A&M University.

Rhonda K. Lewis is associate professor of psychology in the College of Liberal Arts and Sciences at Wichita State University, Wichita, Kansas.

Barbara C. Maddox is a budget coordinator at George Mason University in northern Virginia. She has coauthored publications and presentations on trends and implications of the increased diversity of the workforce.

Audrey Mathews is associate professor of public administration and director of the Social Entrepreneurship /IECE Institute in the College of Business and Public Administration at California State University, San Bernardino. She is author of *The Sum of the Differences: Diversity and Public Organization*.

Wilbur C. Rich is professor of political science at Wellesley College in Wellesley, Massachusetts. Among his books are *The Politics of Urban Personnel Policy*, *Coleman Young and Detroit Politics,* and *Black Mayors and School Politics*. He has served as a visiting scholar at the Russell Sage Foundation.

Floydette C. Cory-Scruggs is associate dean in the College of Architecture, Urban and Public Affairs at Florida Atlantic University.

Jacqueline Smith-Mason is an instructor in the School of Government and Public Affairs at Virginia Commonwealth University. Her areas of interest are organizational behavior and management theory, diversity and human resources management, accountability, and performance measurement.

Mfanya Donald Tryman is a professor of political science at Mississippi State University. He is author of five books including *The Encyclopedia of Malcolm X* (2002) and more than fifty articles, book chapters, and book reviews. He has researched and published extensively in the areas of African-American politics, school desegregation, African-Americans and public policy, affirmative action, and racial profiling.

Daphne C. Watkins is a doctoral student in health education and a graduate research assistant in the Center for the Study of Health Disparities at Texas A&M University.

Mylon Winn is associate professor and MPA coordinator at the University of Arkansas at Little Rock.

Harvey L. White is full professor and special assistant to the president of the University of South Alabama. He is also a member of the faculty of the Graduate School of Public and International Affairs at the University of Pittsburgh.

Blue Wooldridge is an associate professor in the School of Government and Public Affairs at Virginia Commonwealth University. His articles have appeared in: *International Review of Administrative Sciences, International Journal of Public Administration, National Productivity Review, Public Administration Review, American Review of Public Administration, Public Personnel Management, Public Productivity and Management Review*, and the *Review of Public Personnel Administration*. His research interests include design of instruction for public administration, learning styles, high-performing organizations, productivity improvement, and workforce diversity.

Index